Biometrics, Surveillance and the Law

The use of biometric identification systems is rapidly increasing across the world, owing to their potential to combat terrorism, fraud, corruption and other illegal activities. However, critics of the technology complain that the creation of an extensive central register of personal information controlled by the government will increase opportunities for the state to abuse citizens. There is also concern about the extent to which data about an individual is recorded and kept.

This book reviews some of the most current and complex legal and ethical issues relating to the use of biometrics. Beginning with an overview of biometric systems, the book goes on to examine some of the theoretical underpinnings of the surveillance state, questioning whether these conceptual approaches are still relevant, particularly the integration of ubiquitous surveillance systems and devices. The book also analyses the implementation of the world's largest biometric database, Aadhaar, in detail. Additionally, the identification of individuals at border checkpoints in the United States, Australia and the EU is explored, as well as the legal and ethical debates surrounding the use of biometrics regarding: the war on terror and the current refugee crisis; violations of international human rights law principles; and mobility and privacy rights. The book concludes by addressing the collection, use and disclosure of personal information by private-sector entities such as Axciom and Facebook, and government use of these tools to profile individuals.

By examining the major legal and ethical issues surrounding the debate on this rapidly emerging technology, this book will appeal to students and scholars of law, criminology and surveillance studies, as well as law enforcement and criminal law practitioners.

Sara M. Smyth is an Associate Professor of Law at La Trobe University, Melbourne, Australia.

Routledge Research in the Law of Emerging Technologies

Biometrics, Surveillance and the Law
Societies of Restricted Access, Discipline and Control
Sara M. Smyth

Biometrics, Surveillance and the Law

Societies of Restricted Access, Discipline and Control

Sara M. Smyth

Routledge
Taylor & Francis Group
LONDON AND NEW YORK

First published 2019
by Routledge
2 Park Square, Milton Park, Abingdon, Oxon OX14 4RN

and by Routledge
605 Third Avenue, New York, NY 10017

First issued in paperback 2021

Routledge is an imprint of the Taylor & Francis Group, an informa business

British Library Cataloguing-in-Publication Data
A catalogue record for this book is available from the British Library

Library of Congress Cataloging-in-Publication Data
Names: Smyth, Sara M. (Sara Melissa), 1974–, author.
Title: Biometrics, surveillance and the law: societies of restricted access, discipline and control / By Sara M. Smyth.
Description: New York: Routledge, 2019. |
Series: Routledge research in the law of emerging technologies | Includes bibliographical references and index.
Identifiers: LCCN 2018054357 | ISBN 9780367077198 (hardback)
Subjects: LCSH: Biometric identification—Law and legislation. | Electronic surveillance—Law and legislation. | Technological innovations—Law and legislation. | Information technology—Government policy. | Privacy, Right of.
Classification: LCC K5479 .S69 2019 | DDC 345/.052—dc23
LC record available at https://lccn.loc.gov/2018054357

Typeset in Galliard
by codeMantra

ISBN 13: 978-1-03-224142-5 (pbk)
ISBN 13: 978-0-367-07719-8 (hbk)

DOI: 10.4324/9780429022326

For my mother

Contents

Acknowledgements

I am particularly grateful to Emma Tyce, at Routledge UK, whose support and commitment to this project was invaluable. Nicola Sharpe also provided helpful assistance with the manuscript and publishing agreement. I am also indebted to the peer reviewers who took the time to review the proposal and manuscript and who provided helpful advice and recommendations, particularly in suggesting a number of valuable sources for me to consider. I am grateful to LaTrobe Law School for giving me the time and space to pursue this project in 2018. Special thanks are due to Head of School Patrick Keyzer and Associate Head of School Anne Wallace for their support and mentorship. I also want to thank PTB for the gift of inspiration and for thoughtful discussions around the issues explored in this book.

O LORD, thou hast searched me out and known me: thou knowest my down-sitting and mine up-rising, thou understandest my thoughts long before. Thou art about my path, and about my bed: and spiest out all my ways.

– Psalm 139

I give the fight up! let there be an end,
A privacy, an obscure nook for me.
I want to be forgotten even by God!

– Robert Browning[1]

1 *Paracelsus* (London: Effingham Wilson, 1835) 174.

1 Introduction

Introduction to biometrics, surveillance, discipline and control

Biometric technology (from the Greek: *bios*, life and *metron*, measurement) identifies individuals automatically using their biological or behavioural characteristics. In many jurisdictions, it's routinely deployed for passports, voting and access to secure premises – all cases where personal identity plays an essential role. It has yet to gain wide-spread acceptance in what may be considered everyday areas of our lives; but this is changing, particularly when it comes to the retail sector.

Formal identification and authentication systems are becoming ever more crucial for people's dealings with both public and private institutions. The relationship between the individual and the state, as well as his or her wider social and economic environment, will inevitably change as a result of these systems. The process of collecting and organizing information is now a tremendous source of economic, political and cultural power. Data makes us more malleable, easier to predict and highly prone to influence. For retailers and marketers, being able to understand their customers' habits, preferences and aversions – so that they can predict their needs and provide more targeted sales pitches – is the Holy Grail.

The leading organizations are the ones that have tracked us most extensively, have profiled us most accurately and have the power to anticipate our next move. Governments are also claiming access to a growing number of biometric identification systems. These schemes involve considerable expenditure and the financial implications for both government and business are substantial. Biometrics is a global growth industry; and the worldwide market for these services is said to have reached $16.5 billion by 2017.[1]

Proponents argue that formalized identity management systems offer the potential to combat terrorism, fraud, corruption and other illegal activities. Such systems also offer the means to establish strategic partnerships between the state and citizens.[2] Failure to register people and provide identity documents is

1 Alan Gleb & Charles Kenny, 'The Case for Big Brother (Foreign Policy)', *CGD in the News*, 4 March, 2013.

2 International Telecommunications Union (ITU), *Review of National Identity Programs*, 2016 at 9.

thought to have detrimental effects for both the individual and the state; thus, many countries are establishing national ID systems and exploring the role they play in political, economic and social development (ITU, 8). Modern biometric technologies offer the promise of improved authentication, establishing confidence in individual claims about identity.

Critics complain that the creation of an extensive central register of personal information controlled by government will increase opportunities for the state to abuse citizens, for example by searching health records for evidence of genetic diseases to deny benefits or targeting immigrants and other minorities. It's apparent that any such scheme is fraught with enormous challenges and risks. At a minimum, many fundamental concepts such as privacy, autonomy and government accountability will shift. Indeed, contemporary society has already witnessed a substantial shift in the responsibility for public order away from the centralized administrative state towards global corporations and systems.

Yet the complexity of government administration in the modern world is now a major problem for most countries.[3] Governments in developing states are expected to carry out many of the same functions as first-world countries, including 'providing universal access to healthcare and education, implementing know your customer (KYC) rules for financial institutions, and administering a wide variety of transfer programs'.[4] Digital technologies can mitigate some of the problems caused by paper-based registers, including duplications, forgery, false acceptances and false rejections.

As identification technology evolves, so do identification systems. Many of these programs link identities with biometric data across all sectors – nationwide and even globally – to create powerful 'big data' **systems and networks** of identity. 'Big data' refers to very large data sets and the tools and procedures used to manipulate and analyse them.[5] The market sees big data as a way to target advertising, insurance providers use it to optimize their offerings, and Wall Street bankers use it to read the market. Incorporating biometric technologies in big data systems is useful for the growth of e-government, as well as providing public and private services, including voter verification, government transfers and banking. The electronic capture and storage of data can also reduce costs and human error, while increasing administrative efficiency.

Generally speaking, there are three ways in which authentication technologies operate: by assessing something that somebody knows, like a password; by assessing something that somebody has, like a key card; or, by assessing something that somebody is, or is not, which is where biometrics comes into play.[6]

3 Ibid.

4 Gleb & Kenny, *supra*, note 1.

5 danah boyd & Kate Crawford, 'Critical Questions for Big Data', (2012) 15(5) *Information, Communication & Society* 662 at 664.

6 Joseph N. Pato & Lynette I. Millett (eds), *Biometric Recognition: Challenges and Opportunities* (Washington, DC: The National Academic Press, 2010) at 5.

Biometrics can be defined as the automated method of identifying or authenticating the identity of an individual based on physical or behavioural characteristics. It relies on the notion that the human body is its own identifier.[7] It's more reliable than traditional authentication techniques, like passwords, tokens, and PIN-based methods, because it can't easily be lost, damaged, forgotten or stolen.[8]

Biometrics is at the centre of an evolving set of policies and practices related to determining one's identity; and establishing one's identity is central to achieving any number of contemporary policy goals, from stopping criminals to increasing efficiencies within the welfare system.[9] Widespread fingerprinting is controversial in most Western nations but in developing countries where births are routinely undocumented, people often lack official identification, and many can't sign their names, so fingerprints can be a person's only opportunity to secure a bank account.[10] A fingerprint can therefore become a person's PIN, or signature, for depositing money into savings accounts, taking out loans, and even buying funeral insurance, life insurance or crop insurance.[11]

Security concerns are a fundamental impetus behind the implementation of identification systems in many nations. In this context, we see them deployed for border management (i.e. to control immigration/migration flows or to monitor travel); law enforcement (i.e. for use by police or other enforcement officials for purposes of identification, investigation or reporting); and to curb the ability of extremists and criminals to conduct illicit activities.[12] Not only are they assisting governments to track criminal activity, in some jurisdictions they're even helping bystanders to detect and report on crime.

The use of biometric identification can pose significant privacy problems; and the interests of governments and citizens often conflict. Perhaps, for example, the government wants to be able to identify and track the movements of certain people using biometrics. Yet citizens might not be comfortable with the government collecting and storing this information in a database. Similarly, DNA evidence could be collected and used to make determinations about whether or not to provide a person with health-care insurance, based on genetic conditions.[13] In each case, there is a conflict between the ability of private and

7 Joe Celko, *Joe Celko's Complete Guide to NoSQL* (Burlington, NJ: Elsevier Science, 2013) at 129.

8 Richa Singh, Mayank Vatsa & Phalguni Gupta, 'Biometric's', in Margherita Pagani (ed.), *Encyclopedia of Multimedia Technology and Networking* (2nd edn) (Hershey, PA: Information Science Reference, 2008) 121–127 at 121.

9 Pam Dixon, 'A Failure to "Do No Harm" – India's Aadhaar Biometric ID Program and its Inability to Protect Privacy in relation to measures in Europe and the U.S.', (2017) 7(4) *Health & Technology* 539 at 540.

10 Douglas Fox, 'Villages Leapfrog the Grid with Biometrics and Mobile Money', *The Christian Science Monitor*, April 14, 2011.

11 *Ibid.*

12 ITU, *supra*, note 2 at 53.

13 Luther Martin, 'Biometrics', in John R. Vacca (ed.), *Cyber Security and IT Infrastructure Protection* (Waltham, MA: Elsevier, 2014) 151 at 153.

public-sector entities to collect, use, store and share this information, and the individual's interest in keeping it private.

Privacy can be broadly divided into three zones: physical privacy as it relates to the person (i.e. the body); territorial or spatial privacy; and informational privacy, or the freedom of an individual to limit certain information about himself. All three are engaged when it comes to biometrics. The first of these, physical privacy, protects our right to be free from non-consensual contact with another. Liberal assumptions about privacy presume that individuals have a right of dignity, autonomy and bodily integrity and thus are able to decide who and what can have access to their physical selves, and in what manner. Yet these expectations are challenged by biometric systems that can capture personal information from a distance, without the knowledge or consent of the subject.

The second domain of privacy recognizes that individuals must have the right to private spaces within which they can engage in intimate personal acts. This right has a long history in American constitutional law; and the courts have continued to locate the privacy doctrine in real property protections, particularly when it comes to the notion of physical intrusion, and respect for the sanctity and privacy of the home.[14] Furthermore, a person's expectation of privacy will only be deemed 'reasonable' when it is supported by the right to exclude others, which evolves directly from real property law.[15]

The boundaries of the third zone of privacy, informational privacy, are the most difficult to define. Informational privacy protects the right of an individual to limit access to personal information about herself. Thus, it relates to secrecy, and the idea that an individual has a reasonable expectation of privacy in personal information that may tend to reveal intimate details about her lifestyle and personal choices. Profiling – whereby one captures information about an individual and then uses it to anticipate who may pose a security threat and thus who should be subject to further monitoring or other pre-emptive measures – not only threatens the person's right to 'informational self-determination' but it also jeopardizes a linchpin of our legal system: the presumption of innocence and the right to equal treatment under the law.[16]

Technological innovation has meant that the amount of personal information that can be recorded, stored and shared is virtually limitless. In addition, private actors are now playing a critical role in the collection and aggregation of personal information. As a result, our concerns about privacy now centre on personal information that is not necessarily intimate and that may be collected at any time

14 Orin Kerr, 'The Fourth Amendment and New Technologies: Constitutional Myths and the Case for Caution', (2003) 102 *Michigan Law Review* 801 at 809–810; Daniel Solove, 'Digital Dossiers and Dissipation of Fourth Amendment Privacy' (2001) 75 *Southern California Law Review* 1083 at 1129.

15 *Ibid.* at 810.

16 Malcom Thorburn, 'Identification, Surveillance and Profiling: On the Uses and Abuses of Citizen Data', in I. Dennis and G. R. Sullivan (eds), *Seeking Security: Pre-empting the Commission of Criminal Harms* (Oxford: Hart Publishing, 2011) 15 at 18.

by *either* the private sector or the state.[17] Moreover, information collected in one context can easily migrate to others.[18] This understanding of privacy is highly contextual in the sense that myriad factors influence whether we consider it necessary, or even appropriate, to control or limit access to personal information.

This is problematic when one considers the common-law approach to privacy, which largely focuses on the question of whether one has a 'reasonable expectation of privacy' in the information itself. This approach can be criticized for treating data privacy as an 'all-or-nothing affair'.[19] One either has a reasonable expectation of privacy – in which case, the state is restricted from collecting the data – or one does not – whereby the state may do what it will.[20] Yet because there is no bright-line test for how, and to whom, information should be disclosed in the modern world, the common law framework for privacy protection in the management of personal information is outdated. There is no longer the overriding concern of protecting some particular class of information, or even the specific place in which it may be collected; but rather the need to regulate the context in which data can be accessed, shared and used.[21]

At the same time, though we must not lose sight of the fact that there is still a connection between electronic surveillance, biometric systems, and the infringement of one's reasonable expectation of privacy. For example, the potentially lifelong association of biometric traits with an individual, and their connection with identity records, can lead to the conclusion that the individual belongs to a group with certain access rights and benefits, or to a group that should be denied those benefits.[22] This means that people can be denied access to systems and resources, like jobs, health care or insurance; and that the failure to enrol, or be identified, may render an individual unable to leave the country, homeless or even stateless.

This phenomenon is facilitated by persistent closed-circuit television (CCTV) monitoring, inter-agency databases linked to national identity cards, and biometric measurements used for international travel, among other things. A major threat, which has not yet fully materialized, is omnipresent, around-the-clock surveillance that is not only 'always on' but is 'always with us' because the technology is linked with the human body.[23] Furthermore, the systematic use of biometric systems for the monitoring and identification of individuals has enabled segregation by public officials in the name of 'national security' and the support of racism, xenophobia and extremist views worldwide.

17 Lisa Austin, 'Privacy and the Question of Technology', (2003) 22 *Law and Philosophy* 119 at 122–123.

18 Thorburn, *supra*, note 15 at 29.

19 *Ibid.* at 19–20.

20 *Ibid.*

21 *Ibid.* at 29.

22 Pato & Millett, *supra*, note 5 at 10.

23 Katina Michael & M. G. Michael, *Innovative Automatic Identification and Location-Based Services: From Bar Codes to Chip Implants*, (Hershey, PA: IGI Global, 2009) at 464.

Art can be an effective mirror, reflecting the social concerns and problems of the day. With the rise of ubiquitous surveillance and the continuous monitoring of identity, various artists have satirized this technology and the consequences it creates. For example, there's a *New Yorker* cartoon, dated 12 November 2014, showing a couple in bed together. The woman is lying on her side, and the man is sitting upright, holding what appears to be a tablet computer. On the wall overhead, just above the headboard, are two surveillance cameras. The man asks the woman, 'If you're not planning to break the law, why should you care?'

The joke is built around the notion that the bedroom is off-limits to surveillance because it's a sacred space, exclusively reserved for highly personal functions like sleep, sex and self-care. And most of us would consider it a major affront to our dignity and privacy that surveillance cameras should be employed in the toilet, shower or bedroom area of our homes. This goes back to the tripartite definition of privacy explored above.

The cartoon also portrays surveillance as being 'watched.' For most people the very idea of surveillance comes to light when they realise they're *being watched*, such as through a CCTV camera.[24] Yet surveillance need not always be so obvious. Think about all the places where we're surreptitiously observed, monitored and tracked every minute of each day. Think of airport check-ins and supermarket check-outs. Merchants and marketing companies also routinely install cookies into our Internet web browsers, which – along with tracking software – helps them sell us their products.[25] And most of us are photographed or video-recorded by tens of thousands of cameras – many of which are designed to be undetectable – as we move around our cities.

Most North Americans would agree that every individual is entitled to perform his or her actions in private. In other words, she is entitled to be in a state of tranquility and to not have to worry about being watched. The expectation of one's entitlement to such a condition is not confined only to intimate spaces – such as the bedroom or the bathroom – but goes with a person wherever he is.

Yet with technological change, the space between what has traditionally been considered 'private' and 'public' has been eroded. It's no longer clear where 'public' versus 'private' – much less the 'self' versus 'other' – begins and ends. The US and Canadian Constitution's protection against unreasonable search and seizure only provides protection against certain intrusions by the state – notably, those in which the individual has a 'reasonable expectation of privacy', like the home.[26] In contrast, the individual has no such expectation in public. For this reason, there is no protection for citizens against CCTV monitoring by the state – even if that amounts to around-the-clock surveillance of every activity outside the home.[27]

24 David Lyon, 'Globalizing Surveillance', (2004) 19(2) *Comparative and Sociological Perspectives* 135 at 135.

25 Kenneth Ryan, 'Introduction', in Peter P. Swire and Kenesa Ahmad (eds), *Privacy and Surveillance with New Technologies* (New York: International Debate Education Association, 2012) 1 at 1.

26 Thorburn, *supra*, note 15 at 30.

27 *Ibid.* See also: *United States v. Jones*, 132 S. Ct. 945 (2012) discussed in Chapter 4.

Surveillance is more than watching, snooping, or eavesdropping on others.[28] It is a dominant organizational practice that results in people being categorized in ways that facilitate different forms of treatment. Surveillance has become integral to the mediation of risk, which is dependent on software codes and algorithmic methods. Bits of data are extracted from human bodies (biometrics does this accurately; other forms of surveillance rely on behavioural markers) by a variety of agencies to be processed and profiled.[29] These are used as the basis of discrimination and to facilitate disparate treatment.

People make these security trade-offs instinctively, choosing more or less security as situations change. Only later do we realize what we've lost for sake of 'protecting the people'. This reminds us that while information technologies may enable surveillance to occur, they certainly do not cause them to do so. In the realm of crime control, for example, for more than 50 years, surveillance technologies have been embraced by the government as a means of anticipating and pre-empting illegal activities.

Recall, for example, how in the late sixties and early seventies, under J. Edgar Hoover, domestic intelligence and law enforcement agencies, like the FBI, used wiretaps and remote listening devices to conduct warrantless surveillance on anyone deemed a threat to national security. Despite Supreme Court rulings against this sort of unauthorized eavesdropping, like *Olmstead* and *Katz*, similar kinds of privacy violations continued during the Nixon regime.[30]

The dangers posed by new surveillance technologies became a significant public concern during the Watergate scandal. The Senate Select Committee to Study Governmental Operations with Respect to Intelligence conducted extensive investigations of foreign and domestic surveillance programs. This Committee – which is often referred to as the "Church Committee" after its chairman Senator Frank Church – released a report which found that:

> Too many people have been spied upon by too many Government agencies and to[o] much information has been collected. The Government has often undertaken the secret surveillance of citizens on the basis of their political beliefs, even when those beliefs posed no threat of violence or illegal acts on behalf of a hostile foreign power.
>
> The Government, operating primarily through secret informants, but also using other intrusive techniques such as wiretaps, microphone "bugs", surreptitious mail opening, and break-ins, has swept in vast amounts of information about the personal lives, views, and associations of American citizens. Investigations of groups deemed potentially dangerous – and even of groups suspected of associating with potentially dangerous organizations – have

28 Colin J. Bennett & David Lyon, 'Playing the ID Card – Understanding the Significance of Identity Card Systems', in Colin J. Bennett and David Lyon (eds), *Playing the Identity Card: Surveillance, Security and Identification in Global Perspective* (New York: Routledge, 2008) 3 at 6.

29 Lyon, *supra*, note 23 at 138.

30 Ryan, *supra*, note 24 at 7.

> continued for decades, despite the fact that those groups did not engage in unlawful activity. Groups and individuals have been harassed and disrupted because of their political views and their lifestyles.[31]

The Church Committee concluded that these activities undermined the constitutional rights of Americans; and, in an effort to restore those rights, Congress passed a series of measures designed to bring executive agencies involved in intelligence-gathering back in line.

At the heart of these efforts, the *Foreign Intelligence Surveillance Act* of 1978 (*FISA*) was enacted to ensure that the president could never use 'national security' to justify the electronic surveillance of political opponents or citizens.[32] The Act set strict limits on the surveillance of American citizens, established a means of Congressional oversight and required the government to obtain a warrant to conduct national security surveillance against foreign agents. They were entitled to defend against foreign threats, not spy on their citizens.

Yet following the attacks on the World Trade Center and the Pentagon in 2001, the Bush administration passed the *PATRIOT Act*, which significantly expanded the scope of the government's surveillance power. Section 215 (*Access to records and other items under the Foreign Intelligence Surveillance Act)* allows the National Security Agency (NSA) to collect 'any tangible things (including books, records, papers, documents, and other items)' – about anyone, not just foreigners – 'for an investigation to protect against international terrorism or clandestine intelligence activities'. A secret court interpreted the last part to include the continuing collection of telephone metadata for every American.[33] And, as part of the ongoing War on Terror, governments around the world, like those within the 'Five Eyes' partnership of nations (i.e. the United States, Great Britain, Canada, Australia, and New Zealand) have used 'dragnet surveillance' to collect vast amounts of personal data and make predictions about behaviour.[34]

The Edward Snowden revelations about NSA surveillance, starting in June 2013, illustrate the ways in which big data has a cooperative relationship with surveillance.[35] Snowden famously uncovered that, as part of a secret surveillance partnership between the NSA and telecommunications companies, the US government directly – and indirectly through its Five Eyes partners – was able to reach into the servers and pipes of the largest Internet companies in the world and take whatever information they wanted, without judicial oversite or accountability. As part of this top-secret surveillance program, the US government compelled

31 Final Report of the Select Committee to Study Governmental Operations with Respect to Intelligence Activities (Church Committee Report), 26 April 1976. Available online at: www.bibliotecapleyades.net/sociopolitica/esp_sociopol_mj12_22.htm.

32 Ryan, *supra*, note 24 at 8.

33 Bruce Schneier, Data and Goliath: The Hidden Battles to Collect Your Data and Control Your World (New York: W. W. Norton & Co., 2015) at 65.

34 William J. Mitchell, *ME* ++ (Cambridge, MA: MIT Press, 2004).

35 David Lyon, 'Surveillance, Snowden, and Big Data: Capacities, Consequences, Critique', (2014) 1(2) *Big Data & Society* 1 at 1.

some of the biggest technology companies, including Apple, Facebook, Google, Microsoft, Skype, Yahoo, and YouTube, to give them our data.[36]

The central process of securitization is an essentially social process; and, a securitizing system is either accepted or rejected by its audience.[37] Yet the omnipresent nature of all this data-gathering – and the public's tolerance of it throughout virtually all regions and political systems – are both astounding and bewildering, especially when compared with the situation only decades ago.[38] Think, for example, of how profoundly Americans' faith in their government was shaken during the Watergate scandal.[39] But these privacy invasions – and the surveillance that triggered them – were small and sporadic. The occasional privacy breach caused by warrantless wiretaps could – for the most part – be dealt with effectively by the legal system. This is nothing compared with the nearly five billion cell phone records collected by the NSA each day by tapping into cables that connect mobile networks globally.[40]

Over the past 17 years or so, since the September 11, 2001 attacks, surveillance has expanded exponentially. In the immediate aftermath of 9/11, there was a clear shift in political priorities towards reasserted nationalism, the return to geopolitics, the hardening of state power and the closing of national borders.[41] As well, the American military was mobilized and powerful new surveillance agencies were created as a key element in the 'war on terror'. In the most powerful regions of the world, 'fortress continents' are under construction, whereby territorial borders are being sealed to maintain the flow of trade and capital while limiting the possibility of attack or penetration from the outside.[42]

Those in the more-surveillance-is-better camp proclaim, 'If you have nothing to hide, you have nothing to fear!' Yet this is irrelevant if we agree that the government's use of new technologies in the ongoing war on terror, including dragnet surveillance without court approval or oversight, has gone beyond the rule of law.[43] America, along with many other nations, has become a nation tormented by fear – fear of a faceless global enemy bent on destroying its democratic values and way of life.[44] Of course, the very same argument was made to justify military

36 *Ibid.*

37 Mark B. Salter & Geneviève Piché, 'The Securitization of the US–Canada Border in American Political Discourse', (2011) 44(4) *Canadian Journal of Political Science* 929 at 935.

38 The Economist, 'Learning to Live with Big Brother', in Peter P. Swire and Kenesa Ahmad (eds), *Privacy and Surveillance with New Technologies* (New York: International Debate Education Association, 2012) at 23.

39 Michael Hardy, 'Watergate Scandal: Public Distrust of Government Begins', *Federal Times*, 1 December 2015.

40 Lyon, *supra*, note 34 at 3.

41 David Lyon, 'National IDs in a Global World: Surveillance, Security, and Citizenship', (2010) 42 *Case Western Reserve Journal International Law* 607 at 612.

42 David Lyon, 'Filtering Flows, Friends and Foes', in Mark B. Salter (ed.), *Politics at the Airport* (Minneapolis: University of Minnesota Press, 2008) 29 at 33.

43 Ryan, *supra*, note 24 at 15.

44 Glenn Greenwald, 'The Surveillance State Thrives on Fear', in Peter P. Swire and Kenesa Ahmad (eds), *Privacy and Surveillance with New Technologies* (New York: International Debate Education Association, 2012) 62 at 64.

crusades throughout the twentieth century – from the fight against the Nazis to the communists in Vietnam and the USSR – but never before has it been used to defend such far-reaching powers of warrantless surveillance.[45]

Technologies are more advanced now than they were in the past. And neo-liberal ideologies have helped create a world in which we glorify technologies of disruption, even those which the general public fears and largely doesn't understand. Closely related to this trend is the emphasis on risk management, and in particular on statistical analyses of risk to guide public policy. Policing has been transformed by new technologies designed to identify and track people according to the level of risk they might pose. Yet surrendering our privacy to technology doesn't necessarily make us safer; in fact, the very things we think are keeping our fears at bay may actually be doing more harm than good.[46]

Part of the problem is that the law has yet to fully catch up with technology; and in fact, even the legal concept of privacy is still evolving. On the other hand we can observe that, when it comes to many forms of technological innovation, the case for privacy often comes too late. Suddenly, the horse is out of the barn – Facebook has your photos tagged and Google knows where you live. This is not the time to start debating which privacy and civil liberties principles you agree with, and which ones you don't.

Any surveillance technology must be viewed in terms of how it might be abused by a more unethical power than today's. Coming back to the *New Yorke*r cartoon mentioned above, what if the man was viewing child pornography on his computer tablet? Is it acceptable for the state to spy on him in bed to catch him committing this appalling criminal act? What if the government were to make it illegal for all non-married couples to sleep together? Is it still okay to spy on people in bed to enforce the law? Either way, it's a case of '…Big Brother, on the inside looking out'.[47] It bears mentioning that this scenario is not entirely fictitious. Recently, in an effort to find faces, the Pentagon's Optic Nerve program recorded webcam sex by its targets — in fact, up to 11 percent of the material the program collected was 'undesirable nudity' that employees were warned not to access, and which targets didn't know was being recorded.[48]

If governments now have the ability to store, organize and mine massive amounts of data about everyone, without oversight or accountability, they will also be able to draw conclusions in the dark, which may mean, for example, compiling dossiers on people, or looking for illicit activity where none has been suspected from the outset. The risk is that people will start behaving in certain ways to avoid being identified and 'red-flagged'. And banks, telecommunications

45 *Ibid.*

46 Glen Greenwald, 'The Digital Surveillance State: Vast, Secret, and Dangerous', in Peter P. Swire and Kenesa Ahmad (eds), *Privacy and Surveillance with New Technologies* (New York: International Debate Education Association, 2012) 35 at 41.

47 Michael & Michael, *supra*, note 22 at 465.

48 Kyle Chayka, 'Biometric Surveillance Means Someone Is Always Watching', *Newsweek*, 17 April 2014.

companies, insurance companies, credit card companies and other private entities are already amassing a vast treasure trove of information about us, which they are free to use for a wide array of purposes.[49] Once again, the growth of these systems has greatly outpaced the development of laws, ethics or policies regarding their use.[50]

Using another cartoon analogy, we can observe that aspects of the vast data trove have been compared with the comical version of heaven in which St. Peter stands before the 'Pearly Gates' with a ledger. The dearly departed had better be on the 'authorized list' to gain admission to paradise; otherwise, he might find himself 'blacklisted' and condemned to perpetual punishment in hell. Another comparison has been made with the movie adaptation of Philip K. Dick's short story, 'Minority Report', about a futuristic society in which everyone is continually biometrically identified. The main character (Tom Cruise), a Washington DC police officer in the year 2054, strolls through a crowded shopping mall where interactive billboards scan his irises and call out his name, bringing up ads based on his prior purchase history.

With respect to the first example, we know that if we want to access many places, systems and services in everyday life, we had better be authorized to do so – think, for example, of the key-card used to secure an office or a hotel room; the airline passenger no fly list; and the secure website, all of which may be regulated by access control lists and corresponding blacklists.[51] More importantly, if you don't have access to ATM cards and machines, or if you have no electronic device or cannot get reception, you may find yourself without access privileges in contemporary society.

With regard to the second scenario given, we can readily identify many examples in our current societies in which we are automatically self-identifying. And targeted advertising is now commonplace online. From the consumer's point of view, this ease of access can be a good thing, such as when it allows us to drive our vehicles on to toll roads by simply passing by a checkpoint without needing to stop and/or otherwise self-identify. This has the benefit of getting us what we want, when we want it, with very little effort.

But the new mode of electronic commerce is more than simply the substitution of physical facilities with digital telecommunications; rather, it's the 'sophisticated integration of digital networks with physical supply chains'.[52] For individuals, this means that we are increasingly mobile and distant from one another, as electronic information flows have not only replaced traditional bricks and mortar but have also extended the boundaries of person-to-person relationships far beyond the tangible and immediate. As social relations are stretched,

49 Ryan, *supra*, note 24 at 14.

50 Stewart T. Fleming, 'Biometrics: Past, Present and Future', in Rasool Azari (ed.), *Current Security Management and Ethical Issues of Information Technology* (Hershey, PA: IRM Press, 2003) 111 at 112.

51 Mitchell, *supra*, note 33 at 189.

52 *Ibid.* at 3.

courtesy of the new communication technologies, increasingly interactions and transactions become abstract and disembodied, which undermines the trust that once depended upon physical and temporal connectivity.[53]

Overview of the contents

This book straddles two spheres: biometrics and surveillance theory; and biometrics and surveillance law. By 'surveillance', we mean, *any systematic focus on personal information in order to influence, manage, entitle, or control those persons whose information is collected.*[54] In many aspects of our daily lives, our data are collected, stored, classified, revealed or sold to others in ways that influence our purchases, guide our choices, restrict our movements, ensure that we are fairly or unfairly treated and reward or punish our behaviour. As organizations become more digital, they seek more personal data in order to increase efficiency, productivity, oversight and control.

Thus, surveillance has to do with the efficient management of data within modern organizations, and involves the systematic monitoring of people or groups in order to regulate or govern their behaviour.[55] Surveillance is linked to economic and technological development, national security, colonial pasts and globalization. Surveillance processes occur differently in a variety of cultural contexts, as they are embedded within, brought about by and generative of social practices in a range of different environments.[56]

In countries of the global north, surveillance expanded with computerization from the 1970s onwards, especially from workers to consumers and travellers.[57] Since the 1980s, surveillance has become increasingly globalized as populations have become more mobile; and digital advancements greatly multiplied opportunities for surveillance. The impetus behind globalized surveillance was also greatly enhanced by the events of 9/11. Around the world, there is a growing demand for security, which drives much surveillance; and public and private agencies are increasingly linking up and sharing information within that arena.

The chapters explore not only the technical and administrative dimensions of biometric technologies, but also the historical, international, legal and political economy aspects. In particular, the book aims to understand how new identification processes contribute to surveillance practices through the classification of individuals, thus affecting their life experience, status and prospects. It provides an overview of biometric identification technologies and the impact of biometric surveillance (Chapters 2 & 3). Surveillance is understood as a cultural practice rather than as a peripheral tool mobilized by actors to deal with perceived

53 Lyon, *supra*, note 23 at 139.

54 Lyon, *supra*, note 34 at 2.

55 Lyon, *supra*, note 23 at 135.

56 Torin Monahan, 'Surveillance as a Cultural Practice', (2011) 52 *The Sociological Quarterly* 495 at 495.

57 *Ibid.*

problems or needs. This approach includes elements of popular culture, media, art, experience and relationships.

The next four Chapters (Chapters 4–7) offer multiple case studies on the growing reach of biometric surveillance in our lives, and the policy and market forces driving this expansion. Again, the focus is extended from those doing the surveillance to those subjected to it – evaluating these systems on a case-by-case basis and acknowledging that they are shaped by social practices in specific cultural contexts. A surveillance system is thus an instrument of control, social sorting, selection, exclusion and mobilization. The effects and experiences of surveillance differ by population and setting and the monitoring and control of people – the consequence of social sorting – results in the unequal treatment of individuals in just about every area of contemporary society (e.g. from accessing social services to travel to police and security). Not only does this stigmatize and marginalize those considered 'risky', it advantages those perceived to be 'at low risk', augmenting existing social inequalities.

Following this **Introduction, Chapter 2** begins with the history of biometric systems. Biometric security is a vast, global, multi-billion-dollar industry that offers seemingly simple solutions to many of the world's most vexing problems. Whether the motivating force is immigration control, anti-terrorism, electronic government or rising rates of identity theft, security technologies are playing a vital role. Biometrics is yet another tool in the arsenal of technologies aimed at securitizing mobile individuals – with scientific and mechanical objectivity – both inside and outside the nation-state. Biometrics thus comprises a whole administrative and technological regime, and a complex series of social and policy choices.

However, efforts to theorize biometrics have tended to overstate the degree to which these solutions are new. Biometric technologies are the latest development in a long line of mechanisms to measure the human body – from anthropometry to fingerprinting. Such technologies were used in late nineteenth-century colonial contexts in which identities and mobility were a persistent problem for foreign administrators and missionaries. So too in nineteenth-century European cities, when anthropometric science, fingerprinting, photography, coding and filing were means to 'fix' populations considered unruly and dangerous. In this sense, biometric security was intrinsic to the establishment of an orderly and disciplined society.

While historic uses have important lessons to teach, the contemporary world of biometric security has advanced rapidly. Biometric technologies are at the centre of securitization, industrialization and commodification; and they increasingly permeate everyday modern life.[58] Apple began implementing fingerprint-recognition software into its consumer products and it's now experimenting with the use of facial identification. Cars are also being fitted with biometrics. For commercial entities, and many consumers, these systems are simple, smart

58 Shoshanna Amielle Magnet, *When Biometrics Fail: Gender, Race and the Technologies of Identity* (Durham, NC: Duke University Press, 2011) at 8.

and secure. Through the use of a camera in store, for example, I can be identified through facial recognition, and if I can pay with my fingerprint, I don't need the intermediary of a phone.

However, the assessment of the effectiveness of any biometric system's processes should be measured against other criteria, including its trustworthiness and suitability within the larger social context in which it is used. Biometric science largely assumes that the human body is a stable, neutral repository of personal information from which we can collect and store data about identity.[59] It aims to turn the bodies of defendants, inmates, migrants, vagrants and elite travellers into discernible data. This has profound implications for an individual's ability to work, travel, collect benefits and more. As organizations find that they save money or increase their efficiency through digital means, they intensify their use of new technologies and techniques to identify specific categories of people; the result is that that some people are treated differently from others.

All identity systems carry consequential dangers as well as benefits. Various failures, including technical malfunction, the lack of objectivity and neutrality, and their link to contemporary societies of securitization and fear, render them highly questionable.[60] In the worst case, they undermine democratic principles, exacerbate racial disparity/tensions and threaten to harm large swathes of vulnerable people. The case studies explored in this book highlight these concerns and call into question the policy and market forces that fuel the expansion of biometric technologies in all aspects of our lives.

In **Chapter 3**, we examine some of the theoretical underpinnings of the surveillance state and question whether these conceptual approaches are still relevant in the modern age. We also consider the nexus between surveillance technology and popular culture. It has been widely argued that the collection of individual biometric data without adequate safeguards violates privacy rights. Yet the term 'privacy' is vast and amorphous – it has many complex meanings and implications, many of which rest on legal and cultural norms.

How a society chooses to define the 'right to privacy' and give legal meaning to the phrase is an important issue for both governments and individuals, particularly as advances in communications technology are dramatically improving information-gathering techniques. The protection and promotion of the right to privacy in the context of surveillance and the collection, use and disclosure of personal data is a matter of great interest and importance worldwide. Yet the 'right to privacy' remains ill-defined and has been subject to continuous re-evaluation since its legal conception in the late nineteenth century.

In **Chapter 4**, we look at how automated and information-based technologies are being used in the criminal justice system. Two components of actuarial justice feature strongly in the ongoing expansion of biometric identification systems. The first is the movement of extraordinary powers – usually reserved for

59 *Ibid.* at.2.
60 *Ibid.* at 4.

border areas such as airports – to interior parts of the nation-state.[61] The other is the use of profiling in the application of algorithmic risk-assessment tools and the search for pre-emptive justice.

Take, for example, the use of algorithms to decide a defendant's potential recidivism. Courts across the United States are already using this tool. There are a lot of factors that go into making the determination and the exact formula is proprietary. What we do know is that the technology promises to bring uniformity, fairness and scientific discipline to an area of law that has always been arbitrary and capricious.

Proponents argue that the software is ground-breaking and revolutionary. More importantly, an algorithm isn't biased. It appears to be efficient, precise and immune to lapses in judgement. Yet many have argued that the data is biased – it sentences African Americans and Latinos disproportionately compared to whites for the same crimes. Yet so do judges. So, the algorithm is said to be an improvement – a check on an already flawed system. But the algorithm has no historical context. It can't account for the factors that influence disproportionately high rates of incarceration for minorities across the United States. Algorithms also can't understand nuance and empathize.

Recent innovations have opened up new opportunities for both industry and governments to develop comprehensive identity-management systems that link individuals' identities throughout their entire lifetimes, in order to authenticate their interactions with different public and private agencies. In the next two chapters, we examine how states have cultivated this power to define who may move within and across their borders. Systems are now used to discern citizens from non-citizens at the borders of nation-states through biometric passports and visas, as well as through biometric registration and national identity cards. The 'actuarial logic of risk management' has pushed border controls outwards, both legally and physically, through E-passports, transnational interception, detention and deportation, all aimed at preventing unwanted arrivals before they occur.

In **Chapter 5**, we look at the implementation of the world's largest biometric database. The scheme is known as Aadhaar. Its aim is to assign everyone in India a random twelve-digit number that is unique to him or her and to link the person to the number with a photograph, fingerprints and iris scan. Aadhaar's logo is a red fingerprint, in the appearance of a rising sun, which symbolizes a promise that shines on all equally. This is appropriate considering that it had to collect and match not only demographic information but also fingerprints and iris scans for a population of 1.2 billion, the majority of whom are poor, uneducated and without any form of identification. And the technology undertaken for this scheme was previously untested on such a scale anywhere else in the world.

61 Dean Wilson, 'Biometrics, Borders and the Ideal Suspect', in Sharon Pickering and Leanne Weber (eds), *Borders, Mobility and Technologies of Control* (Dordrecht: Springer, 2006) 87 at 102.

Aadhaar is creating an entirely new segment of 'included' residents for the first time in history – those who are attaining portable ID. Citizen identification is, of course, one of the critical responsibilities of the modern state. All modern societies have developed systems to establish that their citizens 'are who they say they are'.[62] Those systems have evolved over time as new technologies and the demands of a complex, mobile and interconnected world have provided more sophisticated identity management systems, which are now often designed with high-tech biometric identifiers. These schemes can provide significant benefits both to citizens in their everyday affairs and to government in the administration of programs and services.[63] To this end, the United Nations Convention on the Rights of the Child provides that everyone has the right to have his or her identity registered at birth.[64]

But if you're shut out of that system, you can lose access to everything. For example, according to a report by activists from the non-profit Right to Food Campaign, there have been at least seven alleged starvation deaths in the eastern state of Jharkhand after a central government order in February 2017 made Aadhaar identification mandatory for accessing subsidized food grain through the Public Distribution System. In March of that year, the state ordered that it would nullify ration cards not linked to Aadhaar. And, as a result, many had their ration cards – linked to subsidized food and fuel – cancelled and were denied food for months on end when the Aadhaar-enabled point-of-sale machine at their local ration shop failed to authenticate their biometrics.

India's plunge into national biometric identification comes as the drive towards secure identity is happening all over the world. Indeed, many countries are seeking to improve their identity infrastructures, largely owing to global fears about terrorism and long-term trends towards e-Government. The Aadhaar experiment is therefore being studied by governments in other countries, eager to see if the creation of a national biometric database solves many of their border security and crime problems.

The World Bank estimates that one in seven people – an estimated 1.1 billion people globally – can't prove their identity, most of whom are in Africa and Asia and are under the age of 18.[65] We have seen that certain populations, such as people living in poverty, and minority groups, are particularly vulnerable to exclusion from essential programs and benefits. Inclusion and access, rather than ownership and autonomy, are the essential means of structuring human rela-

62 Colin J. Bennett & David Lyon, 'Preface and Acknowledgements', in Colin J. Bennett and David Lyon (eds), *Playing the Identity Card: Surveillance, Security and Identification in Global Perspective* (New York: Routledge, 2008) xi at xi.

63 Thorburn, *supra*, note 15 at 19.

64 Article 7(1).

65 Joseph J. Atick, Alan Harold Gelb, Seda Pahlavooni, Elena Gasol Ramos & Zaid Safdar, 'Digital Identity Toolkit – A Guide for Stakeholders in Africa', (Washington, DC: World Bank Group, 2014). Available online at: http://documents.worldbank.org/curated/en/147961468203357928/Digital-identity-toolkit-a-guide-for-stakeholders-in-Africa.

tionships today. Access control lists, which are just one example of this phenomenon, confer enormous amounts of wealth and power on some, while excluding others.

As discussed in **Chapter 6**, the identification of individuals at border checkpoints like airports, roads and sea ports, is vital for any country's sovereignty and national security. Yet today, the 'problem' of uncontrolled borders signals the emergence of a tide of 'global vagrants' who represent disorder and embody the many insecurities arising from globalizing trends in late modernity. This forms part of a larger political process focused on risk mitigation, exclusion and fortification, whereby entire populations are labelled suspicious and preventatively immobilized. National borders are strengthened, as citizens define themselves as distinct from, and even superior to, outsiders.

The technologically enhanced monitoring of suspect populations lies at the heart of contemporary surveillance societies, where rights and freedoms, otherwise considered essential for liberal democracies, are routinely challenged. The boundaries of national borders in the Western liberal states are increasingly ill-defined – it is not clear how far they extend inside and outside the territories of the states themselves.

Chapter 7 looks at global marketplaces of surveillance. While the global marketplaces that flourish on the Internet appear to be expansive, free-flowing and limitless – the very opposite of border enclosures – we can identify many of the same control mechanisms at work. We live so much of our lives online, and share so much of our personal data, that we no longer know where our real *selves* begin and end. Without physical ownership of the networks, end points, or data, and without a clear sense of exposure, we are like the border migrant – lost and aimless, even though we are under surveillance at all times.

The notion of total visibility has its origins in religious devotion and had its darkest moments in the Totalitarian regimes of the twentieth century. Yet the fascination with extensive transparency has been thoroughly absorbed and fetishized in modern capitalist systems which promote reality television, celebrity-obsessed confessional culture and rampant yet clandestine data collection. With the global rise of social media and an explosion in online communications, consumers now provide a handful of tech giants all the information they need to create and sustain powerful markets. Surveillance is becoming ubiquitous, not only for its commercial sway, but for its capacity to influence and undermine so many aspects of democratic life, as well as the innate capacity for human flourishing.

The proliferation of data and access nodes means that there are ever-greater numbers of vulnerabilities, through which identifications may be stolen, and we now live in constant fear of the network infiltrator – whether he be a homicidal terrorist or a rogue insider. The truth be told, there isn't a database that hasn't been misused by the very people entrusted with keeping that information safe: police officers have looked up the criminal records of their neighbours; state employees have sold driving records to private investigators; motor vehicle bureau employees have sold fake driving licences.[66] And this kind of abuse doesn't require the malicious actions of an insider if the information stored in the database is not secure.[67] Indeed, the cost of keeping all this data secure is likely to swell into billions upon billions of dollars.

And, as high as the financial costs may be, the social costs are potentially astronomical. These databases may be consolidated, creating wide-ranging electronic activity records that can be used to track our activities and hold us accountable for our behaviour. Indeed, our data *is* under constant surveillance, not only by governments, but also by corporations that make enormous amounts of money exploiting it. The notion of discrimination features broadly as a global surveillance issue in areas of policing, migration and national security; but increasingly we're seeing it in the domain of consumer capitalism. We're watched so that we can be manipulated; and behind the scenes, algorithms are quietly making choices for us every day. Thus, the costs to our personal freedom are potentially greater than the amount spent on ongoing security and maintenance of these systems.

In conclusion, in **Chapter 8**, we look at the way forwards. Why should we be concerned about the lack of oversight, statutory restriction, and the inadequacy of constitutional principles in the area of biometric identification? The reason is that these technologies pose a unique challenge to liberty and privacy. The level of intrusiveness is entirely different from what has come before. It alters the type of surveillance that can occur; and it allows for prolonged, widespread surveillance to an extent not previously contemplated.

It is clear that increased regulation is needed to deal with the social realities of widespread biometric identification systems, and the ubiquitous surveillance and data-sharing practices they facilitate. Experience tells us that one of the principal ways that we increase transparency is through increased oversight – we need to impose rules, but first we need to ensure that the rules we're imposing are the correct ones. In addition to furnishing users with powerful rights, lawmakers also need to impose responsibilities upon information-gathering entities. Both public- and private-sector entities will be less inclined to abuse their power and misuse our data if they have to be accountable for these practices.

On the other hand, the big tech giants such as Facebook have been lobbying for a more liberal interpretation of privacy laws. But recent events have caused people to realize just how vulnerable their personal data is, and many are becoming more forthright in their demands for the highest level of privacy protections. It remains to be seen how these pressures will be brought to bear on the largely unlimited surveillance and data-gathering practices of big tech companies, which have been allowed to operate with regulatory impunity and little or no competition in the marketplace.

66 Bruce Schneier, *Beyond Fear: Thinking Sensibly About Security in an Uncertain World* (New York: Springer, 2003) at 205.

67 *Ibid.* at 206.

Bibliography

Joseph J. Atick, Alan Harold Gelb, Seda Pahlavooni, Elena Gasol Ramos & Zaid Safdar, 'Digital Identity Toolkit – A Guide for Stakeholders in Africa', (Washington, DC: World Bank Group, 2014). Available online at: http://documents.worldbank.org/curated/en/147961468203357928/Digital-identity-toolkit-a-guide-for-stakeholders-in-Africa.

Lisa Austin, 'Privacy and the Question of Technology', (2003) 22 *Law and Philosophy* 119.

Colin J. Bennett & David Lyon, 'Playing the ID Card – Understanding the Significance of Identity Card Systems', in Colin J. Bennett & David Lyon (eds), *Playing the Identity Card: Surveillance, Security and Identification in Global Perspective* (New York: Routledge, 2008) 3.

Colin J. Bennett & David Lyon, 'Preface and Acknowledgements', in Colin J. Bennett & David Lyon (eds), *Playing the Identity Card: Surveillance, Security and Identification in Global Perspective* (New York: Routledge, 2008) xi.

Danah Boyd & Kate Crawford, 'Critical Questions for Big Data', (2012) 15(5) *Information, Communication & Society* 662.

Joe Celko, *Joe Celko's Complete Guide to NoSQL* (Burlington, NJ: Elsevier Science, 2013).

Kyle Chayka, 'Biometric Surveillance Means Someone Is Always Watching', *Newsweek*, 17 April 2014.

Pam Dixon, 'A Failure to "Do No Harm" – India's Aadhaar Biometric ID Program and its Inability to Protect Privacy in Relation to Measures in Europe and the U.S.,' (2017) 7(4) *Health & Technology* 539.

Final Report of the Select Committee to Study Governmental Operations with Respect to Intelligence Activities (Church Committee Report), 26 April 1976. Available online at: www.bibliotecapleyades.net/sociopolitica/esp_sociopol_mj12_22.htm.

Stewart T. Fleming, 'Biometrics: Past, Present and Future', in Rasool Azari (ed.), *Current Security Management and Ethical Issues of Information Technology* (Hershey, PA: IRM Press, 2003) 111.

Douglas Fox, 'Villages Leapfrog the Grid with Biometrics and Mobile Money', *The Christian Science Monitor*, 14 April 2011.

Alan Gleb & Charles Kenny, 'The Case for Big Brother (Foreign Policy)', *CGD in the News*, 4 March 2013.

Glen Greenwald, 'The Digital Surveillance State: Vast, Secret, and Dangerous', in Peter P. Swire & Kenesa Ahmad (eds), *Privacy and Surveillance with New Technologies* (New York: International Debate Education Association, 2012) 35.

Glenn Greenwald, 'The Surveillance State Thrives on Fear', in Peter P. Swire & Kenesa Ahmad (eds), *Privacy and Surveillance with New Technologies* (New York: International Debate Education Association, 2012) 62.

Michael Hardy, 'Watergate Scandal: Public Distrust of Government Begins', *Federal Times*, 1 December 2015.

International Telecommunications Union (ITU), *Review of National Identity Programs*, 2016.

Orin Kerr, 'The Fourth Amendment and New Technologies: Constitutional Myths and the Case for Caution', (2003) 102 *Michigan Law Review* 801.

David Lyon, 'Globalizing Surveillance', (2004) 19(2) *Comparative and Sociological Perspectives* 135.

David Lyon, 'Filtering Flows, Friends and Foes', in Mark B. Salter (ed.), *Politics at the Airport* (Minneapolis: University of Minnesota Press, 2008) 29.

David Lyon, 'National IDs in a Global World: Surveillance, Security, and Citizenship', (2010) 42 *Case Western Reserve Journal of International Law* 607.

David Lyon, 'Surveillance, Snowden, and Big Data: Capacities, Consequences, Critique', (2014) 1(2) *Big Data & Society* 1.Shoshanna Amielle Magnet, *When Biometrics Fail: Gender, Race and the Technologies of Identity* (Durham, NC: Duke University Press, 2011).

Luther Martin, 'Biometrics', in John R. Vacca (ed.), *Cyber Security and IT Infrastructure Protection* (Waltham, MA: Elsevier, 2014) 151.

Katina Michael & M. G. Michael, *Innovative Automatic Identification and Location-Based Services: From Bar Codes to Chip Implants* (Hershey, PA: IGI Global, 2009).

William J. Mitchell, *ME* ++ (Cambridge, MA: MIT Press, 2004).

Torin Monahan, 'Surveillance as a Cultural Practice', (2011) 52 *The Sociological Quarterly* 495.

Joseph N. Pato & Lynette I. Millett (eds), *Biometric Recognition: Challenges and Opportunities* (Washington, DC: The National Academic Press, 2010).

Mark B. Salter & Geneviève Piché, 'The Securitization of the US–Canada Border in American Political Discourse', (2011) 44(4) *Canadian Journal of Political Science* 929.

Bruce Schneier, *Beyond Fear: Thinking Sensibly About Security in an Uncertain World* (New York: Springer, 2003).

Bruce Schneier, *Data and Goliath: The Hidden Battles to Collect Your Data and Control Your World* (New York: W. W. Norton & Co., 2015).Richa Singh, Mayank Vatsa & Phalguni Gupta, 'Biometrics', in Margherita Pagani (ed.), *Encyclopedia of Multimedia Technology and Networking* (2nd edn) (Hershey, PA: Information Science Reference, 2008) 121.

Daniel Solove, 'Digital Dossiers and Dissipation of Fourth Amendment Privacy' (2001) 75 *Southern California Law Review* 1083.

The Economist, 'Learning to Live with Big Brother', in Peter P. Swire & Kenesa Ahmad (eds), *Privacy and Surveillance with New Technologies* (New York: International Debate Education Association, 2012).

Malcom Thorburn, 'Identification, Surveillance and Profiling: On the Uses and Abuses of Citizen Data', in I. Dennis & G. R. Sullivan (eds), *Seeking Security: Pre-empting the Commission of Criminal Harms* (Oxford: Hart Publishing, 2011) 15.

Dean Wilson, 'Biometrics, Borders and the Ideal Suspect', in Sharon Pickering & Leanne Weber (eds), *Borders, Mobility and Technologies of Control* (Dordrecht: Springer, 2006) 87.

Case Law

U.S. v. Jones, 132 S. Ct. 945 (2012).

2 Historical uses of biometrics

Introduction

The term *biometrics* refers to the measurement of physical features of the human body.[1] Put differently, biometrics is, '[t]he science of automatic identification or identity verification of individuals using [unique] physiological or behavioural characteristics'.[2] It's an *automated* process that doesn't require another human being to make a comparison. Biometric systems can also function without active input, cooperation or even knowledge on the part of the subject.

With all the fascinating applications of this technology, it's no wonder that biometrics has been a source of inspiration for sci-fi movies and television for decades. Your iris scan unlocks the door of your house. Your fingerprint lets you into your office. In essence, you are your own key.[3] Although biometrics may seem like the stuff of the future, it's actually the oldest form of identification.[4] From a very young age, most humans can recognize a familiar face, voice or movement.[5] When we recognize people, we recognize their physical features. Our ancestors used this type of authentication even before they fully evolved into humans.[6]

The first known examples of biometric identification occurred in Ancient Egypt at the time of Pharaoh Khaefre (2558BC–2532BC) – these early Egyptians used body measurements to ensure people were who they claimed to be.[7] Administrators developed a system to identify workers and ensure that they received their allocated food allowance, and no more.[8] The system recorded the

1 Marcus Smith, Monique Mann & Gregor Urbas, *Biometrics, Crime and Security* (New York: Routledge, 2018) at 2.

2 John R. Vacca, *Biometric Technologies and Verification Systems* (Burlington, MA: Butterworth-Heinemann, 2007).

3 Bruce Schneier, 'Biometrics: Uses and Abuses', *Communications of the ACM*, August 1999. Available online at: www.schneier.com/essays/archives/1999/08/biometrics_uses_and.html.

4 *Ibid.*

5 Pato & *Millett*, *supra*, note 5 at 15.

6 Schneier, *supra*, note 65 at 187.

7 Smith et al., *supra*, note 68, at 3.

8 *Ibid.*

distinctive physical and behavioural characteristics of the workers, along with their name, age and place of residence.[9]

Fingerprints were used as early as AD 700 in ancient China, as well as India and Japan, as signatures for contracts.[10] In those cases, fingerprints were pressed in clay to form a distinctive mark that could then be used to identify a person. Fingerprint technologies were further developed in Europe in the nineteenth century for law enforcement.[11] Early digital biometric research also focused on fingerprinting; and one of the first of such technologies on the market was a hand geometry reader developed during the 1960s.[12] Biometric retinal scanning evolved soon thereafter, making its commercial debut in the 1970s.[13] The sophistication of the techniques used have vastly increased over time. Yet the core principle remains the same: biometric recognition, even if replicated by machines, only works for people who are known to us – it can't help identify strangers.

Biometric security follows a standardized set of criteria – the so-called 'seven pillars' – by which to judge the suitability and efficacy of particular characteristics and systems.[14] These include: (1) *universality*, i.e. that all humans share the characteristic, (2) *distinctiveness*, that for each person these features are unique to a significant degree and (3) *permanence*, that the characteristics are permanent and will remain largely unchanged throughout life.[15] The pillars also include standardized ratings according to (4) *collectability*, i.e. that the biometric may be efficiently collected, (5) *performance*, or the accuracy of matching, (6) *acceptability*, the acceptability of the system to users and finally, (7) *security*, the degree to which the system is open to circumvention or 'spoofing'.[16] Some biometrics, such as fingerprints, rank very high; other biometrics may score well in terms of some of the pillars but not others.

Any biometric system has to address two fundamental problems: verification ('is this person who he claims to be?'); and identification ('who is this person?').[17] The differences between these two types of systems can affect how quickly the system operates and how accurate it is. Under a *verification system*, an individual presents herself as a specific person (i.e. 'I am Alice').[18] The system checks that person's biometric data, such as a fingerprint, against the data that it already has on file for Alice to try and find a match. Instead of answering the general

9 *Ibid.*

10 Celko, *supra*, note 6 at 132.

11 Angela Liberatore, 'Balancing Security and Democracy, and the Role of Expertise: Biometrics Politics in the European Union', (2007) 13 *European Journal on Criminal Policy and Research* 109 at 113.

12 Magnet, *supra*, note 57 at 53.

13 *Ibid.*

14 Mark Maguire, 'Vanishing Borders and Biometric Citizens', in Gabriella Lazaridis (ed.), *Security, Insecurity and Migration in Europe* (London: Routledge, 2011) at 32.

15 *Ibid.*

16 *Ibid.*

17 Jennifer Lynch, 'From Fingerprints to DNA: Biometric Data Collection in U.S. Immigrant Communities and Beyond', (22 May 2012) at 5.

18 *Ibid.*

question, 'Who is this person?' the system only has to answer the much easier question: 'Is this person who she claims to be?' And since it only has to compare the biometric to the reference stored in the database, it can generate accurate results relatively quickly, even when the size of the database increases.[19]

When it comes to an *identification system*, it has to answer a much more difficult question: 'Who is this random person?'[20] It seeks to identify who generated the biometric; and thus must check the biometric presented against all others in the database. This makes the decision trickier and less accurate. Forensic databases, such as those whereby a government agent tries to identify a latent fingerprint or DNA discarded at a crime scene, are examples of an identification system.[21] Essential to both types of biometric systems are the capture and storage of biometric samples in some sort of 'reference database' and the comparison of new biometric data to make what's called a 'recognition decision'.[22]

Once the 'recognition decision' is made, certain actions are taken based on the inference that one is dealing with a person who is known or unknown. The outcome is that the person genuinely belongs to a group with certain access rights, or that they don't belong to such a group, and should thus be denied access. In many systems, these processes are perceived as being the same thing; but knowing who someone is and identifying what she is permitted to do are completely different.[23]

Types of biometric systems

Early digital biometrics systems centred on access control; and they were used in banks and other secured spaces, such as US military facilities and prisons.[24] Today, these systems are increasingly used to regulate access to information, services, benefits and places. Not all biometrics are equally suitable for use in each possible application; yet new forms of physical and behavioural biometrics are emerging all the time.

Biometric-based identification or identity verification systems can collect and analyse 'hard biometrics', which are also known as 'primary biometrics'.[25] 'Hard', or 'primary', biometrics include 'hand or finger images, facial characteristics, and iris recognition'.[26] In contrast, 'soft' or 'secondary' biometrics are anatomical or behavioural characteristics that provide some information about the identity of a person, but do not provide sufficient evidence to precisely determine

19 *Ibid.*
20 *Ibid.*
21 *Ibid.*
22 Pato & Millett, *supra*, note 5 at 2.
23 Schneier, *supra*, note 65, at 184.
24 Magnet, *supra*, note 57 at 53.
25 Margaret Hu, 'Bulk Biometric Metadata Collection', (2018) 96 *North Carolina Law Review* 1425 at 1440.
26 Vacca, *supra*, note 69 at 590.

identity.[27] Such systems can use digital analysis of age, height, weight, race or ethnicity, skin and hair colour, scars, birthmarks and tattoos.[28]

Fingerprint identification

Fingerprints are one of the oldest and most trusted forms of biometrics, especially for law enforcement. This technique was first developed in the late eighteenth century to identify individuals based on the unique patterns of their fingertips.[29] The advantage is the inherent uniqueness of fingerprints. Fingerprints are developed within the first seven months of gestation and are uniquely held by every human, even identical twins.[30] Today, fingerprint scanning accounts for at least half of the biometric market worldwide.[31]

Automated fingerprint identification systems have been recognized as one of the most important forensic science advances in the twentieth century – next to DNA typing.[32] Today, the fingerprint-extraction devices commonly used are ten print slap live scans, on which the user places the four fingers from each hand and then the two thumbs.[33] For authentication, single finger readers are sufficient; however, accuracy is dependent on the need to ensure high-quality capture which may be affected by external factors, such as dirt or moisture, as well as the fingerprint sensor, and image quality.

Another drawback is that fingerprints can change over time with age, injury, heavy labour or damage. Given that many of world's poorest people work in manual labour, relying on fingerprints in developing countries such as India substantially increases the error rates.[34] In such cases, multiple biometrics promote inclusion and foster accuracy.

Facial recognition

Facial recognition is another non-invasive method, which relies on algorithms to identify similarities in facial features, such as geometry and appearance.[35] At the initial enrolment stage, a digital photograph is taken of the subject's face. An algorithm then converts the photograph into a digital template by comparing the distances between features of the subject's face, such as eyes, nose, lips

27 Karthik Nandakumar & Anil K. Jain, 'Soft Biometrics' in Stan Z. Li and Anil K. Jain (eds), *Encyclopedia of Biometrics* (New York: Springer, 2009) 1235 at 1235.

28 *Ibid.*

29 Smith et al., *supra*, note 68 at 1.

30 *Ibid.* at 6.

31 *Ibid.* at 24.

32 Magnet, *supra*, note 57 at 55.

33 Frances Zelazny, 'The Evolution of India's UID Program', Center for Global Development, 8 August 2012 at 13.

34 *Ibid.* at 8.

35 Singh et al., *supra*, note 7 at 123.

and chin.[36] When a verification is sought, the system takes a photograph of the subject's face and compares it with the image on file to determine if the two are spatially and geometrically similar to constitute a match. By 2014, face recognition algorithms were already outperforming people.[37] Facial recognition has thus been integrated into all sorts of documents and verification systems, including passports, identity cards and CCTV.[38]

It is widely used for border control and police have also been using smart CCTV technologies to scan the faces of attendees at concerts and sporting matches, comparing them to large databases of known criminals and persons of interest.[39] Law enforcement are also harvesting images of people from the Internet, particularly social media. Facial recognition technologies are similarly being integrated into police body-worn cameras, drones and police robots.[40] For these purposes, it's an ideal technique because it's highly unobtrusive and can be carried out from a distance without the knowledge or consent of the subject. However, given that individuals' appearances can change significantly over time, for example through age, illness, weight gain and surgery, facial recognition is an imperfect form of measurement.

Iris recognition

Iris scans are useful because iris patterns are unique for each individual. However, they are restricted by the need for expensive imaging technologies.[41] For iris enrolment, the devices are typically handheld and mobile, which allows the user to hold one up to his or her eyes like binoculars – this helps to ensure that light doesn't filter through and the iris is captured properly.[42]

The iris is fully formed by the eighth month of gestation and remains the same throughout one's lifetime.[43] Every iris is unique, even those of identical twins, and since iris recognition technology is not sight-dependent, even the blind can be enrolled. India's population contains 15 million of the world's 37 million blind people, their condition often related to cataracts.[44] While blindness does not prohibit iris capture *per se*, cataracts do affect the ability to properly capture the iris; and a substantial number of people in India lack eyes as a result of disease or accidents.[45]

From a security perspective, iris recognition is beneficial because the iris cannot be altered in the way that facial features can, and it cannot be masked in

36 Smith et al., *supra*, note 68 at 7.
37 Schneier, *supra*, note 32 at 29.
38 Smith et al., *supra*, note 68 at 7.
39 *Ibid.* at 57.
40 *Ibid.*
41 Singh et al., *supra*, note 7 at 123.
42 Zelazny, *supra*, note 100 at 13.
43 *Ibid.* at 9.
44 *Ibid.* at 15.
45 *Ibid.*

a way that fingerprints may be.[46] It is also becoming increasingly common in national security, military and border control applications, and having a database with these biometrics can prove very valuable over the long term. However, like fingerprints, irises are metrics that can change with circumstance and age.

DNA identification

DNA can be recovered from most biological material. The most common human biological materials submitted for testing are blood and semen, as well as hair, saliva, skin and sweat.[47] Collecting and analysing DNA evidence is now well established in the field of criminal forensics, and the extensive use of this technique in television crime dramas has vastly increased public awareness about it. Through their exposure to these fictional accounts, people have come to think of DNA as a foolproof means of identifying criminals.[48] Clearly, the need to identify and 'de-anonymize' the individual has long been essential to solving crime. Yet the techniques that make it possible to identify a suspect using his or her DNA have only been around since 1985.[49]

DNA is intrusive because it requires a form of tissue, blood or bodily sample to be collected and analysed. Yet devices that can be connected to a smartphone and provide analysis and a DNA profile within ten minutes have been developed and are expected to be widely available within the next five years.[50] DNA has exonerated many people convicted and awaiting execution on death row. It's now routinely used in criminal investigations, particularly sexual assault cases and homicides, where the offender can easily deposit DNA at the scene of the crime or directly on the victim.[51]

Yet there have been cases of DNA mistakenly implicating someone in a crime. Researchers have come across a phenomenon known as 'secondary transfer'. Once it's out in the world, DNA doesn't always stay put; and hence some people's DNA has appeared on things that they've never touched.[52] The slippery nature of DNA has serious implications for forensic investigations. After all, if traces of our DNA can make their way to a crime scene we never visited, aren't we all possible suspects? Forensic DNA has other faults: complex mixtures of many DNA profiles can be wrongly interpreted, certainty statistics are often miscalculated, and DNA analysis robots have sometimes been worked past the limits of their sensitivity.[53]

46 *Ibid.* at 9.

47 Smith et al., *supra*, note 68 at 38.

48 The Economist, 'The "CSI Effect"' 22 April 2010.

49 William Harris, 'How DNA Evidence Works' *HowStuffWorks.com*, 18 January 2001. Available online at: https://science.howstuffworks.com/life/genetic/dna-evidence.htm.

50 Smith et al., *supra*, note 68 at 49.

51 *Ibid.* at 7.

52 Katie Worth, 'Framed for Murder by His Own DNA', *Frontline*, 19 April 2018. Available online at: www.pbs.org/wgbh/frontline/article/framed-for-murder-by-his-own-dna/.

53 *Ibid.*

Radio-frequency identification (RFID)

Innovative sensors, such as RFID, have brought new capabilities to crime, national security, terrorism, warfare and privacy. RFID was patented in 1983 and is a wireless low-energy device that can be embedded into any object to make it intelligent and able to interact with RFID readers.[54] There are many ordinary uses of RFID technologies, such as the security card you swipe to access your office or a hotel room, your subway pass, the box you use to pay for highway tolls, and so on – it has become one of the most convenient gateways to the omnipresent Internet of Things[55] There is nothing more powerful – in terms of its potential for the continuous tracking and monitoring of identity and location in real time – than the tiny RFID chip implanted in the body of a human being.[56]

Why would someone want an RFID chip embedded in their body? As with many of the biometric tools discussed here, convenience and ease of access are the overriding motivators. In 2017, a Sydney man had the chip from his train pass inserted into his hand and is now using the technology – tapping the card implanted under his skin – to make riding public transit easier.[57] Others have had chips implanted to enable access their front door and car door and to log into their computer.[58] Yet there are other more sinister examples of chip implants being forced upon people for the purpose of segregation and surveillance, leading to concerns about the potential for 'electronic apartheid'.[59]

In Papua New Guinea, the legislative council debated a proposal that would have seen people living with HIV/AIDS forced to have microchips implanted under their skin so authorities could monitor their actions; and similar proposals have been raised in the European Union around the need to register and 'tag' asylum-seekers and illegal immigrants.[60] Singapore has explored the idea of using microchips to contain those with Severe Acute Respiratory Syndrome (SARS), and proposals have been discussed in other parts of the world for using RFID tags to identify victims of natural disasters or terrorist incidents.[61] The US Defense Advanced Research Projects Agency (DARPA) is already working on microchips that can be implanted into soldiers' brains to make them more resilient in warfare.[62]

Not only have these devices been proposed for managing 'national security risks', some parents have been thrusting wearable tracking devices upon

54 Marc Goodman, *Future Crimes* (New York: Doubleday, 2015) at 230.

55 *Ibid.* at 231.

56 Michael & Michael, *supra*, note 22 at 465.

57 Nick Dole, 'Sydney Man Has Opal Card Implanted Into Hand to Make Catching Public Transport Easier', *ABC News*, 27 June 2017.

58 Michael & Michael, *supra*, note 22 at 465.

59 *Ibid.* at 468.

60 *Ibid.*

61 *Ibid.*

62 Richard Gray, 'Is the US Navy Planning to Implant People with Microchips? Officials Consult Presidential Candidate on 'Merging Humans and Machines'. *Daily Mail*, 17 June 2016.

their children in an attempt to keep them safe from predators. In the United Kingdom, a woman had her seven-year-old daughter implanted with a chip to track her movements.[63] One can easily see that in the hands of overprotective parents, these surveillance controls might become a digital umbilical cord they refuse to let go, with potentially tragic consequences.

Other forms of biometric identification

Other forms of biometric data, such as gait, which can be measured unobtrusively at a distance, are still in development; but increasingly, everything from your palm print to veins inside your hand, to the shape of your ears, to your body odour could be used to identify you. Companies like the online education platform Coursera are using keystroke dynamics – measuring the variances with which an individual types characters on his or her keyboard – to ensure the same student 'attends' each virtual class before a certificate of completion is issued.[64]

Yet to date no biometric system has been shown to be foolproof or known to be completely stable across all individuals and groups.[65] The technologies are different, and some are more reliable than others, although they will all improve in the very near future.[66] Direct biometric data are better than others – think of an iris scan, or fingerprint, or even a heartbeat. They usually have a better probability than indirect biometric data of establishing a direct correlation between the identity of the individual and the biometric.[67]

Voice recognition involves reading the acoustic signals of a person's voice and converting it to a unique digital code that can be stored in a template. It's not very reliable, however, because voices can change over time and be altered by environmental factors, like background noise.[68] Despite the fact that voice recognition is not without its problems, companies are already building vast recorded-voice databases of consumers – in an effort to fight fraud – that can be used to ensure the person on the phone matches the original biometric voiceprint collected.[69]

Some kinds of biometric data are more secure than others because they can't easily be mimicked, stolen or given away. An iris scan, for example, would be difficult to forge; but then again, some people could mimic a voice relatively easily, and with sophisticated computer software, it's possible to make a face that looks a lot like someone else.[70] Biometrics are unique but in many cases they're easy to figure out – I leave my fingerprint on everything I touch, my voice has

63 Michael & Michael, *supra*, note 22 at 470.
64 Goodman, *supra*, note 121 at 282.
65 Pato & Millett, *supra*, note 5 at 4.
66 Schneier, *supra*, note 70.
67 Fleming, *supra*, note 49 at 112.
68 Singh et al., *supra*, note 7 at 123.
69 Goodman, *supra*, note 121 at 282.
70 Schneier, *supra*, note 70.

been heard by countless individuals and my face is visible to millions of potential viewers online. As Bruce Schneier has stated, 'biometrics aren't secrets'.[71]

On the other hand, some biometric measurements, such as the human heartbeat, are extremely private and therefore difficult to replicate. The Nymi Band now offers a way for the consumer to use her unique electrocardio rhythm as a secure payment and unlocking technique: the wearable band uses a biometric authentication technology that lets it confirm the user's identity by monitoring the unique rhythm of her heartbeat and matching it to an enabled device through Bluetooth Low Energy (BLE).[72] The company has teamed up with Mastercard to test its product commercially. The Nymi Unlock App also allows users to unlock a computer, smart phone, car or house using the band instead of a password.[73]

Motivations for using biometrics

In the drive to secure identity in our increasingly complex and interconnected world, biometric technologies are thriving. Billions of people around the globe now share this data as part of their daily lives. Yet biometric technologies that enable widespread surveillance are likely to cause a shift in social norms. If everyone's bad behaviour is broadcast to everyone else, we may become accustomed – and therefore desensitized – to seeing people misbehave; or conversely, we may become paranoid and obedient automatons.[74] Furthermore, as biometric systems become increasingly commonplace, and are used for securing ever more personal transactions, they are likely to be targeted for attack, with the potential for the underlying data to be stolen, corrupted or misused.

The history of identification reveals both inclusionary and exclusionary features; and yet there are many examples in recent history when human data has been used for offensive means. During the British administration of India, in 1858, William Herschel pioneered the use of fingerprints in Bengal so that white officials could 'tell the difference' between their Indian subjects.[75] Later, after Belgium established control over the African Ruanda-Urundi territory, they employed a system of rule based on the principles of racial hierarchy. The implementation of the 'ethnic' identity card in 1933 has been cited as an instrument of the process of racialization by the Belgian colonial authorities.[76]

71 *Ibid.*

72 eeDesignIt Editorial Team, 'Ditch the Credit Cards and Fingerprints, Pay with Your Heartbeat Instead', 7 September 2017. Available online at: www.eedesignit.com/ditch-the-credit-cards-and-fingerprints-pay-with-your-heartbeat-instead/.

73 *Ibid.*

74 Matthew Hutson, 'Even Bugs Will Be Bugged', *The Atlantic*, November, 2016.

75 David Lyon, 'Biometrics, Identification and Surveillance', (2008) 22(9) *Bioethics* 499 at 504.

76 Rosamunde van Brakel & Xavier Van Kerckhoven, 'The Emergence of the Identity Card in Belgium and its Colonies', Available online at: www.researchgate.net/publication/258763996_The_emergence_of_the_identity_card_in_Belgium_and_its_colonies at 8.

Before the colonial era, Rwandans were identified by their nationality and every person belonged to a clan comprised of three social groups: the Tutsi, Hutu and Twa.[77] By adding the ethnic category to the identity card, Belgian leaders constructed separate races; thus, 'their usage by colonial and postcolonial governments ... helped to transform the manner in which Rwandans regarded identity'.[78] The colonial authorities also used blood tests and measurements, including weight, nose width, nasal and facial characteristics, to conclude that the Tutsi were thinner, taller and appeared more European. It was official policy that Tutsi were given preference when appointing domestic political authorities. Assuring a Tutsi monopoly of power created a crucial element in sorting and controlling the population, and produced distinct social and political categories.

The Belgians also set the stage for future conflict in Rwanda. However, they were not implementing a 'divide and rule' strategy so much as putting into effect the racist convictions common to most early-twentieth-century Europeans.[79] Still, the identity cards in Rwanda's colonial past played a significant role in the 1994 genocide, which was mainly conducted by Hutus and resulted in the death of between 500,000 and one million Tutsis.[80]

Identity cards provided an easy way to identify Tutsi. Death squads guarding barricades demanded that everyone show their card before being allowed to pass.[81] Those with 'Tutsi' marked on their card were generally killed on the spot; and those without cards were assumed to be Tutsi and murdered.[82] To escape the genocide, many Tutsi used official connections or bribes to receive false identity cards that marked them as Hutu.[83] By 1996, the Rwandan identity card was formally abolished.[84]

During the Nazi regime, many legal and medical professionals supported the compulsory sterilization and euthanasia of the physically and mentally ill, and subsequently, the killing of 'inferior' races. They did this by applying scientifically invalid conclusions from evolutionary biology; yet many felt that what they were doing was correct from a moral and scientific position. Their actions were a colossal error based on what today we may characterize as 'pseudoscience', but which at the time was considered accurate by many.

For example, in 1865, Sir Francis Galton maintained that physical appearance could indicate criminal tendency. He saw fingerprints as a way of classifying 'hereditary' criminals. Galton coined the term 'eugenics' (a term rooted in the Greek 'good in birth' or 'noble in heredity'), which is the study of or belief in

77 *Ibid.*

78 Timothy Longman, 'Identity Cards, Ethnic Self-Perception, and Genocide in Rwanda', in Jane Caplan and John C. Torpey (eds), *Documenting Individual Identity: The Development of State Practices in the Modern World* (Princeton, NJ: Princeton University Press, 2001) 345–358 at 347.

79 van Brakel & Van Kerckhoven, *supra*, note 143 at 10.

80 *Ibid.* at 1.

81 Longman, *supra*, note 145 at 355.

82 *Ibid.*

83 *Ibid.*

84 Lyon & Bennett, *supra*, note 30 at 8.

the possibility of improving the qualities of the human population, especially by discouraging reproduction among those presumed to have inheritable undesirable traits. Galton also first used the term 'biometry' in 1901 to 'describe the application of biology to the modern world of statistics' and made contributions to fingerprint and facial biometric analysis.[85]

For much of the nineteenth century, European criminology did not examine the criminal body for individual identity but rather for anthropological type. The Italian 'positive school' of psychiatrist Cesare Lombroso developed a theory about the 'born criminal'. Over the course of undertaking some three thousand anthropometric measurements, he claimed to have found biological traits of criminals, including unusual size or shape of the head, facial asymmetry, long arms, too big or too small ears, skin colour and many others.

The British strain of eugenics – originating with Galton – was also embraced by American practitioners during the nineteenth century, with the focus on eliminating what they saw as negative characteristics of the poor, including low intelligence, criminality and uninhibited sexuality.[86] From a Carnegie-Institution-funded laboratory in New York state, and eugenics offices throughout the United States, social scientists filled out lengthy questionnaires, took photographs and fingerprints, measured heads, plotted family trees and filled logbooks with descriptions like 'imbecile,' 'feeble-minded', and 'harlot'.[87] Eugenics also provided an underpinning for the wave of white supremacy – and the Jim Crow laws legalizing racial segregation – that swept the nation in the 1880s.

Restrictive immigration laws were passed to protect whites from 'outside threats', and the movement blended elitist fears about white poverty and immigration with racist notions that African Americans were inferior.[88] Popular manifestations of eugenics characterized white northern Europeans as eminently superior, African Americans at the bottom and everyone else somewhere in-between.[89] Both eugenics and pseudoscience were used to amass hundreds of thousands of 'family case studies' in an effort to classify people according to intellect, development and other characteristics – each with a label ready for indexing and filing.

Proponents of eugenics in the early twentieth century argued that modern medicine interfered with Darwinian natural selection by keeping the weak alive; that mentally ill persons were reproducing at a much faster rate than the 'valuable'; and that costs were soaring for maintaining 'defectives' in special homes, hospitals, schools and prisons.[90] Eugenicists in the United States maintained that

85 Smith et al., *supra*, note 68 at 3.

86 Virginia Eubanks, *Automating Inequality: How High-Tech Tools Profile, Police, and Punish the Poor* (New York: St. Martin's Press, 2018) at 22.

87 *Ibid.* at 23.

88 *Ibid.*

89 *Ibid.*

90 Susan Bachrach, "In the Name of Public Health – Nazi Racial Hygiene," (2004) *New England Journal of Medicine* 351.

African Americans, American Indians, poor people, criminals, prostitutes and alcoholics all suffered from inferior genes, a theory that lent scientific credibility to assumptions about white supremacy and informed Virginia's *Act to Preserve Racial Integrity* (1924).

In *Buck v. Bell*,[91] the US Supreme Court, by a vote of 8 to 1, affirmed the constitutionality of that law, which allowed state-enforced sterilization. Justice Oliver Wendell Holmes wrote the following in that case:

> It is better for all the world if, instead of waiting to execute degenerate offspring for crime or to let them starve for their imbecility, society can prevent those who are manifestly unfit from continuing their kind. The principle that sustains compulsory vaccination is broad enough to cover cutting the Fallopian tubes ... [t]hree generations of imbeciles are enough.

Thus, Carrie Buck, a 17-year-old rape victim who was committed to the Virginia State Colony for Epileptics and Feebleminded, was sterilized against her will. Buck had been diagnosed with 'feeblemindedness', a catch-all term for a multitude of mental and social problems as well as promiscuity. Her mother, Emma, had been committed for the same offences. Evidence was used to prove that Carrie was promiscuous – she had given birth to a daughter without being married, notwithstanding that she was raped.

Eugenicists helped to pass sterilization laws in many parts of the US, and about 30 states in total, including Virginia, passed legislation that made it legal to forcibly sterilize any person, male or female, who was deemed mentally defective and committed to a state institution. Before 1933, German racial hygienists cited this to support their own proposals for a sterilization law.[92] Between 1907 and 1945, 40,000 eugenic sterilization operations were recorded in the United States, half of them in California, where patients in state mental hospitals were the main targets.[93]

In 1946–1947, the American military tribunal at Nuremberg tried 20 German physicians and 3 lay accomplices for medical experiments on prisoners in Nazi concentration camps. The defendants cited the *Buck* case in defence of their sterilization experiments.[94] Globally, the Holocaust helped to discredit eugenics and the term became taboo in the scientific community. Even so, the sterilization of mentally ill persons continued in some parts of Scandinavia and Canada after the war, and sterilization remained part of social policy in Virginia, North Carolina and Georgia well into the 1970s.[95]

The Nazis, for their part, perfected the creation of a compulsory registration system for the tracking and profiling of virtually every sector of society.[96]

91 274 U.S. 200 (1927).
92 Bachrach, *supra*, note 157 at 418.
93 *Ibid.*
94 Virginia repealed the law in 1974 and in 2002 apologized to its victims.
95 Bachrach, *supra*, note 157 at 418.
96 Gotz Aly & Karl Heinz Roth, *The Nazi Census – Identification and Control in the Third Reich* (Philadelphia, PA: Temple University Press, 2004) at ix.

Copious amounts of data were gathered and used to determine the social and demographic composition of the entire population, which led to the restructuring of society on the basis of heredity.[97] It's safe to say that the entire Nazi campaign would not have succeeded to the extent that it did without the help of technology, in the form of raw data and punch cards (using an IBM Hollerith card-sorting machine), as well as quasi-scientific analysis.[98]

Statistical information was used to classify and segregate people on the basis of traits like family name, religion, race, language/dialect, health, physical and mental characteristics, and so on. The incessant counting, selecting, and 'singling out' of people into superior and inferior ranks eroded social unity, which was essential to the Nazis' campaign of social division.[99] Indeed, the enemy needed to be 'identified and localized, named and depicted, in order to be made into an accessible target'.[100] This paved the way for violent and sadistic leaders, along with millions of otherwise rational men and women, to engage in a systematic crusade of discrimination, deportation and ultimately, the murder of stigmatized minorities across Europe.

In the interests of preserving the future quality and purity of the Aryan race, 'racial hygiene' became a central goal of the German nation. Beginning in the early 1930s, German Jews, 'Jewish half-breeds' and 'Aryan' adults were identified during a census and registered with the Reich.[101] Under the Nazi eugenics program, which was known more broadly as 'racial hygiene', many other sorts of individuals were identified and targeted for sterilization or death, including prisoners, those with cognitive or physical disabilities, Gypsies, 'antisocials', homosexuals, criminals and more.

The concept of racial hygiene had deep roots in Germany. In the late nineteenth and early twentieth centuries, medical and public health professionals criticized Germany's declining birth rate and the perceived biological 'degeneration' of the nation.[102] Echoing those concerns, in *Mein Kampf*, Hitler wrote that, 'the national state ... must see to it that only the healthy beget children' using 'modern medical means'.[103] This objective underpinned Nazi policies aiming to 'cleanse' German society of people viewed as biological threats to the nation's health. Yet the Nazi's resolve to create a healthy German population was also tied to larger goals: countless fit workers, farmers and soldiers were needed for the country to expand its territory and become a prevailing world power.[104]

97 *Ibid.* at 8.
98 *Ibid.* at 1.
99 *Ibid.* at 24.
100 Louise Amoore, 'Governing by Identity' in Colin J. Bennett and David Lyon (eds), *Playing the Identity Card: Surveillance, Security and Identification in Global Perspective* (New York: Routledge, 2008) at 31.
101 Aly & Roth, *supra*, note 163 at xi.
102 Bachrach, *supra*, note 157 at 417.
103 *Ibid.*
104 *Ibid.*

While the racial-hygiene measures began with the mass sterilization of the 'genetically diseased', they ended with the near-annihilation of European Jewry. And for the first time in history, physicians sought to systematically exterminate their patients.[105] Information to determine who should be considered 'genetically unwanted' was gathered from data supplied to doctors' offices and welfare departments, among other institutions; and it was carefully registered and indexed.[106] The Reich also established hundreds of 'hereditary and racial care clinics' that examined people's family histories.[107]

Staffed by thousands of physicians, the clinics operated under the auspices of regional public health offices, which were responsible for registration and carding, as well as the creation of vast hereditary databanks for the regime's future use.[108] In addition, 'hereditary health courts' were created so that physician-judges could make 'informed' decisions about sterilization based on the index cards, family charts, examination forms, filing systems, and so on.[109] By 1945, some 400,000 Germans had been forcibly sterilized. The flexible diagnosis of 'feeblemindedness' provided legal grounds in most cases.[110]

It's astonishing that the Nazis established such a coordinated and systematized process of population cleansing before the advent of modern computer technologies. Critical to the success of Nazi policy was their penchant for efficiency, methodology and bureaucracy, which enabled them to carry out such an efficient process of registration, evaluation and 'biological diagnosis' throughout the entire population.[111] Not only was the abstraction of individuals into numbers and 'raw data' a fundamental assault on human dignity; it made it easier for the Nazis to streamline, rationalize and pervert their findings and techniques through appeals to 'pseudoscience'.[112]

Clearly, this provides a horrifying example of how both science and law may be perverted by external forces, laying the groundwork for unethical and heinous practices. Yet the Nazis weren't the only ones using biometric data for discriminatory purposes during the Second World War. In November 1941, two weeks before the Japanese attack on Pearl Harbor, President Roosevelt ordered that a list be made of the names and addresses of all foreign and American-born Japanese living in the United States.[113] To compile the list, the President's staffers used census data from the years 1930 and 1940. Although they didn't have the benefit of computers, they compiled the list in only one week. By the spring of 1942,

105 Rael D. Strous, 'Psychiatry During the Nazi Era: Ethical Lessons for the Modern Professional', (2007) 6(8) *Annals of General Psychiatry* 1.

106 Aly & Roth, *supra*, note 163 at 104.

107 Bachrach, *supra*, note 157 at 419.

108 *Ibid.*

109 Aly & Roth, *supra*, note 163 at 104.

110 Bachrach, *supra*, note 157 at 418.

111 Aly & Roth, *supra*, note 163 at 105.

112 *Ibid.* at 6–7.

113 John D. Woodward, 'Biometrics: Privacy's Foe or Privacy's Friend?' *Proceedings of the IEEE*, 85(9), September 1997 at 1486.

the US government forced persons of Japanese descent, including US citizens, to leave their homes on the West Coast and report to 'relocation centers'.[114]

In light of this dreadful historical experience, we need to question the use of any seemingly objective process for mapping and measuring biological data for legal and policy-related decisions. Although those behind a certain technology might not have malicious intentions from the outset, the implementation of the technology by some means that it can be used for a whole array of nefarious purposes by others. In fact, the nightmare biometrics-based scenario rarely happens instantly. Rather, when first deployed, the data is commonly used for a very narrow, clearly specified, sensible purpose; yet over time, the systems spread to additional purposes not announced or even intended when they were first implemented. This becomes evident when looking at the way identity census and biometric data were used in the early part of the twentieth century and during the Second World War.

Current issues and problems with biometrics

For more than 50 years, biometric systems have intrigued us across a variety of platforms, from science to science fiction. Technological advances have suggested that biometrics can solve a range of pressing problems, from border security to the provision of public benefits and services. Many have been amazed by the potential of this field, only to find their investments dwindling faster than the rate of development of new biometric devices. The reasons behind these failures – and the limitations inherent in these systems – fluctuate, depending on the context in which they are used.

Biometrics do not deal in absolute certainty but in probabilities. A biometric system establishes a probabilistic assessment of a match indicating that a person is probably the same person for whom the corresponding data is stored.[115] For example, a match between crime-scene DNA and a defendant's DNA profile is presented as a *match probability* in court.[116] This refers to the probability that if another individual was selected from the population at random, they would have the same profile. Only one person in a million will have a DNA profile which matches that of a crime stain.[117] So, if a defendant has that DNA profile, there is a million to one probability that he left the crime stain.

There is also a temporal aspect to some biometric data. Consequently, there are hurdles to overcome when it comes to changes in age, environment, stress and disease. Biometric systems also require distinctive 'features' to be extracted from sensors; and it's actually the correlation, or relationship, between our physical characteristics that makes each of us unique: the edges of my eye, to my chin, to the corner of my mouth; or, particular parts of my fingerprint in relation to others.

114 *Ibid.*
115 Pato & Millett, *supra*, note 5 at 22.
116 Smith et al., *supra*, note 68 at 45.
117 *Ibid.*

Yet when I put my finger on a fingerprint reader, the image may be affected owing to presentation angle, dirt, moisture, the previous persons' fingerprints, and so on. Even in the best-case scenario, the biometric system can only provide us with probabilistic results; and individuals attempting to thwart or manipulate recognition bring another source of uncertainty to biometric systems. For example, researchers have demonstrated that it's possible to fool a fingerprint-reading device using a fake finger with a mould of the original fingertip imbedded in gelatin.[118]

The story behind CLEAR – a privately owned biometric-based service that pre-screens travellers for an annual fee – illustrates what can happen when these systems fail, and when their uptake in society outpaces the legal, ethical and even practical considerations regarding their use. The CLEAR program, which was first owned by Verified Identity Pass, Inc. (VIP), was initially used at the Orlando International Airport in July 2005, to let subscribers pass through security checkpoints faster than other travellers.[119] However, the program was declared bankrupt in June 2009, and the company shut down its operations.

In a single day, VIP ceased offering CLEAR in all US airports in which it was operating, shut down its offices in New York, discontinued its website presence – except for a single page announcing its closure – terminated all of its employees, and cut off all avenues of communication with it.[120] Without warning, up to 260,000 CLEAR subscribers, and even high-profile investors like General Electric, which invested about $16 million (USD) in the program, were left wondering about refunds and the fate of the sensitive data held by the company.[121]

Each individual enrolled in CLEAR had given the company digital images of their fingerprints, irises and faces, along with their date and place of birth, social security number, gender, address, phone numbers, e-mail addresses, employer, driver's license number, height and credit card numbers. The day after the company shut down, no one knew what would happen to all that sensitive biometric data. Not surprisingly, this led to an interesting legal question: would the company's biggest asset – the personal information of more than a quarter of a million CLEAR members – become the property of its creditors; or could the company sell it to a third party to pay off its debts?

A class action lawsuit was brought by CLEAR subscribers against VIP. A Manhattan federal court judge ordered VIP to 'take affirmative steps' to preserve the data; and further, issued an injunction preventing it from 'selling or

118 Tsutomu Matsumoto, Hiroyuki Matsumoto, Koji Yamada & Satoshi Hoshino, 'Impact of artificial "gummy" fingers on fingerprint systems', Tsutomu Matsumoto, Hiroyuki Matsumoto, Koji Yamada, Satoshi Hoshino Yokohama National Univ. (Japan) (2002) 4677 *Optical Security and Counterfeit Deterrence Techniques* IV.

119 Bruce Schneier, 'Life in the Fast Lane', *The New York Times*, 21 January 2007.

120 *Perkins, et al. v. Verified Identity Pass Inc., and Doe Defendants 1–25*, United States District Court Southern District of New York (Case # 09-CV-5951).

121 Ryan Singel, 'Clear Promises to Delete Sensitive Flier Data, but No Refunds', *Wired*, 23 June 2009.

otherwise transferring, disclosing to third parties or maintaining in any unsecure way any personal biographic or biometric data that was provided to it…' by its members. One of the compelling factors behind the decision was that the contracts the members signed with CLEAR forbid it from selling their data.

What caused CLEAR to collapse? The company ran out of cash after it failed to attract enough subscribers to pay to staff its fast-track security lanes, which were then available in twenty of the nation's busiest airports.[122] But this wasn't the only problem the company faced. In order to get a card to pass through airport security checkpoints faster, CLEAR members had to undergo federal background checks. Based on this 'pre-screening', the company wanted its travellers to pass through security checkpoints faster than everybody else – avoiding additional screening and keeping their shoes and coats on.

However, the Transportation Safety Administration (TSA) refused to let CLEAR members bypass its inspection process and avoid the security checks that other passengers faced. Likewise, security experts ridiculed the idea that any American could apply for a CLEAR card. To 'verify' a person's status, his or her name was compared against government watch lists, as well as citizenship or legal immigrant status, and the presence or absence of any relevant criminal record.[123] In other words, the background check only verified whether or not someone was already in a 'bad guy' database.

But what about previously unknown villains, like the Unabomber or Timothy McVeigh? Taking things one step further, it wouldn't be difficult for a terrorist organization to find ostensibly 'clean' hijacking contenders who could get the cards and then walk freely on to a plane.[124] So, in the world of airport security, where life and death truly are a matter of first priority, it makes sense to insist on physically screening someone to make sure he's not carrying a knife or a bomb, notwithstanding the fact that he hasn't been 'red flagged' by background checks. In practice, though, this meant that the security background check CLEAR members underwent as part of their registration process was simply for show.

Still, like a Phoenix rising from the ashes, CLEAR was born again in 2010. In May of that year, Alclear, LLC announced that it acquired the assets of VIP out of bankruptcy protection. The Company relaunched CLEAR, its Trusted Traveler program, in major airports in the fall of 2010. The subscription terms of nearly 160,000 previous members were honoured by the company; and it now claims to have a membership base of over 1.5 million people.[125] The company has continued to expand its partnerships with airports throughout the United States – currently, they have services at 24 airports – and they have also

122 Ryan Singel, 'Defunct Airport Fast-Pass Company Banned from Selling Customer Biometrics', *Wired*, 19 August 2009.

123 Schneier, *supra*, note 186.

124 *Ibid.*

125 Shivani Voranov, "How Clear Can Speed Up the Airport Screening Process," *The New York Times*, November 17, 2017.

provided screening services at sports stadiums in the US.[126] But even after passing through a CLEAR kiosk at the airport, members must still go through TSA screening, just like everybody else – the only difference is that CLEAR members get to go straight to the front of the queue, ahead of other travellers.

Delta SkyMiles members who are enrolled in CLEAR now have the option to use their fingerprints instead of their boarding pass to board any Delta aircraft at Regan Airport in Washington, DC, and to enter that airport's Delta Sky Club lounge.[127] For everyone else, it seems as if CLEAR membership only gives you 'front of the line' privileges at some airport security checkpoints throughout the US. And as the TSA get better at keeping their queues moving, the benefits of paying $200 for CLEAR status, and giving up so much personal and highly sensitive data to a private company that might go bankrupt again, or be hacked, are less than clear.

This case illustrates that the security and integrity of data are fundamental – this is where the greatest security and regulatory oversight should be focused, especially after a company holding our biometric data goes broke. It also shows that biometrics are not a one-stop shop, in terms of the solutions and capabilities they provide. Biometrics might be useful for someone to pay or get where they're going more conveniently. We already have scores of biometric data items on our bodies at all times, so there's no need for a chip to be inserted, such as an RFID tag, or something else even more ominous and chilling.

My biometric data might also be used to identify me before I board my local subway, for example; and by linking my fingerprint to my credit card, I could easily pay for my trip. The same technologies might be useful at my local movie theatre ('would you like popcorn or M&Ms with your movie tickets?'), or, perhaps, my local grocery store where automatic checkout tills could read my fingerprint and link it to my prior purchases, providing me with convenience ('do you want to add bananas to your purchase today?') and the store with cost-savings (i.e. checkout staff won't be needed any more).

But these same technologies, by themselves, are not very well-suited to identifying those who pose a national security threat – in crowded places such as airports, shopping malls and concert stadiums – particularly, if thousands of people are converging on the venue in a short period of time. So, while I might conveniently show my iris or fingerprint before being asked if I want to pre-order food or drinks on the plane; I'm not comfortable with the same technologies being used to wave me past security before I board my flight.

The reason is that there's only a limited amount of information that can be stored about me in the database, and it's often not the right kind of data, or not good enough data, to determine whether I'm likely to carry a knife or a gun on to an airplane. At best, information about my date and place of birth, gender, address, phone numbers, e-mail addresses, employer, driving licence number,

126 *Ibid.*
127 *Ibid.*

height/weight, credit card numbers, fingerprints or even irises, can only be matched to existing data to identify whether I've previously committed a crime, or am an immigrant, or possess some other characteristic that *may* be used to determine my propensity to carry out a terrorist act. But there are too many other variables that make this determination extremely difficult, if not impossible, especially on the fly.

And while there have been several instances of someone applying for entry to a country under one name, being denied, applying under another name, and again being denied (owing to biometrics records), which may prevent criminal activity, the biometric system cannot 'predict' if I'm a terrorist if my identity is unknown. If I'm an ordinary law-abiding citizen who happens to self-radicalize and tries to board an aeroplane with a gun, a biometric system is not likely to flag me as a potential threat, no matter how sophisticated it is. Determining the impact of metal fatigue, the frequency of bird strikes and the impact of environmental threats is a science; but predicting the likelihood of a terrorist attack is not.[128] There is no database for terrorist activities that can serve as a reliable prognosticator for the future because these dangers are vastly unpredictable, unquantifiable and cannot be precisely ranked.[129] That's why I'm far happier if we adhere to physically searching people, or using tools that can replace, or even augment, a physical search.

It also bears mentioning that the way most of us use biometrics today is still pretty old-school – you put your finger on a fingerprint reader or you allow someone to take a picture of your eyeball – thus, gathering biometric data generally requires the cooperation or coercion of the subject.[130] But that won't be the case for very much longer. Imagine this: You walk into a car dealership of the future and before you open your mouth, the dealer knows your name, employment status, car-buying history and credit score.[131] This sort of future isn't far off. Data brokers already compile masses of data about all of us; and clients can purchase information about our consumer, criminal and marital pasts.[132] It's not long before data brokers begin gathering information from online-dating profiles and social-media posts; and eventually, someone might be able to point a phone at you and see a bubble over your head marking you as unemployed or recently divorced.[133]

Face-reading algorithms have already been used to predict people's sexual orientation,[134] political persuasion and other psychological traits, based on

128 Mark B. Salter, 'The Global Airport', in Mark B. Salter (ed.), *Politics at the Airport* (Minneapolis: University of Minnesota Press, 2008) 1 at 21.

129 *Ibid.*

130 Scientific American, 'Biometric Security Poses Huge Privacy Risks', 1 January 2014.

131 Hutson, *supra*, note 141.

132 *Ibid.*

133 *Ibid.*

134 Sam T. Levin, 'New AI can Guess Whether You're Gay or Straight from a Photograph', *The Guardian*, 8 September 2017.

their facial photos, with an extremely high degree of precision – even better, researchers claim, than that of our closest companions.[135] So, when it comes to the commercial entity I visit in the future, they'll have little difficulty determining what sort of sales pitches I'm most susceptible to, and how profitable a customer I am likely to be – and of course, they're going to interact with me on that basis.[136] We'll no longer be able to separate our work lives from our personal lives; our histories will come bundled as a pop-up on strangers' screens.[137]

Everything needed to authenticate me is already right out in the open, and readily available to anyone, at any time. We don't need to sign up or give our consent for this – it has already been realized, and it's steadily improving with personal information we've willingly given away. For example, with its database of two hundred and fifty billion user photos, Facebook has developed a facial-recognition algorithm that is more reliable than those created for the F.B.I.[138] Companies with large databases of tagged photos and personal information are now selling that information and facilitating all kinds of new surveillance and data-recognition services for private businesses and governments. The underlying technologies are being developed and implemented at this very minute, and there are few rules limiting their use.

Biometric tools are even being introduced to children as a matter of convenience. As part of a Cashless Schools initiative, Fredericton High School in New Brunswick, Canada, now allows students to pay for lunch in the cafeteria simply by leaving a thumbprint.[139] Such systems are being sold widely in Canada, to both universities and high schools. In the case of Fredericton High School, parents must register with Cashless Schools, a Canadian-based company that specializes in payment systems for schools, make a deposit in their account and sign a consent form confirming that their child may use the biometric scanner.[140]

But just how comfortable are we with the growth and development of technologies that use biometric data to identify us? For some people, this 'convenience' breeds deep suspicion and paranoia. What about the fear that there's going to be no escape from all the scanning and screening in our future lives?

Like the fictional character in the sci-fi movie *Minority Report*, we could be walking down the street and a facial recognition system might spot who we are and put out an ad just for us. This is no longer science fiction. Billboards and store displays are already being designed to track the movement and focus of customers'

135 The Guardian, 'Your Computer Knows You Better than your Friends do, say Researchers', 13 January 2015.

136 Bruce Schneier, 'The Era of Automatic Facial Recognition and Surveillance Is Here', *Forbes*, 29 September 2015.

137 Hutson, *supra*, note 141.

138 Patrick Radden Keefe, 'The Detectives Who Never Forget a Face', *The New Yorker*, 22 August 2016.

139 Bennett et al., *supra*, note 27 at 160.

140 *Ibid.*

eyes, generating data about individual attention and tastes of which the person may be completely unaware and which he or she may be unable to disclose accurately even if he or she were cooperative.[141] The Venetian hotel in Las Vegas, for instance, has implemented billboards that draw on the technology to advertise bars, clubs and restaurants appropriate for the demographic identified.[142] Similarly, Adidas and Intel are working together to instal digital walls in stores, with plans to target passers-by with shoe displays appropriate to their age and gender.[143]

With all the data being collected, questions inevitably arise regarding who 'owns' the data, and the extent to which they can use it. We already saw how this issue has come before the courts with respect to CLEAR. Having this data on hand will make investigations a lot easier for law enforcement. But it also makes it easier to build maps of social networks, or to engage in profiling. And it creates enormous potential for misuse.

Conclusion

It's a matter of convenience versus security when it comes to biometrics – and it's a personal question for each of us to decide how much convenience we want, or need, and how much we're willing to risk. Perhaps what should worry us most is the transfer of our biometric data to a devious individual or authority. Criminal organizations, for example, could steal biometric data and then sell it on the online black market. This is quite likely, especially considering that cases of identity theft have skyrocketed in recent years, and it's now possible to purchase someone's entire digital identity – bank account information, passwords and other valuable information – on the dark web for less than a dollar.

When it comes to something as precious as my thumbprint – of which I only have two – if someone steals it, I will lose it for ever.[144] Unlike a password, I can't simply 'make up' another one and reclaim my privacy and security. And while this may sound like something from a dystopian nightmare, it's not. A motorist in Germany had his finger chopped off by thieves to steal his car which used a fingerprint reader instead of a key lock.[145]

Clearly, there are important questions to be asked around secrecy, randomness, the ability to update or destroy our biometric data, and who has access to it. The concern is that the drive towards the adoption of biometric technologies is happening faster than laws and policies to protect this data are being created. While the systems are omnipresent and ubiquitous, they are largely being implemented below the radar, without public discussion, oversight or accountability.

141 Torin Monahan, 'Built to Lie: Investigating Technologies of Deception, Surveillance, and Control', (2016) 32(4) *The Information Society* 229 at 229.

142 Laura K. Donohue, 'Technological Leap, Statutory Gap', (2012) 97 *Minnesota Law Review* 407 at 513.

143 *Ibid.*

144 Schneier, *supra*, note 70.

145 The Economist, 'The Difference Engine: Dubious Security', 1 October 2010.

Bibliography

Gotz Aly & Karl Heinz Roth, *The Nazi Census – Identification and Control in the Third Reich* (Philadelphia, PA: Temple University Press, 2004).

Louise Amoore, 'Governing by Identity', in Colin J. Bennett & David Lyon (eds), *Playing the Identity Card: Surveillance, Security and Identification in Global Perspective* (New York: Routledge, 2008) 21.

Susan Bachrach, 'In the Name of Public Health – Nazi Racial Hygiene', (2004) *New England Journal of Medicine* 351 (5).

Colin J. Bennett & David Lyon, 'Playing the ID Card – Understanding the Significance of Identity Card Systems', in Colin J. Bennett & David Lyon (eds), *Playing the Identity Card: Surveillance, Security and Identification in Global Perspective* (New York: Routledge, 2008) 3.

Joe Celko, *Joe Celko's Complete Guide to NoSQL* (Burlington, NJ: Elsevier Science, 2013).

Nick Dole, 'Sydney Man Has Opal Card Implanted into Hand to Make Catching Public Transport Easier', *ABC News*, 27 June 2017.

Laura K. Donohue, 'Technological Leap, Statutory Gap', (2012) 97 *Minnesota Law Review* 407.

eeDesignIt Editorial Team, 'Ditch the Credit Cards and Fingerprints, Pay with Your Heartbeat Instead', 7 September 2017. Available online at: www.eedesignit.com/ditch-the-credit-cards-and-fingerprints-pay-with-your-heartbeat-instead/.

Virginia Eubanks, *Automating Inequality: How High-Tech Tools Profile, Police, and Punish the Poor* (New York: St. Martin's Press, 2018).

Stewart T. Fleming, 'Biometrics: Past, Present and Future', in Rasool Azari (ed.), *Current Security Management and Ethical Issues of Information Technology* (Hershey, PA: IRM Press, 2003) 111.

Marc Goodman, *Future Crimes* (New York: Doubleday, 2015).

Richard Gray, "Is the US Navy Planning to Implant People with Microchips? Officials Consult Presidential Candidate on 'Merging Humans and Machines'," *Daily Mail*, 17 June 2016.

William Harris, 'How DNA Evidence Works', *HowStuffWorks.com*, 18 January 2001. Available online at: https://science.howstuffworks.com/life/genetic/dna-evidence.htm.

Margaret Hu, 'Bulk Biometric Metadata Collection', (2018) 96 *North Carolina Law Review*, 1425.

Matthew Hutson, 'Even Bugs Will Be Bugged', *The Atlantic*, November, 2016.

Patrick Radden Keefe, 'The Detectives Who Never Forget a Face', *The New Yorker*, 22 August 2016.

Sam T. Levin, 'New AI can Guess Whether You're Gay or Straight from a Photograph', *The Guardian*, 8 September 2017.

Angela Liberatore, 'Balancing Security and Democracy, and the Role of Expertise: Biometrics Politics in the European Union', (2007) 13 *European Journal on Criminal Policy and Research*, 109.

Timothy Longman, 'Identity Cards, Ethnic Self-Perception, and Genocide in Rwanda', in Jane Caplan & John C. Torpey (eds), *Documenting Individual Identity: The Development of State Practices in the Modern World* (Princeton, NJ: Princeton University Press, 2001) 345–358.

Jennifer Lynch, 'From Fingerprints to DNA: Biometric Data Collection in U.S. Immigrant Communities and Beyond', 22 May 2012.

David Lyon, 'Biometrics, Identification and Surveillance', (2008) 22(9) *Bioethics* 499.

Shoshanna Amielle Magnet, *When Biometrics Fail: Gender, Race and the Technologies of Identity* (Durham, NC: Duke University Press, 2011).

Mark Maguire, 'Vanishing Borders and Biometric Citizens', in Gabriella Lazaridis (ed.), *Security, Insecurity and Migration in Europe* (London: Routledge, 2011).

Tsutomu Matsumoto, Hiroyuki Matsumoto, Koji Yamada & Satoshi Hoshino, 'Impact of Artificial "Gummy" Fingers on Fingerprint Systems'.

Tsutomu Matsumoto, Hiroyuki Matsumoto, Koji Yamada & Satoshi Hoshino, Yokohama National Univ. (Japan) (2002) 4677. Rudolf L. van Reness (ed.), *Optical Security and Counterfeit Deterrence Techniques IV*, Thursday–Friday 24–25 January 2002 (http://www.spie.org/Conferences/Programs/02/pw/confs/4677.html).

Terrence McNally, 'Alone Together: Why We've Started Expecting More from Technology and Less from Each Other', *AlterNet*, 18 March 2011. Available online at: www.alternet.org/story/150295/alone_together%3A_why_we%27ve_started_expecting_more_from_technology_and_less_from_each_other.

Katina Michael & M.G. Michael, *Innovative Automatic Identification and Location-Based Services: From Bar Codes to Chip Implants* (Hershey, PA: IGI Global, 2009).

Torin Monahan, 'Built to Lie: Investigating Technologies of Deception, Surveillance, and Control', (2016) 32(4) *The Information Society* 229.

Karthik Nandakumar & Anil K. Jain, 'Soft Biometrics', in Stan Z. Li & Anil K. Jain (eds), *Encyclopedia of Biometrics* (New York: Springer, 2009) 1235.

Joseph N. Pato & Lynette I. Millett (eds), *Biometric Recognition: Challenges and Opportunities* (Washington, DC: The National Academic Press, 2010).

Mark B. Salter, 'The Global Airport', in Mark B. Salter (ed.), *Politics at the Airport* (Minneapolis: University of Minnesota Press, 2008) 1.

Bruce Schneier, 'Biometrics: Uses and Abuses', *Communications of the ACM*, August 1999. Available online at: www.schneier.com/essays/archives/1999/08/biometrics_uses_and.html.

Bruce Schneier, *Beyond Fear: Thinking Sensibly About Security in an Uncertain World* (New York: Springer, 2003).

Bruce Schneier, 'Life in the Fast Lane', *The New York Times*, 21 January 2007.

Bruce Schneier, *Data and Goliath: The Hidden Battles to Collect Your Data and Control Your World* (New York: W. W. Norton & Co., 2015).

Bruce Schneier, 'The Era of Automatic Facial Recognition and Surveillance Is Here', *Forbes*, 29 September 2015.Ryan Singel, 'Clear Promises to Delete Sensitive Flier Data, but No Refunds', *Wired*, 23 June 2009.

Ryan Singel, 'Defunct Airport Fast-Pass Company Banned from Selling Customer Biometrics', *Wired*, 19 August 2009.

Marcus Smith, Monique Mann & Gregor Urbas, *Biometrics, Crime and Security* (New York: Routledge, 2018).

Rael D. Strous, 'Psychiatry During the Nazi Era: Ethical Lessons for the Modern Professional', (2007) 6(8) *Annals of General Psychiatry* 1.The Economist, 'The "CSI Effect",' 22 April 2010.

The Economist, 'The Difference Engine: Dubious Security', 1 October 2010.

The Guardian, 'Your Computer Knows You Better than your Friends do, say Researchers', 13 January 2015.

John R. Vacca, *Biometric Technologies and Verification Systems* (Burlington, MA: Butterworth-Heinemann, 2007).

Rosamunde van Brakel & Xavier Van Kerckhoven, 'The Emergence of the Identity Card in Belgium and its Colonies'. Available online at: www.researchgate.net/publication/258763996_The_emergence_of_the_identity_card_in_Belgium_and_its_colonies.

Shivani Voranov, 'How Clear Can Speed Up the Airport Screening Process', *The New York Times*, 17 November 2017.

John D. Woodward, 'Biometrics: Privacy's Foe or Privacy's Friend?' *Proceedings of the IEEE*, 85(9), September 1997.

Katie Worth, 'Framed for Murder by His Own DNA', Frontline, 19 April 2018. Available online at: www.pbs.org/wgbh/frontline/article/framed-for-murder-by-his-own-dna/.

Frances Zelazny, 'The Evolution of India's UID Program', *Center for Global Development*, 8 August 2012.

Case Law

Buck v. Bell 274 U.S. 200 (1927).

Perkins, et al. v. Verified Identity Pass Inc., and Doe Defendants 1–25, United States District Court Southern District of New York (Case # 09-CV-5951).

3 Privacy, surveillance and the self

Introduction

Before the dial phone was introduced in 1919, callers were connected through operators, who could listen in on their calls; and until after World War II, most Americans used shared (party) lines for their phone services, which meant that their neighbours could listen to their conversations.[1] While most Americans probably found this annoying, they did not consider it excessively intrusive.[2] In fact, before the proliferation of modern technologies, people usually assumed that what they said or did would remain private.[3] And, as a general rule, they were right. But this belief began to change with the rise of both the public eye – think of the curious citizen and the press – and the private eye – think of the government's ability to conduct electronic eavesdropping.[4]

In the 1930s, the advent of electronic surveillance, or wiretapping, produced uncertainties about the extent to which private conversations were free from government intrusion. The data-gathering and surveillance capabilities of new information technologies – and their potential for the creation of large computerized databases – began to arouse concern among policy analysts, journalists and fiction writers.[5] New and emerging surveillance technologies now allow the government to track us wherever we go, monitor our activities and gather massive amounts of data about our communications, financial transactions and social networks. These systems enable privacy violations that would make those observed less than a century ago seem superficial by comparison.

How a society chooses to define the 'right to privacy' and give legal meaning to the phrase is an important issue, particularly as advances in technology are dramatically improving information-gathering techniques. The protection and promotion of the right to privacy in the context of surveillance and the

1 Ryan, *supra*, note 24 at 4.

2 *Ibid.*

3 *Ibid.* at 3.

4 Jill Lepore, 'The Prism – Privacy in an Age of Publicity', *The New Yorker*, 24 June 2013.

5 Helen Nissenbaum, 'Protecting Privacy in an Information Age: The Problem of Privacy in Public', (1998) 17 *Law and Philosophy* 559 at 561.

collection, use and disclosure of personal data, including on a mass scale, is a matter of great interest and importance worldwide. Yet the 'right to privacy' remains ill-defined and has been subject to continuous re-evaluation since its legal conception in the late nineteenth century.

Privacy as a theoretical construct

Theories about individual privacy were first elucidated by classical philosophers and great liberal scholars, such as Aristotle, John Locke and John Stuart Mill. These debates hark back to the early traditions of liberal individualism, which define the long-established notion of 'the self' – the free and autonomous individual – that privacy is assumed to protect.[6]

Over time, privacy debates shifted towards the 'right to be let alone', whereby the individual was said to have both abstract liberty and the capacity to carve out a space of seclusion in which to engage in solitary acts of self-determination.[7] Although these debates are important for their historical significance, they no longer cover the full extent of the need for privacy in our information age.[8]

Nonetheless, if the values that underlie our modern understanding of privacy are ancient ones, we need to understand what is meant by privacy in the context of its historical roots. Some of our earliest notions of privacy come from Ancient Greece. Aristotle wrote about the division between the public sphere of political affairs (which he termed the *polis*) and the personal sphere of human life (termed *oikos*). This dichotomy may provide an initial recognition of 'a confidential zone on behalf of the citizen'.[9] The term 'private' indicated the realm of familial and other personal or intimate relations, while the term 'public' indicated the civic or community realm outside this personal one.[10]

In 1690, John Locke made similar observations in his *Second Treatise of Government*.[11] For Locke, this right was rooted in a right of all humanity to private property. His argument rests on the notion that '...every man has a property in his own person: this no body has any right to but himself.'[12] While Locke didn't specifically mention the word 'privacy', he gave expression to the idea that all men are born free, and that they are separate and autonomous from the 'distinct separate government'.[13] In other words, he recognized two discrete spheres: in the private realm, human beings are independent and free 'to dispose

6 Julie E. Cohen, 'What Privacy is For', (2013) 126(7) *Harvard Law Review* 1904 at 1906.
7 *Ibid.* at 1906–1907.
8 Nissenbaum, *supra*, note 218 at 565.
9 Michael C. James, 'A Comparative Analysis of the Right to Privacy in the United States, Canada and Europe', (2014) 29(2) *Connecticut Journal of International Law* 257 at 261.
10 Nissenbaum, *supra*, note 218 at 567.
11 John Locke, 'Second Treatise of Government', in Michael Morgan (ed.), *Classics of Moral and Political Theory* (Indianapolis, IN: Hackett, 1992) 736.
12 *Ibid.* at para.27.
13 *Ibid.* at para.113.

of [their] person and possessions'; yet in the public domain, they are subject to government interference and control.

John Stuart Mill, in his essay, 'On Liberty', also wrote about the need to preserve a zone within which the liberty of the citizen would be free from the authority of the state. Indeed, he argues that the individual has exclusive power over his own thoughts, his own body, in effect, over his own autonomous self. According to Mill: 'Over himself, over his own body and mind, the individual is sovereign'.[14]

Though, like Locke, Mill did not use the term 'privacy', he recognized that the liberal self is inherently autonomous and possesses both intangible liberty rights and the capacity for rational thought and freedom of choice. Liberty necessarily depends upon an individual's having sovereignty over an intimate realm to engage in the basic freedoms that underpin the democratic values of most leading nations. The significant element in defining privacy thus lies in one or another overarching principle (i.e. liberty, autonomy, speech, association, and so on).

American philosopher James Madison also wrote about the inalienable rights of citizens and the necessity of safeguarding these liberties from governmental authority.[15] Madison played a crucial role in the chronicles of American history as the architect of the United States Constitution and the Bill of Rights.[16] Madison's writings about the sanctity of property and his expansive definition of that term suggests that he felt strongly about protecting the values of seclusion and control. It's no coincidence that in the early years of Fourth Amendment jurisprudence, the focus was on property and protection of physical spaces that would be considered private, such as an individual's home.

This framework emerged in America in 1890 when the *Harvard Law Review* published an article written by two alumni, Samuel D. Warren, Jr. and Louis D. Brandeis, entitled the 'Right to Privacy'.[17] Warren and Brandeis conceived the right of privacy as one of the natural, fundamental rights which form part of an individual's basic individuality. But for Warren and Brandeis, the right to privacy also had another vital aspect – technology was increasingly threatening to invade the personal sphere. Warren and Brandeis wrote that:

> [t]he intensity and complexity of life, attendant upon advancing civilization, have rendered necessary some retreat from the world, and man, under the refining influence of culture, has become more sensitive to publicity, so that solitude and privacy have become more essential to the individual; but modern enterprise and invention have, through invasions upon his privacy, subjected him to mental pain and distress, far greater than could be inflicted by mere bodily injury.

14 John Stuart Mill, "On Liberty," in Michael Morgan (ed.), *Classics of Moral and Political Theory* (Indianapolis, IN: Hackett, 1992) 1044 at 1050.

15 James, *supra*, note 222 at 264.

16 *Ibid.*

17 Samuel D. Warren & Louis Brandeis, 'The Right to Privacy', (1890) 4 *Harvard Law Review* 193.

The right to privacy developed by Warren and Brandeis was set against the backdrop of dense urbanization on the East Coast of the United States.[18] Between 1790 and 1890, the US population rose from four million to sixty-three million.[19] The population of urban areas grew over a hundredfold after the end of the civil war; and, by 1890, over eight million people had immigrated to the US.[20] Urbanization and economic growth led to the replacement of traditional social structures – as well as the tranquility of rural life – with urban ghettos which seemed to 'submerge the individual into a seamless web of interconnected lives'.[21]

Technological progress necessarily led to the private realm being placed under stress:

> By 1890 there were also telegraphs, fairly inexpensive portable cameras, sound recording devices, and better and cheaper methods of making window glass...these advances in technology, coupled with intensified newspaper enterprise, increased the vulnerability of individuals to having their actions, words, images, and personalities communicated without their consent beyond the protected circle of family and chosen friends.[22]

Modern life was becoming a spectacle of itself; and Warren and Brandeis echoed the concern of their contemporaries by proclaiming that '[i]nstantaneous photographs and newspaper enterprise have invaded the sacred precincts of private and domestic life; and numerous mechanical devices threaten to make good the prediction that "what is whispered in the closet shall be proclaimed from the house-tops".'[23] And true to prediction, it wasn't long after the invention of the telephone that police began secretly wiretapping people's conversations.[24]

Brandeis was appointed to the United States Supreme Court in 1916; and he was there when, in 1928, in *Olmstead v. United States*,[25] the Court considered the constitutionality of police wiretapping for the first time. Roy Olmstead was the head of a bootlegging ring who appealed his conviction of conspiracy to violate the *National Prohibition Act*, which then prohibited the import and sale of alcohol. He argued, among other things, that the gathering of evidence of his private conversations by federal wiretap violated the Fourth Amendment, which protects '[t]he right of the people to be secure in their persons, houses, papers and effects, against unreasonable searches and seizures'.

18 Dorothy J. Glancy, 'The Invention of the Right to Privacy', (1979) 21(1) *Arizona Law Review* 1 at 7.
19 *Ibid.*
20 *Ibid.*
21 *K. S. Puttaswamy v. Union of India*, Writ Petition (Civil) No. 494 of 2012 at para.39.
22 Glancy, *supra*, note 231 at 7–8.
23 Warren & Brandeis, *supra*, note 230 at 195.
24 Ryan, *supra*, note 24 at 5.
25 277 U.S. 438 (1928).

In a five-to-four decision, the Court affirmed Olmstead's conviction and held that the warrantless wiretaps were legal because they did not involve 'a search'. Since 'there was no entry of the houses or offices of the defendants',[26] the federal authorities didn't trespass on the defendants' property when they installed the wiretaps.[27] Clearly, the Court was relying on the notion of physical intrusion to determine whether there was an invasion of Fourth Amendment privacy.

Justice Brandeis famously dissented and wrote that the warrantless tapping of Olmstead's phone constituted a violation of his right to be let alone. The focus of the decision is clearly on the potential abuses of new technologies by agents of the state. In the twentieth century, he cautioned,

> subtler and more far-reaching means of invading privacy have become available to the Government. Discovery and invention have made it possible for the Government, by means far more effective than stretching upon the rack, to obtain disclosure in court of what is whispered in the closet.

Brandeis warned that, notwithstanding the fact that, with the Fourth Amendment, the Framers 'conferred, as against the government, the right to be let alone...'[28] the '...progress of science in furnishing the Government with means of espionage is not likely to stop with wiretapping'. He went on to predict that, '[w]ays may someday be developed by which the Government, without removing papers from secret drawers, can reproduce them in court, and by which it will be enabled to expose to a jury the most intimate occurrences of the home'. Given its recognition of the powerful relationship between privacy and intimate information about an individual, the 'right to be let alone' concept of privacy underpins a subsequent body of case law intended to protect communications from state surveillance.

Yet it wasn't until almost 40 years later that the Supreme Court shifted the focus of the Fourth Amendment away from property to privacy in another landmark surveillance case. In *Katz v. United States*,[29] the Court held that F.B.I agents violated the Fourth Amendment when, without judicial authorization, they attached an electronic listening and recording device to the outside of a public telephone booth used by the defendant to place calls transmitting illegal gambling information. Justice Stewart found that it was no longer necessary to determine whether a trespass occurred but rather whether the use of the device violated the expectation of privacy upon which the individual reasonably relied.[30]

Justice Stewart observed that an individual who enters a telephone booth, 'shuts the door behind him, and pays the toll that permits him to place the call is surely entitled to assume that the words he utters into the mouthpiece

26 *Ibid.* at 464.
27 *Ibid.* at 457.
28 *Ibid.* at 478.
29 389 U.S. 347 (1967).
30 *Ibid.*

will not be broadcast to the world'.[31] In the words of Justice Harlan, at that moment, the telephone booth became a 'temporarily private place whose momentary occupants' expectations of freedom from intrusion are recognized as reasonable'.[32] Thus, the Court held that the government's actions, which were undertaken without a warrant, constituted an unreasonable 'search' in violation of the Fourth Amendment.

This shift away from trespass towards the individual expectation of privacy harkens back to original conceptualizations of privacy as a form of protection for the liberal self – one which postulates our capacity for autonomous choice and self-determination above all else.[33] Privacy therefore is an indispensable feature of liberal democratic political systems.[34] Yet, as privacy law scholar Julie Cohen has pointed out, the notion of 'privacy as a defensive bulwark for the autonomous self' is both outdated and incorrect.[35] Privacy is not a fixed condition, but rather is inherently subjective, relational and responsive to its surroundings. It's socially constructed and inherently malleable; thereby, its boundaries shift dynamically over time in response to culture and experience.[36]

There is no question that ubiquitous computing and data surveillance threaten to undermine these values. In literature and in the popular press, the idea of a surveillance society is frequently linked to totalitarian systems. And, as we shall see in Chapter 4, totalitarian regimes such as that governing China openly encourage citizens to spy on one another, and these measures pose a chilling threat to human rights and civil liberties. Of course, surveillance cultures have long encouraged individuals to participate. Citizens respond by establishing neighbourhood watch programs; moving into gated communities; and sharing information online. Yet where governments are able to mount systems with little public consultation or approval, it's possible to establish sweeping surveillance against a backdrop of muted dissent.[37]

Biometrics – privacy's friend or foe?

Biometrics has long been eschewed by privacy advocates. This is perhaps because when we collect biometric data from a person, we are not just collecting data *about* a person, but *from* that person. Nothing is more private than an individual's biological property and should this information be corrupted, leaked, stolen or lost, there could be a range of potentially catastrophic outcomes and abuses.

The past 25 years have seen several waves of data privacy regulation around the globe, with many of the world's leading nations revising their legal regimes

31 *Ibid.* at 352.
32 *Ibid.* at 361.
33 Cohen, *supra*, note 219 at 1905.
34 *Ibid.*
35 *Ibid.* at 1908.
36 *Ibid.* at 1908–1909.
37 Lyon, *supra*, note 23 at 142.

and passing new laws. Essentially, these laws regulate how organizations and governments handle personal data and are all based on common principles, such as: consent; transparency; openness; security; purpose limitation; and control. Regulatory oversight also comes in other forms, ranging from data privacy commissioners, to government ministries, to provincial or state-level bodies and financial services authorities.

Various courts have also analysed technological developments which have made surveillance more pervasive and privacy-encroaching. The courts have tried to balance the interests of the individual in maintaining the right to privacy with the interest of the state in maintaining law and order. Yet it is uncertain exactly how biometric technologies interact with privacy rights. Depending on the nature and implementation of any given biometric system, the use of that technology may violate a state's international human rights obligations, as well as domestic privacy protections – or not. Compliance with the law will depend on a proportionality assessment that, in essence, weighs the intrusion against the achievement of a legitimate government aim.

We have seen that both the public and private sectors are making extensive use of biometrics for human recognition. As this technology becomes more economically viable and technologically feasible, the field of biometrics will spark further legal and policy concerns. Such technologies are widely touted as providing the answer to our most pressing security problems. Biometrics – *sine qua non* – is the foremost tool of risk assessment and the guarantor of security. However, as our experiences are increasingly mediated by search engines, social networking platforms and algorithms, the liberal self's capacity for rational thought, critical decision-making, self-actualization and human flourishing is increasingly being redefined and reconfigured by these interfaces.

Paradoxically, there is little willingness to question the reliability and efficacy of these technologies – one is accused of being a Luddite and against progress.[38] Privacy concerns are often dismissed on the grounds that they are antiquated, anti-progressive, overly costly and ill-disposed to the safety and security of the state.[39] The recent advent of social media, mobile platforms, cloud computing, data mining and predictive analytics now threatens to place privacy in opposition to democratic progress. This threat has been reinforced in some cases by the operation of trade secrecy law and obscurity in the internal mechanisms of complex network architectures.[40] Over time, such processes become seamlessly embedded within the normal course of business and government, often with the tacit consent of the ill-informed public.

Once a biometric identifier is captured from an individual, and even if it is captured only once, it can easily be replicated, copied and otherwise shared among countless public- and private-sector entities. This sharing can take place without

38 Elia Zureik & Karen Hindle, 'Governance, Security and Technology: The Case of Biometrics', (2004) 73(1) *Studies in Political Economy* 113 at 133.

39 Cohen, *supra*, note 219 at 1904.

40 *Ibid.* at 1914.

the individual's knowledge or consent. It also creates the potential for personal information from different sources to be linked together to form a detailed personal profile of an individual, unbeknownst to him or her. Thus, the threat to privacy arises not only from the positive identification that biometrics provide, but the ability of third parties to access this data in identifiable form and link it to other information, resulting in secondary uses of the information.

For example, private-sector firms such as Google, Facebook and the data broker Acxiom use information about consumer behaviour to target advertisements, search results and other content. Countless firms rely on this information to maximize their ability to identify high-value consumers and generate profits. The whole purpose is to mould customers into those whose means of self-determination are predictable yet ever more malleable. This is the very opposite of the liberal democratic ideal of individual autonomy, freedom of thought and choice. With little or no regulatory constraint, this model helps to sustain the power of the ruling elites, undermining the informed, critical and vigilant constituency that liberal democratic societies depend upon.[41]

Information from and about individuals also feeds into sophisticated systems of predictive analytics. For example, biometric identifiers are used by various law-enforcement agencies as part of their databases. The process involves mining the data for patterns, distilling the patterns into predictive analytics and applying the analytics to forecast the behaviour of individuals and groups with assumed scientific certainty. The availability of such data raises the question of whether there will inevitably be abuses by law enforcement, such as the unjustified flagging of suspicious behavior or the targeting of minorities. A related issue is 'function creep', whereby systems incorporating biometric data gradually spread to purposes not publicized or not even intended when the identification systems originally were implemented.

Even when the ethical and procedural shortcomings behind practices are exposed and become the subject of critical investigation, we seem unable to contest, much less upend these processes. In his seminal book, *Code and Other Laws of Cyberspace*, Lawrence Lessig argued that systems are regulated by four different regulatory pressures: the market, the law, code (or architecture) and social norms.[42] Most discussions about privacy and surveillance focus on the role that the law can play in curbing abuses of privacy by the market and the government.[43] Social norms are often rationalized through ambiguous expressions like 'Privacy is dead' or 'People do (or don't) care about privacy'.[44] Yet social norms underscore how privacy and surveillance are being challenged by an increasingly networked society – privacy is, after all, a dynamic and socially constructed process.

41 *Ibid.* at 1918.

42 Lawrence Lessig, *Code and Other Laws of Cyberspace* (New York: Basic Books, 1999).

43 danah boyd, 'Dear Voyeur, Meet Flâneur… Sincerely, Social Media', (2011) 8(4) *Surveillance & Society* 505 at 505.

44 *Ibid.*

Theoretical constructs of surveillance and the self

As our 'digital selves' become increasingly interconnected by ubiquitous electronic devices, we live and work within multiple, overlapping digital relationships, moving seamlessly between networked communities and remote links and interacting with persons and places that are spatially and temporally distant.[45] Through digital networks, we can multiply and distribute our points of physical agency through space and time. Geography has largely become irrelevant, as we don't need to know where our physical boundaries lie in the online realm; and yet we can also mobilize and assemble people face to face who would otherwise remain unknown to, and distant from, one another.

These themes have been embraced by social theorists for decades. One of the most pertinent of these accounts is American sociologist Charles Horton Cooley's 'Looking Glass Self'. The theory postulates that a person's self-image is shaped by his or her interactions with others. The view of ourselves comes from the contemplation of personal qualities and impressions of how *we believe* others perceive us. According to Cooley, this process has three steps. First, we imagine how we *appear* to another person. Second, we imagine what *judgements* people make of us based on our appearance. Third, we *imagine* how the person feels about us, based on these judgements. As a result, we often change our behaviour based on how we *feel* people perceive us.

Since we can't ever truly know how we appear to other people, our self-image is always mutable and opaque. In our digital age, with ubiquitous social media, it's easy to see the proliferation of the looking-glass self as exemplifying a society bounded by narcissism and self-preservation. The infinite social spaces we inhabit online make us endlessly beholden to the judgement of others. Conversely, if we're moving anonymously through a space where we are unknown, we are likely to feel autonomous and empowered. In other words, if we are not aware that others are watching us, reacting to us and judging us, we are likely to care less about – and try to shape – the self-impression we give off.

Similar themes were explored in the late eighteenth century by the English philosopher and social theorist Jeremy Bentham. The Panopticon was a model for the control of a large number of people, which became the prototype for a new design of prison architecture – a circular inspection house containing a central observation tower with full view of prisoners' cells populating the prison's outer wall. The effect of the Panopticon was to induce in the inmate a sense of permanent surveillance – unable to view the guards, prisoners had to assume they were being watched at all times. Bentham proposed that this external control would be internalized whereby prisoners would come to regulate their own behaviour to conform to socially desirable expectations and avoid punishment.[46]

45 Mitchell, *supra*, note 33 at 17.

46 Michel Foucault, *Discipline and Punish: The Birth of the Prison*, translated by A. Sheridan (London: Allen Lane, 1977) at 201.

Scholars have argued that this prototype endures in the digital age through the use of surveillance technology.[47] In his 1975 book *Discipline and Punish*, French philosopher Michel Foucault used the Panopticon to examine the cultural, social and theoretical mechanisms behind covert, systematic surveillance of individuals by institutions and organizations, contributing to the production of surveillance societies and reinforcing corresponding degrees of social control.

Foucault's argument is that discipline creates 'docile bodies',[48] ideal for the new economies of the modern industrial age. This requires a particular form of institution, exemplified, Foucault argued, by Bentham's Panopticon. Perhaps the most important feature of the Panopticon was that the prisoner could never be sure whether he was being observed at any moment. This caused the internalization and normalization of discipline, and the docile body required of inmates, without excessive force.

Bentham's concept was not limited to the prison: 'The Panopticon...must be understood as a generalizable model of functioning; a way of defining power relations in terms of the everyday life of men'.[49] Foucault tells us that '[w]henever one is dealing with a multiplicity of individuals on whom a task or a particular form of behaviour must be imposed, the panoptic schema may be used'.[50] Thus, the Panopticon was the ultimate realization of a modern disciplinary institution.

Foucault reflected on the move away from the spectacle of public executions to gentler forms of punishment hidden within various institutions. The systematic use of surveillance was thought to be more effective and humane. Foucault tells us that during the industrial revolution, for example, '[a]s the machinery of production became larger and more complex, as the number of workers and the division of labour increased, supervision became ever more necessary and more difficult'.[51] Just like inmates, the workers did not know exactly when they were under surveillance, which forced them to conform:

> He who is subjected to a field of visibility, and who knows it, assumes responsibility for the constraints of power; he makes them play spontaneously upon himself; he inscribes in himself the power relation in which he simultaneously plays both roles; he becomes the principle of his own subjection.[52]

As William Mitchell has pointed out, distributed control is no longer administered through '...the all-seeing eye (as depicted, for example, on the US dollar bill), but that of a continuous, sensate skin'.[53] It's no secret that Facebook wants

47 Josh A. Hendrix, Travis A. Taniguchi, Kevin J. Strom, Kelle Barrick & Nicole J. Johnson, 'The Eyes of Law Enforcement in the New Panopticon: Police-Community Racial Asymmetry and the Use of Surveillance Technology', (2018) 16(1) *Surveillance & Society* 53 at 53.

48 Foucault, *supra*, note 259 at 135.

49 *Ibid.* at 205.

50 *Ibid.*

51 *Ibid.* at 174.

52 *Ibid.* at 202.

53 Mitchell, *supra*, note 33 at 31.

its two billion-plus users to think of their public image as part of a collective whole that's indistinguishable from their private, autonomous selves. It wants to bind users to a uniform, automated 'self' that uses facial-recognition technology to tag friends in photos, which ultimately form a continuous biometric narrative documenting one's life. Facebook requires each one of its users to sign up using their real name and then it makes their name and photos public by default. The US government regularly mines this data to verify citizenship applications, for evidence in criminal cases, and to look for threats to national safety and security.[54]

For users, the process is self-reflexive, in the manner of the looking glass. What happens when people share so much of themselves that they no longer have any private, autonomous selves left? What if a person's entire record were accessible to any organization or entity at the local, state, federal or international level, including data stored in private security cameras, crowd photos, and posted on Facebook or anywhere else on the Internet? Wouldn't expanding these kinds of systems to incorporate multiple biometrics and allowing entities and organizations to share data with little oversight or restraint risk making the ubiquitous tracking and identification of people both easy and commonplace?

Insight can be gleaned from a 2017 American 'techno-thriller', *The Circle* (2017), adapted from Dave Eggers' 2013 novel and directed by James Ponsoldt. While the movie was panned by audience members – it received only a 16 percent approval rating on Rotten Tomatoes – it deserves praise for its depiction of life in a surveillance society, and for warning us about the dangers of digital observation as a means of social control. Yet the truly scary part is not the Panoptic society the film proposes, it's that most of the technology it showcases already exists – miniature cameras, drones, smartphones, tablets, data-mining, location-based tracking, and so on. And with respect to how we *use* that technology, it's a cautionary tale for the age of social-media vigilantes, witch-hunts and compulsive oversharing.

Emma Watson stars as Mae Holland, a young woman who gets an entry-level job as a 'customer experience' manager at the Circle, a youth-cult-like tech firm based in the Bay Area – think Microsoft meets Apple, meets Facebook. The Circle has a 'campus' where its employees are encouraged to spend almost all their time, complete with a nightclub, an organic farm, and a sky filled with busy drones. Naturally, the Circle stores vast amounts of personal data about its customers worldwide.

Mae attends her first 'Dream Friday', the weekly pep-rally/Ted Talk in which Eamon Bailey (Tom Hanks), the company's co-founder, gets on stage with a lofty sense of self-importance. Bailey is the public face of the Circle's idealistic, progressive, social justice-oriented rhetoric. An apparent mashup of Steve Jobs and Mark Zuckerberg, he's an uber-cool middle-age surfer-dude who wears jeans and a V-neck sweater. He outlines his latest innovation: a tiny camera inside

54 Lynch, *supra*, note 84 at 9.

a transparent glass marble-like enclosure. Placed unobtrusively, the camera, which is practically invisible, can transmit real-time images from anywhere in the world, at any time. Bailey calls it SeeChange – and he uses the moment to wax poetic about society's need for total transparency:

> There needs to be accountability. Tyrants and terrorists can no longer hide. We will see them. We will hear them. We will hear and see everything. If it happens, we'll know...Oh, we'll know the good things, too...We will see it all. Because knowing is good. But knowing everything is better.[55]

The idea of 'total transparency' is a key theme throughout the film, and it's trumpeted alongside other technogiant buzz-words, such as 'integration', which is a thinly disguised way for companies to make us think they're promoting a new way of 'connecting', when, in fact, they're interested in accessing our data so they can peddle products and re-sell our personal information to third parties.

Power isn't contained in the hands of one all-seeing authority who can exercise it single-handedly against others. Instead, it forms part of an apparatus in which everyone is bound together – those who exercise power as much as those over whom it is implemented. As we shall see in Chapter 6, this ambition has a firm footing in Silicon Valley – the tech giants were born out of a culture that disguised its quest for monopoly in idealistic pursuits of 'networkization' for the sake of global harmony and connection.[56] *Transparency* is acceptable when paired with words like 'convenience', 'ease of access' and 'security' – consequences for privacy be damned. That's a world view that has long been defended by the titans of Big Tech – people should invest their faith in the network, and the inherent wisdom of the crowds.[57] Yet the utopian dream of a world brought together by a transcendent, collaborative network has become the basis for surveillance and control.

To illustrate, we can look back to *The Circle.* Before long, Mae, in her ambitious naïveté, fully embraces the cult of 'transparency' and she volunteers to become 'fully transparent' – the first person to wear a micro-camera 24/7, where nothing except the bathroom is hidden from view. She'll wear cameras on herself and plant them all over her apartment and in other locations of her life and embrace 'the Circle' in every way. Her life is online now and millions of followers observe and comment on her every move. She wins supporters throughout the world, the love of her coworkers, the approval of her superiors; and the company, in turn, gets an enthusiastic cheerleader for its pervasive tool of surveillance.

Mae gets up on stage next to Bailey during one of his pep rallies when he reveals that his mission is driven by an arrogant belief in his own goodness and disregard for the effect of his new technology on long-standing social norms

55 Read more at: www.springfieldspringfield.co.uk/movie_script.php?movie=the-circle.

56 Franklin Foer, *World Without Mind – The Existential Threat of Big Tech* (New York: Penguin Press, 2017) at 12.

57 *Ibid.* at 2.

and practices. He tells the company audience – in a manner consistent with Bentham's enlightenment principles – that:

> I am a believer in the perfectibility of human beings. When we are our best selves, the possibilities are endless. There isn't a problem that we cannot solve. We can cure any disease and we can end hunger, and... Without secrets, without the hoarding of knowledge and information, we can finally realize our potential.

That's not simply a claim about dominating an industry – it's a statement of his intention to impose his values and convictions on the world. Here, we see the technical idea of an 'all-seeing' eye combined with the notion that it's possible to prevent wrongdoing by immersing people in a field of total visibility where, through the observation and judgement of others, they would be motivated to transform and refrain from harmful acts. This was Bentham and later Foucault's image of the transparent society, the notion that without darkness, or secrets, our embarrassing or harmful behaviour will be broadcast – and we'll behave better in the long run. The working of the Panopticon is clear from this point of view, as Mae tells the audience:

> Secrets are what make crimes possible. We behave worse when we're not accountable. I was my worst self because I didn't think anyone was watching. I thought...I was alone.

Mae then goes on to demonstrate that anyone on earth can be located in 20 minutes using the global network of over a billion participants that the Circle provides. She starts with a wanted killer (an easy sell to her audience: 'She locked her three children in the closet and went on holiday to Spain'), then – in a nightmarish turn – moves on to 'a regular person'. The ensuing search for Mae's real-life friend Mercer leaves us unsure of whom we can trust.

His pursuit by social-media hordes, armed with mobile phone cameras, and buzzing drones, plays out before the audience of cheering employees who revel in the cat-and-mouse game and the fact that he has nowhere to hide. The incident delves into how, in the event of a hunt, these technologies render innocent people suspects, create a need for justification on their part, and make further finger-pointing and suspicion unavoidable. The film concludes that when it comes to digital technology's capacity for voyeurism and dehumanization, it doesn't matter whether you're innocent or guilty. This is the essence of Panopticon justice and its link to modern forms of surveillance – cameras do not have to be monitored to change behaviour – indeed, they do not even have to be operational.

In the post-9/11 era, we've seen biometric technologies offer up the promise of security and the ability to deal with complex threats with mathematical certainty. Such technologies are part of what Rachel Hall calls 'an aesthetics of transparency', part of the culture of post-9/11 security which aims to render complex phenomena transparent, so that 'there would no longer be any secrets or interiors, human or geographical, in which our enemies (or the enemy within) might find refuge'.[58] The aim is to make individuals visible and knowable at all times, in our quest for security, stable borders, safer communities and more.[59]

One has the feeling of confronting a diabolical force that no one – neither the subject nor the object of the unrelenting gaze – can escape. This society may seem like science fiction, but it isn't. It's been sold to us by big tech companies, of the very sort depicted in *The Circle*, as an urgent social good. What emerged from the hippie counterculture of the 1960s – and profoundly shaped the future of big tech – is the naïve belief that computer networks could transform global society into a single, altruistic 'global village'.[60] While this expression of idealism has all but been lost, private and public actors have been attempting to create a superior version of humanity, in much the same way as *The Circle* portrays.

For example, this theory of 'radical transparency' or 'ultimate transparency' has already been pursued by Facebook. Indeed, Mark Zuckerberg has openly acknowledged that his company has a strong view about what's best for you and how to get you there: '[t]o get people to this point where there's more openness – that's a big challenge. But I think we'll do it', Zuckerberg has said.[61] With its power, size and influence over people worldwide, Facebook clearly has this power within its sites. And indeed, Zuckerberg has stated, '[i]n a lot of ways, Facebook is more like a government than a traditional company. We have this large community of people, and more than other technology companies, we're really setting policies'.[62]

This assumes that these systems are all-knowing and yet the people are in charge, which is clearly not the case. For example, even though Facebook users have access to the largest facial-recognition system in the world, they do not control the algorithms that help classify people into groups for disparate treatment – either as identifiable individuals or as members of whole populations. It is also far more complex and far-reaching than Zuckerberg lets on. These simplistic and self-serving comments fail to grasp the personal, social and political consequences of surveillance.[63]

Although the problem is best defined in terms of surveillance, the social and individual values that are at risk are still best encapsulated by privacy.[64] Surveillance does not just involve the monitoring and tracking of individuals; rather, its far-reaching practices affect the panoply of concerns that we have clustered

58 Rachel Hall, 'Of Ziplock Bags and Black Holes: The Aesthetics of Transparency in the War on Terror', in Shoshanna Magnet and Kelly Gates (eds), *The New Media of Surveillance* (New York: Routledge, 2009).

59 Magnet, *supra*, note 57 at 152.

60 Foer, *supra*, note 269 at 25.

61 Foer, *supra*, note 269 at 61.

62 *Ibid.*

63 Colin J. Bennett, Kevin D. Haggerty, David Lyon & Valerie M. Steeves (eds), *Transparent Lives: Surveillance in Canada (The New Transparency Project)* (Edmonton: Athabasca University Press, 2014) at 4.

64 Priscilla M. Regan, 'Response to Bennett: Also in Defence of Privacy', (2011) 8(4) *Surveillance & Society* 497 at 497.

together under the umbrella of 'privacy'.[65] However, the traditional concept of privacy cannot solve the myriad problems that we now face in the complex, global information-based surveillance society.[66]

Philosophically, privacy is too deeply rooted in individualism and notions of separation between the state, the individual and civil society.[67] Similarly, the 'right to be let alone' concept of privacy first articulated by Warren and Brandeis reinforces the notion that privacy is about seclusion and separation. Indeed, Brandeis wrote, in his dissenting opinion in *Olmstead v. United States*, that the Framers had 'conferred, as against the government, the right to be let alone…'[68] However, this conception of privacy, by itself, is clearly insufficient because privacy is not simply about a 'bubble' around the self but about social, relational and contextual complexity.[69]

The problem with defining the scope of privacy as such was compounded when Justice Stewart famously quipped in *Katz* that the 'Fourth Amendment protects people, not places'.[70] Not surprisingly, this assertion has been described by some commentators as normatively hollow.[71] As Justice Harlan observed in his concurring opinion, the answer to the question of 'what protection it affords to those people' still 'requires reference to a place'.[72] Yet this leaves privacy entangled in spatial metaphors about 'trespass', 'invasion' and 'intrusion', which are no longer appropriate in the modern age.

Privacy isn't a unitary 'space' to be invaded, but rather a symbiotic set of practices through which individuals reveal – and organizations capture – data as part of one's participation in contemporary society.[73] The scale and scope of the problem exist at a systemic level (institutions, social practices, routine transactions) not at the level of private space (invading one's house, taking pictures, eavesdropping on a conversation).[74] The phrase 'privacy invasion', as it is traditionally used and understood, is too limited to encompass what has become a characteristic feature of modern life.[75]

Even if we consider the general ways that biometric data are collected – ranging from highly invasive (e.g. blood samples for DNA) to minimally invasive

65 *Ibid.*

66 Colin J. Bennett, 'In Defence of Privacy: The Concept and the Regime', (2011) 8(4) *Surveillance & Society* 485 at 485.

67 *Ibid.* at 486.

68 *Olmstead, supra*, note 238 at 478.

69 Regan, *supra*, note 277 at 498.

70 *Katz, supra*, note 242 at 351.This is discussed in Kerr, *supra*, note 59 at 817; note that the 'property-based approach' was formulated in *Olmstead, supra*, note 238. See also Andrew E. Taslitz, 'The Fourth Amendment in the Twenty-First Century: Technology, Privacy, and Human Emotions', (2002) 65 *Law and Contemporary Problems* 125.

71 Tracey Maclin, 'Katz, Kyllo, and Technology: Virtual Fourth Amendment Protection in the Twenty-First Century', (2002) 72 *Mississippi Law Journal* 51 at 74.

72 *Katz, supra*, note 242 at 361.

73 Bennett, *supra*, note 279 at 488.

74 *Regan, supra*, note 277 at 497.

75 *Ibid.*

(e.g. fingerprint or iris scan); to non-invasive (e.g. gait, which can be collected without the subject's knowledge) – each of these has different implications for privacy.[76] Moreover, information shared by an individual for one purpose can be acquired by another party and used for a different purpose altogether. These practices allow deeply personal inferences to be drawn about the individual that would not have been possible before the age of big data. Not only do they affect one's privacy rights, but the decisions made and the corresponding actions taken can also be variously privacy infringing.

Other, more recent, conceptualizations of privacy include that of Alan Westin: 'the claim of individuals, groups, or institutions to determine for themselves when, how, and to what extent information about them is communicated to others'.[77] Charles Fried similarly characterized privacy in terms of 'the control we have over information about ourselves'.[78] While these definitions seem to incorporate the informational concerns of the modern world, they are too narrow and reliant on liberal assumptions about the separation between the autonomous 'self' and others which have been largely displaced by omnipresent, decentralized data capturing in which '...the human self is located [in] fragments of personal data [that] constantly circulate within computer systems beyond any agent's personal control'.[79] The insistence that individuals should have a right to *control* the circulation of information that relates to them also fails to deal with the residual discrimination that comes with profiling and categorizing individuals.

Thus, while privacy traditionally protects secrecy, seclusion and individuality, it must be recognized as a much broader societal value that does not exist in a vacuum.[80] Indeed, privacy violations don't just affect individuals in terms of their relationship with the state or other individuals, they can also affect their opportunities, life chances, freedoms and lifestyle.[81] Excessive surveillance also impacts the very nature of society, in the Panoptic sense. The relationships between individuals and modern organizations are enormously complicated and now almost universally are mediated by, or occur within, technological systems. In the age of surveillance, we must look for a more nuanced theory of privacy that considers contextual integrity and technological change.

Conclusion

The extent to which personal information is gathered, processed and retained is unparalleled in human history. Surveillance is a dominant global practice that inevitably results in people being categorized in ways that facilitate different forms

76 Lynch, *supra*, note 84 at 4.

77 Alan Westin, *Privacy and Freedom* (New York: Atheneum, 1970) at 7.

78 Charles Fried, 'Privacy' (1970) 77 *Yale Law Journal* 475 at 475.

79 David Lyon, *The Electronic Eye: The Rise of Surveillance Society* (Minneapolis: University of Minnesota Press, 1994) at 18.

80 Bennett *supra*, note 279 at 487.

81 *Ibid.* at 488.

of treatment for different individuals. Some groups are affected by surveillance more than others, but in all cases the balance of power between individuals and organizations shifts with the growth of surveillance practices and processes. In essence, they 'serve to open and close doors of opportunity and access'[82] for both the privileged and underprivileged.

There is growing awareness and antipathy towards the routine practice of recording, analysing and communicating information about individuals as they move about and transact in the normal course of their commercial and public lives. Moreover, in the context of biometric technologies, we are now seeing the collection of information from the person's body – intrinsic to them – which raises entirely new questions as to what counts as a legitimate violation of privacy. Contemporary constitutional law is not even remotely prepared to handle these developments. The legal status of most kinds of biometric data is uncertain. No court has addressed whether the state can collect biometric data without a person's knowledge, and the case law says nothing about facial recognition. The potential for misuse is patently obvious.

Bibliography

Colin J. Bennett, 'In Defence of Privacy: The Concept and the Regime', (2011) 8(4) *Surveillance & Society* 485.

Colin J. Bennett, Kevin D. Haggerty, David Lyon & Valerie M. Steeves (eds), *Transparent Lives: Surveillance in Canada (The New Transparency Project)* (Edmonton: Athabasca University Press, 2014).

danah boyd, 'Dear Voyeur, Meet Flâneur… Sincerely, Social Media', (2011) 8(4) *Surveillance & Society* 505.

W. J. Clinton, 'Commencement Address at Morgan State University', Baltimore, MD, 18 May 1997.

Julie E. Cohen, 'What Privacy is For', (2013) 126(7) *Harvard Law Review* 1904.

Franklin Foer, *World Without Mind – The Existential Threat of Big Tech* (New York: Penguin Press, 2017).

Michel Foucault, *Discipline and Punish: The Birth of the Prison* translated by A. Sheridan (London: Allen Lane, 1977).

Charles Fried, 'Privacy' (1970) 77 *Yale Law Journal* 475.

Dorothy J. Glancy, 'The Invention of the Right to Privacy', (1979) 21(1) *Arizona Law Review* 1.

Rachel Hall, 'Of Ziplock Bags and Black Holes: The Aesthetics of Transparency in the War on Terror', in Shoshanna Magnet & Kelly Gates (eds), *The New Media of Surveillance* (New York: Routledge, 2009) 41–68.

Josh A. Hendrix, Travis A. Taniguchi, Kevin J. Strom, Kelle Barrick & Nicole J. Johnson, 'The Eyes of Law Enforcement in the New Panopticon: Police-Community Racial Asymmetry and the Use of Surveillance Technology', (2018) 16(1) *Surveillance & Society* 53.

82 David Lyon, 'Surveillance as Social Sorting', in David Lyon (ed.), *Surveillance as Social Sorting – Privacy, Risk and Digital Discrimination* (New York: Routledge, 2003) at 27.

Michael C. James, 'A Comparative Analysis of the Right to Privacy in the United States, Canada and Europe', (2014) 29(2) *Connecticut Journal of International Law* 257.
Orin Kerr, 'The Fourth Amendment and New Technologies: Constitutional Myths and the Case for Caution', (2003) 102 *Michigan Law Review* 801.
Jill Lepore, 'The Prism – Privacy in an Age of Publicity', *The New Yorker*, 24 June 2013.
Lawrence Lessig, *Code and Other Laws of Cyberspace* (New York: Basic Books, 1999).
John Locke, 'Second Treatise of Government', in Michael Morgan (ed.), *Classics of Moral and Political Theory* (Indianapolis, IN: Hackett, 1992) 736.
Jennifer Lynch, 'From Fingerprints to DNA: Biometric Data Collection in U.S. Immigrant Communities and Beyond', 22 May 2012.
David Lyon, *The Electronic Eye: The Rise of Surveillance Society* (Minneapolis: University of Minnesota Press, 1994).
David Lyon, 'Surveillance as Social Sorting', in David Lyon (ed.), *Surveillance as Social Sorting – Privacy, Risk and Digital Discrimination* (New York: Routledge, 2003) at 27.
David Lyon, 'Globalizing Surveillance', (2004) 19(2) *Comparative and Sociological Perspectives* 135.
Tracey Maclin, 'Katz, Kyllo, and Technology: Virtual Fourth Amendment Protection in the Twenty-First Century', (2002) 72 *Mississippi Law Journal* 51.
Shoshanna Amielle Magnet, *When Biometrics Fail: Gender, Race and the Technologies of Identity* (Durham, NC: Duke University Press, 2011).
John Stuart Mill, 'On Liberty', in Michael Morgan (ed.), *Classics of Moral and Political Theory* (Indianapolis, IN: Hackett, 1992) 1044.
William J. Mitchell, *ME ++* (Cambridge, MA: MIT Press, 2004).
Helen Nissenbaum, 'Protecting Privacy in an Information Age: The Problem of Privacy in Public', (1998) 17 *Law and Philosophy* 559.
Priscilla M. Regan, 'Response to Bennett: Also in Defence of Privacy', (2011) 8(4) *Surveillance & Society* 497.
Kenneth Ryan, 'Introduction', in Peter P. Swire & Kenesa Ahmad (eds), *Privacy and Surveillance with New Technologies* (New York: International Debate Education Association, 2012) 1.
Andrew E. Taslitz, 'The Fourth Amendment in the Twenty-First Century: Technology, Privacy, and Human Emotions', (2002) 65 *Law and Contemporary Problems* 125.
Samuel D. Warren & Louis Brandeis, 'The Right to Privacy', (1890) 4 *Harvard Law Review* 193.
Alan Westin, *Privacy and Freedom* (New York: Atheneum, 1970).
Elia Zureik & Karen Hindle, 'Governance, Security and Technology: The Case of Biometrics', (2004) 73(1) *Studies in Political Economy* 113.

Case Law

Katz v. United States, 389 U.S. 347 (1967).
Olmstead v. United States, 277 U.S. 438 (1928).
K. S. Puttaswamy v. Union of India, Writ Petition (Civil) No. 494 of 2012.

4 Biometrics and law enforcement

Introduction

The escalating global insecurity of the last couple of decades has brought with it an equally precipitous rise in the use of sophisticated technologies. Predictive algorithms, risk models, and other sorts of automated decision-making tools are now ubiquitous in the public service.[1] Investments in these systems are often justified by calls for administrative efficiency – doing more with less and making decisions on a fairer and more consistent basis.

Yet, although we devote more and more attention to managing it, risk seems increasingly to be out of our control. Our society's belief that risk is everywhere has prompted ever more determined efforts to control it. And the more we consider and discuss risks, the more this leads to a climate of fear. This, in turn, leads to the demand for more information about risks, creating a vicious circle that helps to justify even more surveillance and profiling in the pursuit of security.

Yet security technologies are not neutral. They produce and reinforce understandings of gender, race, class, authority and criminality (i.e. a larger set of relationships that are politically determined and that raise complex social, economic, political and legal issues). These understandings further contribute to the development and use of the technology. Biometric technologies, thus, categorize individuals with a dangerous logic that cannot be viewed as "true" or 'objective'.

Those lower on the social and economic hierarchy – the poor, working-class and minorities – have often found themselves targets rather than beneficiaries of these systems.[2] Since those who are most vulnerable to risk include those whose actions can contribute to risk, certain groups of people – for example, particular ethnic minorities or poor people – are often seen as risky themselves.[3] Marginalized people are exposed to more risks and are categorized as bad risks; thus, the very people who need our help the most are viewed as a threat, which actually inhibits them from getting the help that they might need.[4]

1 Eubanks, *supra*, note 153 at 9.

2 *Ibid.*

3 Bennett et al., *supra*, note 276 at 47.

4 *Ibid.*

The first part of this chapter examines the use of innovative technologies for policing. Police who were once restricted to naked-eye surveillance can now use high-tech devices to profile individuals in large crowds. Digital tracking and decision-making systems are increasingly commonplace. They are powerful forces for control, manipulation and punishment, which can restrict people's liberty and undermine their civil rights.[5]

The concept of 'predictive policing' is new. It's the logical extension of crime mapping and offender profiling in a world with more available data and processing power. Artificial intelligence tools are being developed to predict a crime before it happens, and to provide authorities with precise information about when and where a crime is about to be committed and who is about to commit it. But should we trust AI to decide who is a criminal and what defines a crime?

Criminal justice algorithms – sometimes called 'risk assessments' or 'evidenced-based methods' – are controversial tools that purport to predict future behaviour of individuals, including defendants and incarcerated persons who are already within the criminal justice system.[6] The focus is on bringing together massive amounts of data and applied mathematics to answer the 'what, when and where' questions that have long puzzled law-enforcement officials and policymakers.

In the late 1980s, Utah became the first U.S. state to adopt biometric retinal scanners to identify prisoners.[7] This technique quickly became a 'booming business' and expanded across the United States throughout the 1990s. This coincided with the massive growth of the U.S. prison system and the corresponding need for innovative surveillance tools to support the prison industrial complex.[8]

The addition of these technologies must also be seen as part of the growth in the privatization of the surveillance state – and the prison industrial complex – with tremendous profits made by companies from the expansion of the U.S. prison system.[9] Indeed, the prison system offered technology manufacturers scores of compliant test subjects, and the industry found the needed research and development funds through government subsidies, grants and public-private partnerships.[10]

New high-tech tools are now being used to win the war *against* mass incarceration by making the physical institution of the prison less essential. For the most part, these developments are positive. However, when these systems begin to inform basic decisions affecting civil liberties, law enforcement agencies must address issues beyond narrow considerations of cost and ease of use. The question is how to harness their potential benefits while addressing difficult questions of fairness, accountability and transparency.

5 Eubanks, *supra*, note 153 at 10.

6 Electronic Information Privacy Center, 'Algorithms in the Criminal Justice System'. Available online at: https://epic.org/algorithmic-transparency/crim-justice/.

7 Magnet, *supra*, note 57 at 57.

8 *Ibid.* at 58.

9 *Ibid.* at 62.

10 *Ibid.* at 62.

Biometric policing

Law enforcement can be seen as the birthplace of biometrics. Fingerprints collected from a crime scene were first leveraged to investigate crime and the people involved by matching them against known prints. Police in the UK are now trialling a mobile fingerprint-matching system, aimed at making it easier for officers to recognize criminals, wanted suspects, and 'persons of interest', in the field.[11] The mobile app, paired with a compact fingerprint scanner device, matches prints against two national databases of known images in less than a minute, and can thus also help officers identify individuals in emergency situations, and contact next of kin.[12]

DNA evidence also continues to play a critical role in criminal investigations worldwide. It has been used in many high-profile cases to prove that suspects were involved in crimes and to free the wrongly convicted. Millions of people have also bought into the new science of consumer genealogy, sending saliva-filled tubes to DNA-testing websites that offer to help them discover their family roots.

After decades as a cold case, police in California recently used DNA to arrest a man they believe to be the 'Golden State Killer'. The killer had mystified authorities for a generation, leaving a trail of unsolved crimes across the state that included at least a dozen killings and as many as 50 rapes.[13] Four decades after the first crimes, and three decades after the killer went quiet, police were finally able to make an arrest.

The killer's DNA eventually led the police to him; but it wasn't as simple as linking him to a match found at a crime scene. Instead, they turned to an online service called GEDmatch that allows people to upload genetic data from private services and make it available to other people interested in finding out more about their family history. The site's operators say they didn't even realize it was being used in the investigation.[14]

DNA recovered from a crime scene in the 1970s or '80s was used to find the killer's great-great-great-grandparents, who lived in the early 1800s.[15] Branch by painstaking branch, the investigative team created about 25 family trees containing thousands of relatives down to the present day. That data eventually pointed them to Joseph James DeAngelo, 72, a disgraced former police officer who matched the age and description of the suspect, and also happened to live

11 Alex Perala, 'UK Police to Use Mobile Fingerprint Scanning System in the Field', *Find-Biometrics*, 12 February 2018.

12 Matt Reynolds, 'UK Police are Now Using Fingerprint Scanners on the Streets to Identify People in Less than a Minute', *Wired*, 10 February 2018.

13 Justin Jouvenal, Mark Berman, Drew Harwell & Tom Jackman, 'Data on a Genealogy Site led Police to the "Golden State Killer" Suspect. Now Others Worry about a "Treasure Trove of Data"' *The Washington Post*, 27 April 2018.

14 *Ibid.*

15 Justin Jouvenal, 'To find Alleged Golden State Killer, Investigators First Found his Great-Great-Great-Grandparents', *The Washington Post*, 30 April 2018.

near where the crimes occurred.[16] He has since been arrested and charged with multiple murders.

Publicly available sites like the one used by police in that case hold lots of intimate genetic information and can potentially connect people to everyone related to them. Our DNA can tell us a lot about ourselves but it can also reveal a lot about our nearest and dearest. Experts have been concerned about the privacy risks of storing this highly sensitive personal information online; and this case highlights what it's possible to do with this vast treasure trove of biological data.

This astonishing case highlights the consumer DNA industry's growing role in resuscitating cold cases and reforming justice in the digital age. But the data's use in policing has also fuelled concerns that people don't truly understand the power of what they're so liberally handing over – the building blocks of identity, both for themselves and their families. It also raises questions about the circumstances in which intimate personal information can be freely shared by DNA genealogy websites with third parties.

Such practices intrude upon norms of contextual integrity when information revealed in one context is transmitted to, and exposed in, another. When you enter your personal data into a database, you have certain expectations about how it will be used; so, when it gets utilized for completely different purposes, like law enforcement, this strikes at the heart of why many people are concerned about violations of their personal privacy. When it comes to DNA, which can identify whole networks of individuals without their knowledge or consent, questions about privacy and contextual integrity become murky.

Of course, police in the United States don't need to rely on privately held DNA databanks such as this. Since 2009, at least 21 states and the federal government have been collecting DNA from any adult arrested for (not just convicted of) a crime and at least 28 states collect DNA from juvenile offenders.[17] As of June 2013, criminal justice databases in the U.S. contained DNA profiles for 10.7 million offenders and 1.7 million arrestees.[18] The United States has used this data to amass the largest DNA database in the world.

All 50 states, the federal government and the District of Columbia collect, share and rely on records through the FBI's central system called the Combined DNA Index System (CODIS) – a system linking information among the different DNA databases around the country – to match crime-scene samples with offender or arrestee DNA profiles.[19] The potential benefits of this system include increased efficiency, cooperation and information-sharing, particularly for cross-jurisdictional investigations.[20]

16 Jouvenal et al., *supra*, note 308.

17 Lynch, *supra*, note 84 at 7.

18 Elizabeth E. Joh, "Policing by Numbers: Big Data and the Fourth Amendment," (2014) 89 *Washington Law Review* 35 at 50.

19 *Ibid.* at 51.

20 Smith et al., *supra*, note 68 at 10.

CODIS includes profiles drawn from crime-scene evidence, unidentified remains, and genetic samples voluntarily provided by relatives of missing persons.[21] Once a government agent collects a genetic sample, it is sent to a lab which isolates the DNA and then processes it to obtain a 'profile', which is then entered into the database and given an anonymized identification number.[22] The DNA profile remains in CODIS permanently and can be continually accessed and searched by police at any level of government without any consent, suspicion or warrant.[23]

A 2016 report by the Georgetown Law Center on Privacy and Technology further noted that law enforcement facial recognition networks include over 117 million American adults, and at least 26 states permit law enforcement to search against driving licence photos.[24] Such biometric data collection methods identify and locate data points around the individual to allow inferences of suspicion that simply weren't possible in the past.[25] For example, the addition of crowd and security camera photos could mean that virtually everyone ends up in the database, and risks being accused of crime just by happening to be in the wrong place at the wrong time, or by fitting a stereotype.[26] The DNA in CODIS could be used at some point in the future to look for genetic predispositions for diseases or for traits that would suggest they are aberrant and need to be disciplined.[27]

Facial recognition on smartphones represents another important step in the evolution of high-tech policing. Beginning in 2010, dozens of law enforcement agencies in the United States were outfitted with a handheld facial recognition device known as MORIS, or Mobile Offender Recognition System, which attaches to an Apple iPhone, enabling an officer to snap a picture of a face from up to five feet away, or scan a person's irises from up to six inches away, and do an immediate search to see if there is a match with a criminal database.[28]

More recently, police departments around the country have begun using body cameras. Small enough to be worn on the head, ear or chest, a body camera can go everywhere officers go, providing an audiovisual recording of what they see when they come into contact with citizens at homes, on foot patrol, while executing search warrants, and more.[29] In Ferguson, Missouri, the shooting of Michael Brown in August 2014 created public uproar and riots; and President Obama subsequently proposed nationwide funding to equip police agencies

21 Lynch, *supra*, note 84 at 7.
22 *Ibid.*
23 *Ibid.* at 8.
24 Margaret Hu, 'From the National Surveillance State to the Cybersurveillance State', (2017) 13 *Annual Review of Law and Social Science* 161 at 175.
25 *Ibid.*
26 Lynch, *supra*, note 84 at 10.
27 *Ibid.* at 11.
28 Emily Steel & J. Angwin, 'Device Raises Fear of Facial Profiling', *The Wall Street Journal*, 13 July 2011.
29 Mary D. Fan, 'Justice Visualized: Courts and the Body Camera Revolution', (2017) 50 *U.C. Davis Law Review* 897 at 901.

across the United States with body-worn cameras.[30] In Canada, the shooting of Sammy Yatim in July 2013 by a Toronto police officer similarly lead to discussions about equipping police officers with body-worn cameras. Stock prices have recently surged for Taser International, the maker of one of the most popular brands of body cameras and a cloud-based service to store the footage.[31]

Police officers throughout the United States are now using these devices to record stops, searches, responses to calls for service, pursuits, uses of force, arrests, and transportation of arrestees.[32] Besides increasing police transparency and accountability, these devices are said to reduce police officer exposure to litigation and unjustified citizen complaints. Supporters also maintain that law enforcement encounters won't have to be reconstructed through what often amounts to biased or otherwise unreliable testimony.[33] Events are now captured on video, giving judges and juries the chance to see for themselves what actually occurred.[34]

Having the benefit of full event replay would seem to do away with the credibility contests that often ensue as defendant and officer dispute each other's recollection of events. Defendants are frequently assumed to be lying villains with dubious credibility; and police are accused of being deceptive power abusers.[35] Courts are caught between conflicting stories in which both sides are discredited. For minority groups alleging unfair treatment, body cameras are also a way to 'police the police', promote transparency and reduce the risk of injuries and deaths.[36]

On the other hand, police officers, police unions and civil liberties groups have expressed concerns, for example about chilling interactions with witnesses and victims and the loss of privacy for the public and police.[37] People face having their most painful, traumatic and embarrassing moments recorded for replay when such encounters are videotaped.[38] The use of video replay also usurps the defendant's right to not take the stand during trial and to remain silent. It gives the court the ability to replay the events and check the story – and perhaps view the encounter from a different perspective, even if the defendant does not speak.

This can be more than just inconvenient or embarrassing for a defendant – it can annihilate his case and his credibility. The video can speak beyond officer accounts, adding a fuller range of details to disputed events. However, if a defendant stays silent and fails to offer evidence contrary to the video, this might increase the likelihood that the jury will draw an adverse inference from his

30 Thomas A. Bud, 'The Rise and Risks of Police Body-Worn Cameras in Canada', (2016) 14(1) Surveillance & Society 117 at 117.

31 Fan, *supra*, note 324 at 927.

32 *Ibid.* at 902.

33 *Ibid.* at 908.

34 *Ibid.* at 905.

35 *Ibid.* at 919.

36 *Ibid.* at 925.

37 *Ibid.* at 922.

38 *Ibid.*

silence. Moreover, the relevant 'truth' may not actually be the camera's depiction of events.

Body cameras and smart glasses worn by law enforcement are also being integrated with facial recognition and other artificial intelligence tools, including automated analytics and database screening capacities. As technologies progress, they are likely to be used to link biometric identity to multidimensional surveillance (e.g., algorithmic-driven biographical screening and behavioural analysis).[39] Body cameras may also one day be used to assess future risk and isolate other data deemed suspicious.[40]

Multidimensional systems are now embracing 'situational awareness' technologies that integrate multiple sensors, including video surveillance and additional image sensors, with the 'web scraping' of social media platforms.[41] In one case, a corporation tested a Smart Surveillance System and Intelligent Video Analytics software for a city to conduct surveillance of a concert. The program assimilated and aggregated information on live video and social media activity through monitoring crowds, pedestrians and vehicles; and, notably, the surveillance had a "People Search" feature that could identify individuals by skin colour, clothing texture, baldness, or whether or not they wear glasses.[42]

Once biometric identifiers are aggregated in databases, they can form the backbone to support all sorts of multidimensional surveillance systems. These technologies inevitably change the relationship between the police and their environment; and they can shift the balance between individual freedom and social control. It goes without saying that individuals – both police officers and members of the public – tend to act differently when they feel they're being watched. In addition, biometric surveillance not only identifies people, but also makes assessments based on identity.[43]

These systems are now so advanced, they can make predictions regarding which individuals are most likely to commit acts of terrorism or other serious crimes. Indeed, terrorism is now largely associated with singling out certain groups who are profiled on the basis of national origin, race and religion. Surveillance is a 'tautological' exercise in which 'everything that moves' is captured on video camera and becomes part of an ordinary or aberrant frame.[44]

Security has become an abstract concept – a not-quite-attainable ideal for which a vast number of procedures, gadgets, systems and institutions are designed and deployed to assess risk and increase safety.[45] It is dominated by experts and professionals who bypass public participation and design 'top down' security solutions. Under certain conditions, surveillance can create a criminogenic

39 Hu, *supra*, note 92 at 1435.
40 *Ibid.* at 1435.
41 *Ibid.* at 1434.
42 *Ibid.* at 1446.
43 *Ibid.* at 1441.
44 Zureik & Hindle, *supra*, note 251 at 115.
45 *Ibid.*

environment that encourages distrust, stigmatizes innocent people and enhances societal division.[46] It's deeply concerning that the legislative and constitutional framework for regulating such practices is sorely lacking.[47]

A prison without bars: life in the surveillance state

With the help of technologies like CCTV cameras and GPS monitoring, the would-be felon and the convict released back into the community need not wonder whether they are being watched – they can be sure that they are, at all times. The prototype lies in the eighteenth century, with the Panopticon – a name that derives from the Greek word for 'all-seeing'.[48] Under the watchful eye of the all-powerful, God-like gaze, the prisoner is transformed from a delinquent rebel – a villain, a traitor, a madman or a monster – into a 'civilized' individual.

From a law-enforcement perspective, anonymity is the enemy. The need to 'de-anonymize' the individual has long been central to solving crime. Panopticon justice aims to place a small voice in each of our heads warning us that someone is watching and that wrongdoing will be punished. Now, imagine living with surveillance cameras on every corner. You're walking home from the subway and the cameras pick up your face. The system runs it through a facial recognition system and your name, age, social media profile and criminal record pops up – your whole identity is revealed from a single source of biometric data – your face.

As disturbing as that might sound, it's not far off from what China has already implemented. If you visit China today, you'll find that you can board a continental flight without a ticket, and even smile to pay at some fast-food places. China's facial recognition technology is among the most advanced in the world, capable of identifying a person from a database of more than two billion people in a matter of seconds. The technology is used widely in retail, finance and transportation, as well as to monitor citizen behaviour.

Banks, hotels, airports and even toilets are all trying to verify people's identities with facial recognition technologies.[49] At the entrance of the public restrooms at Beijing's Temple of Heaven, for example, facial-recognition scanners linked to toilet-paper dispensers dole out 23.6 inches of tissue per person.[50] Want more? Wait nine minutes, or the scanner will recognize you and retort: 'please try again later'.[51]

46 *Ibid.* at 118.

47 Margaret Hu, 'Biometric Cyberintelligence and the Posse Comitatus Act', (2017) 66 *Emory Law Journal* 697 at 711–712.

48 Graeme Wood, 'Prison Without Walls', in Peter P. Swire and Kenesa Ahmad (eds), *Privacy and Surveillance with New Technologies* (New York: International Debate Education Association, 2012) at 295.

49 Simon Denyer, 'China's Watchful Eye', *The Washington Post*, 7 January 2018.

50 Rene Chun, 'China's New Frontiers in Dystopian Tech', *The Atlantic*, April 2018.

51 *Ibid.*

If that's not dystopian enough for you – consider this: at KFC China's 'smart restaurant' in Beijing, customers stand in front of a facial-scanning screen and receive menu suggestions based on their age, sex and facial expressions.[52] A young man might be steered towards a full meal, complete with a chicken burger, fries and drink; but a middle-aged woman might be encouraged to select a healthier option consisting of oatmeal and soy milk.[53] Behind this veil of convenience lies a sinister reality – biometric tools, like facial-recognition software, have quietly enabled China to become the world's most sophisticated surveillance state.[54]

The other trend is the deployment of Artificial Intelligence (AI) technology with object detection, crowd monitoring and feature extraction to filter, collect and analyse the data and create detailed profiles of individuals. The technology can detect people walking down the street and offer information about their identities, including their name, job and online public profiles. The goal is to track and monitor where people are at all times of the day and night, what they're doing, who they associate with and what they believe.[55] It means that just by having a snapshot of someone the watchers suddenly have their entire identity.

In 2015, China's national police force – the Ministry of Public Safety – advocated for the creation of an 'omnipresent, completely connected, always on and fully controllable' national video surveillance network. One hundred per cent of Beijing is now covered with surveillance cameras. This forms part of an ambitious plan, known as Xue Liang, which can be translated as 'Sharp Eyes'. It aims to connect security cameras throughout the country – which already scan roads, shopping malls and transport hubs – with private cameras, and integrate them into a nationwide surveillance and data-sharing platform that uses artificial intelligence to identify and track suspects, pinpoint suspicious behaviour and dispatch emergency services.[56]

In its comprehensive 2014 planning outline, the Chinese Communist Party explains that it wants to 'keep trust and constraints against breaking trust'. And the government plans, by 2020, to ensure that its video surveillance network is 'omnipresent, fully networked, always working and fully controllable'.[57] Yet the result may be that no one will have a clear idea of who they can trust. Not only will these efforts lead to the creation of a vast database of information about every citizen – from travel bookings and hotel stays to medical records, to online purchases, and even social media comments – it will also assign them a numerical 'social credit' score based on whether the government and their fellow citizens consider them popular and trustworthy or not.[58]

52 *Ibid.*
53 *Ibid.*
54 *Ibid.*
55 Denyer, *supra*, note 344.
56 *Ibid.*
57 *Ibid.*
58 *Ibid.*

In Jinan, the capital of Shandong province, traffic-management authorities have been using facial recognition to prevent jaywalking at busy intersections.[59] When the scanner detects a jaywalker, it takes several photos and records a video, which is then cross-referenced against images in a regional police database. Within 20 minutes, photos appear overhead with the individual's ID number and home address. Police have also been known to post names and photos of jaywalkers on social media; which, of course, ties into one's 'social credit score' whereby points might be added for good behaviour like winning a community award and deducted for things like failure to pay a traffic fine.[60] The goal of the programme, as set out in government documents, is to 'allow the trustworthy to roam everywhere under heaven while making it hard for the discredited to take a single step'.[61]

Already, 100,000 Chinese citizens have posted on social media about high scores on a 'Sesame Credit' app operated by Alibaba, in a privately owned forerunner to the government system. While the system was purportedly implemented to deal with the threat of criminal activity by shining a light into dark corners where crime flourishes, it poses a chilling threat to human rights and civil liberties as it may be used by the state to tighten its grip on every aspect of society.[62] Indeed, the name of the project is taken from the Communist slogan, 'the masses have sharp eyes', which harkens back to Mao Zedong's effort to ensure that citizens all spy on one another.[63] It's no surprise that concerns have been raised over the increased ability of police to track citizens' movements and monitor political and religious dissidents, with fears that information linked to the ID programme can be used to target or detain certain groups.

Intrusive surveillance technologies aren't only being embraced by closed societies like China. Even Britain – which used to pride itself on its commitment to democracy, tolerance and respect for liberty – has rushed to install CCTV cameras fitted with loudspeakers to allow staff to censure people spotted dropping litter, urinating in public, not picking up after their dog, vandalizing property or fighting. The objective is to prevent people from acting antisocially – those who misbehave 'face the shame of being publicly embarrassed'.[64] By some estimates, as many as a million CCTV cameras are installed in London, making it the most surveilled metropolis in the world.[65] The plethora of cameras was premised on a coercive principle – the architecture of surveillance would dissuade people from committing crimes. 'There is a friendly eye in the sky', a Home Office minister proclaimed in 1994; 'There is nothing sinister about it, and the innocent have nothing to fear'.[66]

59 Chun, *supra*, note 345.
60 *Ibid.*
61 *Ibid.*
62 Denyer, *supra*, note 344.
63 *Ibid.*
64 Peter Griffiths, "Britain Plans more 'talking' Surveillance Cameras," *The Globe and Mail*, April 4, 2007.
65 Keefe, *supra*, note 205.
66 *Ibid.*

Yet monitoring is a form of power – a power that operates over specifically identified individuals or through the ability to manipulate entire populations. With the contemporary expansion of surveillance, such that monitoring becomes an ever more routine part of our lives, there is also a vast shift in the balance of power between citizens and organizations.[67] The most significant danger is that we are creating a society that is hard-wired for surveillance and that such devices can effortlessly be turned to oppressive uses. This infrastructure can easily be used to monitor people because of their dress, appearance, religious beliefs, skin colour, gender, migration status, and so on.

New processes of surveillance and risk-profiling are already being used to make the ordinary domains of the commute, the office and the marketplace sites of enforcement in the global War on Terror.[68] For example, a Seattle IT company, Town Compass LLC, markets 'personal products to fight the war on terror'[69] to citizens. Their 'Most Wanted Terrorists' database can be downloaded free to smartphones as part of the 'terrorism survival' package. Town Compass promises that 'people can have the photos and descriptions at their fingertips at all times in case they spot a suspicious person, easily comparing the person to the photo without endangering themselves'.[70] Should the honourable foot soldier identify a suspicious-looking person, the download comes complete with one-touch dialling to the FBI and full details of available rewards.[71]

Similarly, in the wake of the recent London bombings, the UK government offered its residents a 'Life Savers' hotline number, which is downloaded to mobile phones with the message that 'people should consider whether the behaviour of those they encounter, through work or socially, gives them any reason to think they might be planning terrorist attacks'.[72] The deployment of such systems, like the biometric border discussed in Chapter 6, implicates us all in the regulating of mobility and the profiling of suspicious behaviour. It also provides a striking example of how surveillance measures are often introduced on the basis of one dramatic and horrifying but statistically unlikely incident that receives a great deal of media, political and public attention.[73] These campaigns do more than just enlist the public to monitor one another – they also reinforce the message that danger is always out there, justifying even more surveillance.[74]

By 2025, it is forecast that there will be a billion AI cameras deployed in cities worldwide; and over a short time, with machine learning, the systems will become faster and more accurate in applying biometric and movement algorithms

67 Bennett et al. *supra*, note 276 at 36.

68 Louise Amoore, 'Biometric Borders: Governing Mobilities in the War on Terror', (2006) 25 *Political Geography* 336 at 346.

69 *Ibid.*

70 Editors, 'Briefs: Hand-held Guide to "Most Wanted Terrorists" Revised', (2004) 15(7) *Military and Aerospace Electronics* at 4.

71 Amoore, *supra*, note 363 at 346.

72 Home Office, *Terrorism: What you can do* (London: HMSO, 2005).

73 Bennett et al., *supra*, note 276, at 45.

74 *Ibid.* at 50.

for people and object matching on a scale never previously thought possible.[75] Studies show that security cameras can reduce street crime in urban areas, but surveillance also tends to suppress non-criminal activity, creating a chilling effect on freedom.[76] There are, of course, many people throughout the world who think it is acceptable to flout society's norms and break its laws. For the rest of us, though, the need to fight the bad guys now seems to mean that we're all confined to prisons without bars.[77]

One could easily imagine that, in the hands of a rogue government, these devices could be used to monitor the movements of people belonging to a particular class or race and to ensure compliance with restrictive terms that could include, for example, staying within a specific area or keeping away from public places, such as shopping malls and parks. In the Warsaw ghetto, Jews wore white armbands with a blue Star of David on their left arms. The band was clearly used to single out this population, fixing their identities and movements. It was also used to mark them for discrimination, segregation and deportation.

Almost a century earlier, Bentham had conceived of combining policing through census-style data with the tattooing of 'proper names' on to individuals' wrists to combat fraud.[78] This was seen as imperative during time in which suspicion could easily fall upon a person who had the wrong name; and the guilty could hide from the law by assuming a new name.[79] Bentham was clear that instruments of control such as identification, or the Panopticon, would fix, locate and identify individuals in order to maximize efficiency and enhance liberty for all.

If one were to design a system with these characteristics in mind, it would be difficult to come up with a more efficient substitute than what we already have today. Rather than inscribing human bodies with distinctive markers, like tattooing, new systems can 'read off' our bodies – their physical description, facial features, fingerprints, irises, and so on.[80] Indeed, technological advances have provided an array of new means by which we can identify people: passwords, DNA, iris scans, fingerprints, photographs and even full-body scans.[81] In many of the new biometric systems, several of these modalities are included for identification, surveillance and profiling purposes.

A talking CCTV camera, for example, can be used to identify people by race (e.g. clothing, facial features, skin colour, and hair length or covering) and emit a warning instructing them to leave an area or face the penalties. Cooperation need not be obtained using old-school police-state thugs like Nazi Germany's Gestapo. A pervasive system of surveillance can achieve more effective results

75 Chris Cubbage, "Creating and Intelligent World," *Australian Security Magazine*, February/March, 2018, 20 at 22.

76 Hutson, *supra*, note 141.

77 Wood, *supra*, note 343 at 294.

78 Maguire, *supra*, note 81 at 40.

79 Thorburn, *supra*, note 15 at 23.

80 *Ibid.* at 24.

81 *Ibid.* at 26.

with less manpower and fewer points of failure (i.e., a CCTV camera can't be bribed or manipulated). Even those not targeted for discrimination and exclusion can be frightened into compliance if they know that they're being watched. These are the sorts of potentials that give civil liberties advocates the creeps.

This raises two significant questions: does the country's due process system protect people from being falsely accused – or worse yet, convicted – on the basis of facial recognition technology? And are the false positives disproportionately skewed towards certain groups? This is particularly important given that the technologies are not foolproof. What, then, of the pervasive rollout of biometric security in regions such as Europe and the United States?

What happens when people start being caught, jailed, or possibly tortured or exterminated as a result of this technology? What if, as in China, it's being used to target anyone who 'threatens to undermine stability' or 'has extreme thoughts' or complains about perceived injustices and advocates for human rights? Again, these are not far-fetched dystopian ideas, but real threats, particularly as the world is increasingly focused on using technology and the sharing of personal data – in the name of safety and national security – and less concerned about privacy.

The use of artificial intelligence to predict crime

Imagine a world where police can predict a crime before it happens. It's already the stuff of science fiction and Hollywood: recall Philip K. Dick's short story turned movie, *Minority Report*, in which there is a special government branch in New York, in the year 2054, called 'Precrime' that apprehends those who have been identified by three mutants – or 'precogs' – as committing murders in the future. While this is clearly fiction, police departments are increasingly deploying data-mining techniques to predict, prevent and investigate crime.

Recall that millions of CCTV cameras are now installed throughout the UK. A major impetus for the concentration of surveillance cameras was the 1993 murder of a toddler named James Bulger, who disappeared from a shopping centre in northwest England.[82] Footage from a security camera showed two older boys leading him away. Both boys were later convicted of Bulger's murder, and the sinister images were played incessantly on the news, hardening the resolve to install even more cameras.

The case underscored both the potential and limits of CCTV. Today, whenever a crime is committed in London, police check to see if any suspects were captured on CCTV. There are now more than a hundred thousand images of unidentified suspects in the database established by London's Metropolitan Police Service.[83] Even the best facial-recognition tool still has trouble identifying a person based on grainy photos and videos — and it's totally useless if an individual's proof of identity is not already stored in computer databases or at

82 Keefe, *supra*, note 205.
83 *Ibid.*

least publicly visible on a social networking site such as Facebook.[84] As with the abduction of James Bulger, CCTV cameras may help solve crime – but they can't prevent it. However, a new generation of algorithms, a growing supply of online and offline databases, and hordes of cameras aim to make facial recognition crucial to preventing crime.

Since 9/11, increased fears about terrorist attacks and other serious crimes have led law enforcement to focus on preventing crimes rather than solving them after the fact. Many police departments use predictive algorithms to determine where crimes might occur, which persons might be at a high risk of victimization or perpetration and what threats are posed by those who officers encounter on the street.[85] Some of these programs are used to predict the geographic locations where crimes might occur. For example, in New York, Los Angeles, Chicago and Miami, software analyses historical crime data to forecast where crime hotspots are most likely to emerge; and the police are directed to those areas.[86]

Cities such as Los Angeles, Atlanta, Santa Cruz and Seattle have used software to predict where property crimes will occur.[87] In Charlotte, North Carolina, police compiled foreclosure data to generate a map of areas that are at high risk of being struck by crime.[88] In New York City, the N.Y.P.D. has partnered with Microsoft to employ a 'Domain Awareness System' that collects and links information from various sources like CCTVs, licence plate readers, radiation sensors and informational databases.[89]

The use of predictions in policing is not a new concept. Crime mapping, which allows the police to allocate more resources to where crime is most likely to occur, has been around for a very long time; and police used to plot crime on a map – with different coloured pins representing various crimes – to see if hot spots emerged.[90] Today's crime-mapping technologies can produce nearly perfect information about the frequency and geographic location of crimes in any given area.[91] Some jurisdictions have almost real-time data collection and daily reports of problematic areas to officers in the field.[92]

Other systems use social network analysis to determine which persons are at a high risk of becoming the victims or perpetrators of violence. Just like

84 Jeremy Hsu, 'Face of the Future: How Facial-Recognition Tech Will Change Everything', *NBC News*, 11 June 2013.
85 Joh, *supra*, note 313 at 35.
86 Kate Crawford, 'Artificial Intelligence's White Guy Problem', *The New York Times*, 25 June 2016.
87 Andrew D. Selbst, 'Disparate Impact in Big Data Policing', (2017) 52 *Georgia Law Review* 109 at 114.
88 Joh, *supra*, note 313 at 35.
89 *Ibid.* at 35.
90 Andrew Guthrie Ferguson, 'Crime Mapping and the Fourth Amendment: Redrawing High-Crime Areas', (2011) 63 *Hastings L.J.* 179 at 184.
91 *Ibid.* at 182.
92 *Ibid.*

crime mapping, offender profiling, in which police examine psychological and environmental factors to predict an unknown suspect's identity or to anticipate the next crime, is another form of prediction that has been around for a very long time. The algorithms themselves are largely secret, but the factors include past criminal history, arrests, parole status and whether the target has been identified as part of a gang. The algorithm ranks these variables to come up with a predictive score of how 'hot' individuals might be in terms of their risk.

In Chicago – as of late 2017 – 1,400 young men were identified through big data techniques as targets for a roster called 'the heat list'.[93] The software generates a list of potential victims and subjects with the greatest risk of violence. Based on an algorithm, the heat list uses 11 variables to create risk scores from 1 to 500. The higher the score, the greater the risk that the individual is a victim or a perpetrator. According to Ferguson, the algorithm has been highly accurate: on a violent Mother's Day weekend in 2016, 80 per cent of the 51 people shot over two days had been identified on Chicago's heat list; and on Memorial Day 2016, 78 per cent of the 64 people shot were on the list.[94]

Ferguson has pointed out that through the heat list, police have prioritized youth violence to intervene in the lives of the most at-risk males. This involves a home visit, usually by a senior police officer, a social worker and a member of the community (such as a football coach or pastor). During the visit, police hand-deliver a 'custom notification letter' setting out what they know about the individual's criminal past, as well as a warning about the future. The letter is used to inform individuals of the arrest, prosecution and sentencing outcomes they may face if they engage in public violence.[95]

The premise behind profiling is that a significant portion of crime occurs in predictable patterns, and if police can find those patterns, they can either prevent crime or catch the criminals.[96] While these predictive technologies are novel, the concerns underlying them are antiquated.[97] Fears of racial bias, a lack of transparency, data error and the distortions of constitutional protections offer serious challenges to the development of workable predictive policing approaches. There are actually *two* separate problems at issue: the fact that predictive policing systems have the potential for discriminatory results; and the lack of awareness about the efficacy and discriminatory impact of these systems.[98]

Data mining is the process of using machine learning to find patterns and relationships among different people or outcomes.[99] It works by exposing a machine-

93 Andrew Guthrie Ferguson, 'Beyond Big Data Policing', (2017) 105(6) *American Scientist* 377 at 380.
94 *Ibid.*
95 *Ibid.*
96 Selbst, *supra*, note 382 at 126.
97 Ferguson, *supra*, note 388 at 380.
98 Selbst, *supra*, note 382 at 168.
99 *Ibid.* at 127.

learning algorithm to examples of cases with known outcomes.[100] The system then builds a predictive model – a set of correlations that determine which associated attributes can serve as useful proxies for an otherwise unobservable outcome.[101] Once those attributes are discovered, the system compares new subjects' traits to those observed attributes to make predictions about the outcome.

Yet data-mining systems also incorporate a series of man-made decisions that can create or exacerbate discriminatory outcomes, independent of any intent to do so.[102] For example, some use data about past criminal activity, such as crime locations and arrest records. In other cases, data-mining companies purchase tools 'largely developed by and for the commercial world', as well as data from social networks such as Facebook and Twitter.[103]

As we will discuss, recent research has uncovered the dangers of hidden bias in AI systems. These biases can lie in the data, algorithms and overall design of the systems themselves, as well as the credibility and weight assigned to their findings.[104] The introduction of such bias should raise alarm when applied to a criminal justice system that has already long imposed disproportionate burdens on racial minorities and the poor.

When police allocate more resources to areas where there has been more crime in the past, crimes in those areas will be over-represented in future data.[105] Furthermore, when predictive policing is used to decipher where to put more officers, this creates a 'positive feedback loop' that skews future data, as the increased police presence will lead to the detection of more crime in that area.[106] These systems can also lead to extra monitoring of individuals, and when a crime occurs, police might be more likely to look at them first.[107]

Over time, the appearance of greater threat levels in minority neighbourhoods could inflame an already adversarial relationship with police and put lives at risk. For example, increased police presence means a greater likelihood of police–citizen encounters. If a high percentage of stop-and-frisks turn out to be erroneous, this results in an unnecessary infringement on personal liberty.[108] Whether they view this as a helpful presence or reject it as an unnecessary interference with their liberty, residents in these areas are forced to endure ongoing police surveillance as an ever-present daily reality.[109] The perception of mistreatment only undermines the legitimacy of the front-line responders in these areas.[110]

100 *Ibid.*
101 *Ibid.*
102 *Ibid.* at 116.
103 *Ibid.* at 128.
104 Elizabeth E. Joh, 'Artificial Intelligence and Policing: First Questions', (2018) *Seattle University Law Review*. Available online at: https://papers.ssrn.com/sol3/papers.cfm?abstract_id=3168779.
105 Selbst, *supra*, note 382 at 135.
106 *Ibid.*
107 *Ibid.* at 137.
108 Ferguson, *supra*, note 385 at 217.
109 *Ibid.*
110 *Ibid.* at 228.

In August 2016, 17 civil rights organizations released a joint statement on the civil rights concerns of predictive policing, emphasizing the possibility of racist outcomes, as well as the lack of transparency, public debate and attention to community needs.[111] The way police are using these technologies means more people of colour are arrested, jailed or physically harmed by police, while the needs of communities are often ignored. We must keep in mind that policing is different from other fields that have embraced AI because the police act with enormous discretion: they choose where to focus their attention, who to detain, who to arrest and even when to use force deadly force.[112] The type of AI utilized thus has significant implications for both power and accountability in policing.

Since all humans exhibit unconscious bias, it's clear that police officers will too. The fact of unconscious bias is widely acknowledged; and thus, it seems to make good sense to take at least some discretion away from unreliable human officers and give it to a seemingly neutral technology. Yet researchers have found that 'seemingly objective' algorithms can reproduce the very same biases of the engineers who designed them – not to mention the officers who are tasked with using them on the street. To illustrate, Andrew D. Selbst provides an example of an arrest scenario based on the recommendation of a suspect-based predictive policing algorithm:

> The arrest would go something like this: police are driving down the street, running a facial recognition program to identify people, and then running those names through their algorithms based on publicly available data to see who matches a profile. Once they find a match, they arrest the person on suspicion of whatever crime they are looking to solve.[113]

An arrestee in the above scenario might argue that he was unreasonably searched or seized because the police methods were discriminatory or the reliance on the algorithm implies a lack of individualized suspicion. Where, for example, reasonable suspicion was lacking because the only evidence was the race of the suspect and one or two other indicators that were not suggestive of criminality, the stop can violate the Fourth Amendment.[114]

Knowledge of crime patterns in a particular area can make an officer's observations appear more reasonable where that knowledge is tied to the suspicion of the observed person.[115] However, if the reference to a high-crime area weighs in favour of reasonable suspicion, this means that the same activity in one neighbourhood (i.e. a high-crime area), but not in another (i.e. a low-crime area),

111 Selbst, *supra*, note 382 at 114.
112 Joh, *supra*, note 399.
113 Selbst, *supra*, note 382 at 144.
114 *Floyd v. City of New York*, 959 F. Supp. 2d 540 at 630.
115 In *Pennsylvania v. Dunlap* 129 S. Ct. 448, 448 (2008), for example, the officer staked out a particular location with a specific crime problem because of an official decision of his police administrators; and the expected type of criminal activity matched what Officer Devlin actually saw – suspected narcotics dealing.

may rise to the level of reasonable suspicion. Yet the same objective standard of reasonable suspicion is assumed to apply in *all* neighbourhoods and to *all* people.[116] Furthermore, some courts have expressed concern or confusion about what a high-crime area is, or how it should be weighed against other factors in the reasonable-suspicion analysis; and courts have developed different standards and solutions to resolve the issue.[117] This raises fairness concerns, including 'issues of race, class, and place'.[118]

Automated decision-making and remote tracking in the American penal system

In 1965, President Lyndon Johnson gave a special message to Congress on Law Enforcement and the Administration of Justice.[119] Criticizing the high crime rate and its fiscal and human costs, the President announced the appointment of a Presidential Commission to: 'probe … fully and deeply into the problems of crime in our nation'.[120] The 1965 Commission established a Science and Technology Task Force which sought, among other things, '[t]o identify and describe crime control problems in a form susceptible to quantitative analysis", and '[t]o suggest organizational formats within which technological devices and systems can be developed, field tested, and rendered useful'.[121]

The Commission also criticized then-current sentencing practice: 'Each year, judges in this country pass roughly two million sentences. Almost all sentencing decisions are made with little or no information on the likely effect of the sentence on future criminal behavior'.[122] That observation also applied to policing practice at the time: 'About 200,000 policemen spend half of their time on "preventive" patrol. Yet no police chief can obtain even a rough estimate of how much crime is thereby "prevented".'[123]

The contemporary solution to both those concerns is big data analytics. New high-tech tools allow for more precise measuring and tracking, better sharing of information, and the possibility of identifying racial bias. In a perfect world, automated decision-making could be used to apply the rules in each case consistently and without prejudice. With this aim, data-driven risk-assessment tools are being used to set bail, determine sentences and even contribute to determinations about guilt or innocence.

116 Ferguson, *supra*, note 385 at 199.
117 *Ibid.* at 203.
118 *Ibid.* at 206.
119 Lyndon B. Johnson, "Special Message to the Congress on Law Enforcement and the Administration of Justice," March 8, 1965.
120 *Ibid.*; see also Exec. Order No. 11,236, 3 C.F.R. 329 (1964–1965).
121 President's Commission on Law Enforcement and Administration of Justice, 'The Challenge of Crime in a Free Society', (Washington, DC: 1967) at 245. Available online at: www.ncjrs.gov/pdffiles1/nij/42.pdf.
122 *Ibid.* at 247.
123 *Ibid.*

These systems operate on the basis that a data subject's expected outcome for some query is similar to those of other people with whom he or she shares relevant attributes, such as age, sex, geography, family background and employment status. As a result, two people accused of the same crime may receive different bail or sentencing outcomes based on inputs that are beyond their control, and which they have no way of assessing or challenging. As criminal justice algorithms have come into more widespread use, they have also come under greater scrutiny. They have been criticized for being unclear, unreliable and unconstitutional. It's evident, for example, that risk assessment scores used in criminal sentencing overestimate black recidivism and underestimate white recidivism.[124]

The Correctional Offender Management Profiling for Alternative Sanctions, or COMPAS, created by the for-profit company Northpointe, aims, and claims, to predict an individual's risk of recidivism. It assesses variables under five main areas: criminal involvement, relationships/lifestyles, personality/attitudes, family and social exclusion. In addition, it evaluates nearly two dozen so-called 'criminogenic needs' that relate to the major theories of criminality, including 'criminal personality', 'social isolation', 'substance abuse' and 'residence/stability'. Defendants are ranked low, medium or high risk in each category. Although these risk categories may be presented in 'neutral' language, often moral evaluations – judgements about who is good and who is bad – are hidden in the technical wording; and riskiness is assessed behind the scenes, by secret algorithms.[125]

Nevertheless, the use of such algorithms in risk assessment is becoming increasingly common in courtrooms across the United States. They are being used to make decisions about who can be released at every stage of the criminal justice system, from assigning bail amounts – as is the case in Fort Lauderdale – to even more significant decisions about defendants' liberty. In Arizona, Colorado, Delaware, Kentucky, Louisiana, Oklahoma, Virginia, Washington and Wisconsin, the results of such assessments are given to judges during criminal sentencing.

Not only do these techniques largely do away with judicial discretion in sentencing matters, they compound racially based harms because they are used to determine an offender's propensity for recidivism based on attributes held by *other* people. In other words, the data relied on to determine a particular offender's level of risk comprises the recidivism rates collected from multiple sample populations of released offenders for a specific period of time.

COMPAS then compares the offender's information with the group data to generate a 'risk score' meant to predict the likelihood that those with a similar history of offending are either more or less likely to commit another crime following release from custody. Moreover, since the system measures not only risk, but also a variety of other vague and spurious criteria, including 'criminal

124 Julia Angwin, Jeff Larson, Surya Mattu & Lauren Kirchner, 'Machine Bias: There's Software Used Across the Country to Predict Future Criminals. And It's Biased Against Blacks', *ProPublica*, 23 May 2016. Available online at: www.propublica.org/article/machine-bias-risk-assessments-in-criminal-sentencing.

125 Bennett et al., *supra*, note 276 at 47.

personality', 'social isolation', 'substance abuse' and 'residence/stability', the results can easily be prone to misinterpretation and manipulation, not to mention false positives.

Wisconsin has been among the most eager and expansive users of Northpointe's risk assessment tool in sentencing decisions. In 2012, the Wisconsin Department of Corrections launched the use of the software throughout the state. It is now used at each step in the prison system, from sentencing to parole. Once a defendant is convicted of a felony anywhere in the state, the Department of Corrections attaches a COMPAS assessment to the confidential pre-sentence report given to judges.[126]

Some judges have cited the scores in their sentencing decisions. In August 2013, Judge Scott Horne in La Crosse County, Wisconsin, found that defendant Eric Loomis had been 'identified, through the COMPAS assessment, as an individual who is at high risk to the community'. He went on to state: '[W]eighing the various factors', the court 'rul[ed] out probation because of the seriousness of the crime and because . . . [Petitioner's] history on supervision, and the risk assessment tools that have been utilized suggest that [Petitioner is] extremely high risk to re-offend'. He then imposed a sentence of eight years and six months in prison.

Loomis, who was charged with driving a stolen vehicle and fleeing from police, challenged the use of the score at sentencing as a violation of his due process rights because he could not contest the scientific validity of the assessment owing to Northpointe's proprietary claim over the software's algorithm. Loomis relied on *Gardner v. Florida*,[127] in which the defendant appealed his conviction for first-degree murder, for which he was sentenced to death. Gardner argued that the trial court erred by deeming certain portions of the pre-sentence investigation report confidential and refusing to disclose the information to counsel. The U.S. Supreme Court held that the defendant was denied due process because the trial court had imposed a sentence 'at least in part, on the basis of information which (Gardner) had no opportunity to deny or explain'.

On appeal in the Loomis case, the state defended the use of the COMPAS score with the argument that judges can consider it in addition to other factors. The Supreme Court of Wisconsin held that the trial court did not violate Loomis's right to due process when it considered the COMPAS report because its decision was based on other considerations and the trial court had properly limited its use of the report. Since the trial court 'considered the appropriate factors', including 'the gravity of offense, the character and rehabilitative needs of the defendant, and the need to protect the public', and only 'considered the COMPAS risk assessment as "an observation" to reinforce its assessment of the other factors it considered', the Court decided that the 'consideration of COMPAS in this case did not violate [Petitioner's] due process rights'. In another case, the Indiana

126 *Ibid.*
127 430 U.S. 349, 351 (1977).

Supreme Court reached the same conclusion, namely, that a court can consider a risk assessment, so long as it does not base the actual sentence on that consideration alone.

The United States Supreme Court further rejected Loomis's appeal and observed the following:

> Gardner does not support Petitioner's case. As a threshold matter, because the present case does not involve the death penalty, it is unclear whether Gardner has any application here at all. In any event, even if Gardner were extended to non capital cases, see App. A-24, ¶ 49 n.26, it would not support Petitioner. This is not a case where "secret evidence [was] given to the sentencer but not to" the convict, O'Dell, 521 U.S. at 162: both the trial court and Petitioner received the same PSI, with the same information about COMPAS. Petitioner was free to question his assessment and explain its possible flaws. See App. A-10, ¶¶ 53, 55–56. And the trial court did not base its sentence on the COMPAS report. The court based its sentence entirely upon independent considerations and would have imposed the same sentence without COMPAS.

The attractiveness of a system such as COMPAS is that it purports to inject objectivity into a criminal justice system that has been compromised, far too many times, by human error through bias, racism, xenophobia, stereotyping and discrimination. However, this seemingly compelling solution overlooks the fact that algorithms, their 'science' notwithstanding, are as fallible as the people, and the institutions, that write them.[128] Furthermore, if private companies like Northpointe can keep their algorithms confidential, by claiming that they are trade secrets, no one will ever truly know how the system calculates risk.

When mental-health professionals and other experts give evidence in court about an offender's risk of reoffending, they are typically cross-examined; and this process provides an opportunity to test the evidence for the truth of its contents, as well as to question the credibility of the witness. Yet since a software program, such as COMPAS, can never be examined or deposed – and neither can its makers be compelled to reveal the 'trade secrets' behind their methods – there is the obvious potential for juries and judges to misunderstand and misuse the results, assigning greater accuracy to predicted outcomes than is warranted.[129] As well, such risk assessments classify individuals within a group as low, medium or high risk; yet they cannot say exactly where in this group the individual lies, and therefore cannot pinpoint the precise risk the individual poses.[130]

Assigning risk to an individual based on group characteristics can lead to inaccurate assessments; and, if these inaccuracies cannot be teased out through

128 Megan Garber, 'When Algorithms Take the Stand', *The Atlantic*, 30 June 2016.

129 Bernadette McSherry & Patrick Keyzer, *Sex Offenders and Preventive Detention: Politics, Policy and Practice* (Leichhardt, NSW: The Federation Press, 2009) at 33.

130 *Ibid*. at 30.

cross-examination, this has the practical effect of turning a tool for the assessment of probabilities for future offending into something relied on as empirically infallible. That seems to upend principles of due process, fairness and the right of the defendant to make full answer and defence. This is particularly true given that these tools give scientific value to estimations that actually perform less well than chance.[131]

In fact, research carried out by ProPublica demonstrated that the results produced by COMPAS *are* dubious and racially biased against minorities. They obtained the risk scores assigned to more than 7,000 people arrested in Broward County, Florida, in 2013 and 2014 and checked to see how many were charged with new crimes over the next two years, the same benchmark used by the creators of the algorithm. The score proved unreliable in forecasting violent crime: only 20 per cent of the people predicted to commit violent crimes actually went on to do so. When a full range of crimes were considered — including misdemeanours such as driving with an expired licence — the algorithm was just slightly more accurate than a coin toss. Of those deemed likely to reoffend, only 61 per cent were arrested for a subsequent crime within two years.

ProPublica also uncovered significant racial disparities. In forecasting who would reoffend, the algorithm made mistakes with African American and white defendants at roughly the same rate but in very different ways: the system was particularly likely to falsely flag African American defendants as future criminals, wrongly labelling them this way at almost twice the rate as white defendants; and white defendants were mislabelled as low risk more often than African American defendants. African American defendants were 77 per cent more likely to be pegged at higher risk of committing a future violent crime and 45 per cent more likely to be predicted to commit a future crime of any kind than whites. Thus, not only may these risk scores be injecting bias into the courts that use them, they may also be increasing the perception of unfair disparities.

Notably, despite ruling against Loomis, even the Wisconsin Supreme Court seemed uneasy about using a secret algorithm to send a man to prison. Justice Ann Walsh Bradley, writing for the court, discussed the ProPublica report about COMPAS that concluded that African American defendants in Broward County, Fla. 'were far more likely than white defendants to be incorrectly judged to be at a higher rate of recidivism'. Justice Bradley noted that Northpointe had disputed the analysis. Still, she wrote, 'this study and others raise concerns regarding how a COMPAS assessment's risk factors correlate with race'.

In the end, though, Justice Bradley allowed sentencing judges to use COMPAS. However, she warned that judges must proceed with caution when using such risk assessments. They must take account of the algorithm's limitations and the secrecy surrounding it, but she said the software could be helpful 'in

131 Frank Farnham & David James, "Dangerousness and Dangerous Law," (2001) 358 *The Lancet* 1926 at 1926.

providing the sentencing court with as much information as possible in order to arrive at an individualized sentence'.

To ensure that judges weigh risk assessments appropriately, the court advised both how these assessments must be presented to trial courts and the extent to which judges may use them. The court explained that risk scores may not be used 'to determine whether an offender is incarcerated' or 'to determine the severity of the sentence'. Therefore, judges using risk assessments must explain the factors other than the assessment that support the sentence imposed.

Furthermore, pre-sentence investigation reports that incorporate a COMPAS assessment must include five written warnings for judges: first, the 'proprietary nature of COMPAS' prevents the disclosure of how risk scores are calculated; second, COMPAS scores are unable to identify specific high-risk individuals because these scores rely on group data; third, although COMPAS relies on a national data sample, there has been 'no cross-validation study for a Wisconsin population'; fourth, studies 'have raised questions about whether [COMPAS scores] disproportionately classify minority offenders as having a higher risk of recidivism'; and fifth, COMPAS was developed specifically to assist the Department of Corrections in making *post*-sentencing determinations. In issuing these warnings, the court made clear its desire to cast doubt upon the tool's accuracy and reliability.

Given that the United States incarcerates a larger share of its population than any other country, and yet the practice of locking up such vast numbers of people each year has proven to be an exorbitant, ineffective and largely counterproductive strategy, it's not surprising that alternatives to incarceration are increasingly being considered. Though the United States tops the charts in prison population, many other countries – from Brazil to Russia – also incur huge economic and social costs from very high incarceration rates. Corporations already anticipate the immense cost savings of building digital prisons, without bars, guards or even walls.[132] A 2012 Deloitte Touche Tomatsu report titled *Public Sector, Disrupted*, sees 'transforming criminal justice with electronic monitoring' as an 'opportunity for disruptive innovation' in public services.[133]

For decades, politicians have assumed that less crime and greater safety mean tougher sentencing laws and more money spent on incarceration. This perspective has dominated criminal justice thinking in much of the world, particularly in the United States: 'With less than 5 per cent of the world's population, America has nearly one quarter of the world's prisoners'.[134] At the end of 2016, there were about 2.2 million people behind bars in the U.S., including 1.5 million under the jurisdiction of federal and state prisons and roughly

132 Eubanks, *supra*, note 153 at 215.

133 Deloitte, 'Public Sector Disrupted: How Disruptive Innovation Can Help Government Achieve More for Less', 2012. Available online at: www2.deloitte.com/content/dam/Deloitte/global/Documents/Public-Sector/dttl-ps-publicsectordisrupted-08082013.pdf.

134 Adam Liptak, 'Inmate Count in U.S. Dwarfs Other Nations', *New York Times*, 23 April 2008.

741,000 in the custody of locally run jails.[135] That amounts to a nationwide incarceration rate of 860 prison or jail inmates for every 100,000 adults of ages 18 and older. Lower-level offenders have accounted for a significant portion of this growth.

This rise in incarceration came at a huge monetary cost. U.S. state corrections costs now top US$50 billion annually and consume one in every 15 discretionary state budget dollars. Prison costs now trump higher education costs in some states; and the social cost for many minority communities, where a large proportion of the young men are now locked up, is astounding. According to the Pew Research Center, 'serving time reduces hourly wages for men by approximately 11 per cent, annual employment by 9 weeks, and annual earnings by 40 per cent'.[136] Since minority populations disproportionately make up the prison population (1 in 87 working aged white men are behind bars compared with 1 in 36 Hispanic men and 1 in 12 African American men), high incarceration rates negatively impact minority populations.[137] Moreover, the impact of incarcerated parents on children is substantial and long-lasting.

Yet of all the millions of Americans currently 'serving time' in the U.S., as many as 5 million of them at any given time are outside the prison system and living relatively 'free' lives on conditional supervised release, as parolees or otherwise. New technologies have the greatest potential to continue this upward trend and disrupt traditional incarceration patterns, and costs, in favour of increasing the numbers of people on some form of supervised release. Today, the technologies involved in electronic monitoring include home monitoring devices controlled by radio, wrist bands and anklets tracked by global positioning systems (GPS), alcohol testing patches and even voice recognition.[138] The criminal justice system uses electronic monitoring technologies primarily for offender tracking, confirming that offenders are where they are supposed to be, or are prevented from approaching identified high-risk areas.

Criminals typically differ from the general population in that they tend to have poor impulse control, addictive personality, and a penchant for short-term gratification.[139] More than a fifth of all incarcerated criminals are there for drug offences, and a substantial proportion of the others also abuse substances.[140] Poor impulse control and other factors mean that many parolees and probationers are likely to transgress and return to their old criminal habits; and this

135 John Gramlich, 'America's Incarceration Rate is at a Two-Decade Low', *Pew Research Center*, 2 May 2018. Available online at: www.pewresearch.org/fact-tank/2018/05/02/americas-incarceration-rate-is-at-a-two-decade-low/.

136 The Pew Charitable Trusts, 'Collateral Costs: Incarceration's Effects on Economic Mobility', 2010 at 4–5. Available online at: http://ezto-cf-media.mheducation.com/Media/Connect_Production/hssl/english/integrated/connectirw/Effect_on_Economic_Mobility.pdf.

137 *Ibid.*

138 Deloitte, *supra*, note 428.

139 Wood, *supra*, note 343 at 299.

140 *Ibid.*

is reinforced by the fact that many believe that if they violate the terms of their release they are unlikely to be caught and punished.

Before the use of technological tools to monitor these individuals, they were largely correct in making that assumption – indeed, it would take an army of probation officers, who are already burdened by limited time and resources, to monitor all those on conditional release on a 24/7 basis. Moreover, asking for a convict's probation to be revoked takes significant time and effort. Besides, it makes little sense to send a person to prison for a relatively minor infraction, like getting drunk or high while on parole.[141]

With the exception of highly dangerous offenders who can't be trusted to circulate in the general population, convicts can now wear inexpensive tracking devices that can not only monitor their movements 24/7, but send out an alert if they, say, loiter around a school yard, or approach the house of the ex-spouse they threatened. An astute parole officer could easily map out a strict weekly routine for his parolee – with specific times when he would have to leave and return home and specific sites that he would have to check into throughout the week (e.g. work, church, drug testing, AA meetings, and so on), along with various "'no-go' zones (e.g. the bar, the casino, the playground, his ex's house, and so on). In this way, parolees and probationers are assured that if they violate the terms of their release, they will certainly – and swiftly – be caught and reprimanded.[142]

When it comes to the suite of law-enforcement gadgets designed to monitor and track convicted offenders, we can see how the classic concepts of deterrence, discipline and punishment are increasingly being imposed on to *the body* itself. Looking back to the time leading up to the Enlightenment, we can point to the use of deeply inhumane forms of physical punishment which were calculated to shock as much as brutalize. They placed the body front and centre in the use of cruelty and public physical castigation as a means of discipline and control.

Historians have also documented the inscription of justice onto the bodies of offenders. During the era of the East India Company, for example, an individual's name and offence were tattooed on to the forehead when a life sentence was handed down.[143] Pillory and branding remained common in many European countries until the early to mid-nineteenth century. In 1828, *Journal des Débats* covered a case of pillory outside the Palais de Justice during which the name of the crime was branded on to an offender's body with a red-hot iron.[144]

In contrast, the technological devices used today – although situated on the body – are well-concealed and unobtrusive. They represent a giant leap forward for the rehabilitation and integration of the prisoner as they are designed to be worn 'freely', out in the open, while remaining hidden from public view. Offenders can remain at home with their families, and continue working and financially

141 *Ibid.* at 301.
142 *Ibid.* at 299.
143 Maguire, *supra*, note 81 at 38.
144 *Ibid.* at 35.

supporting them, thereby mitigating the harmful social and economic impacts of being sent to prison.[145]

The new generation of GPS trackers used to monitor millions of convicted offenders in the United States is largely manned by private companies that specialize in tracking and monitoring offenders across all fifty states.[146] The company's 'clients' (i.e. the felons monitored) wear an unobtrusive radio-frequency-based device around their ankles, which is capable of monitoring real-time locations down to a few metres and sending out an alert notifying the relevant probation officer if he or she steps outside the 'exclusion zone'.[147] Similar sorts of devices can also be used to chemically read sweat for signs of alcohol, which might signal that an individual has violated their probation for drunk driving charges.[148]

Most importantly, by removing low-level offenders from jails and prisons and putting them under house arrest, local, state and federal governments can dramatically reduce their spending on incarceration. Approximately 5.5 offenders can be electronically monitored for the cost of incarcerating a single offender behind bars.[149] It also replaces a one-size-fits-all approach for offenders with one that employs the most appropriate and cost-effective approach for each offender, depending on the crime committed and his or her potential danger to the community.

While the United States is believed to be the biggest subscriber to electronic monitoring – more than 20 different electronic monitoring companies provide monitoring for upwards of 100,000 offenders – other countries are moving rapidly in this direction.[150] In England and Wales, as of 2016/17, about 65,000 offenders annually are subject to electronic monitoring, a number likely to rise considerably in the near future.[151] Significant growth in electronic monitoring also is expected in other European countries, as well as Brazil and South Africa.

The legal framework

What does it mean for the prisoner to have his or her steps monitored at all times – 24 hours per day, 7 days a week – as he moves throughout the world? And what is the significance of the fact that policing and surveillance are increasingly being offloaded on to private third parties by the state? Has there been a shift in accountability? Do we need to worry about the ever-expanding power of government and the mechanization of surveillance? These systems – and the possibilities they provide – topple the traditional relationship between the citizen and the state. The software, algorithms and models are complex, powerful and largely secret.

145 Wood, *supra*, note 343 at 304.
146 *Ibid.* at 296.
147 *Ibid.* at 297.
148 *Ibid.*
149 Deloitte, *supra*, note 428 at 14.
150 *Ibid.* at 15.
151 www.nao.org.uk/wp-content/uploads/2017/07/The-new-generation-electronic-monitoring-programme.pdf.

The United States Supreme Court

The Fourth Amendment's protection against unreasonable searches and seizures provides the baseline protection for Americans versus the police. Decades of police reliance on CCTV cameras, electronic beepers, listening devices, surveillance aircraft and other sense enhancements have prompted concerns that these measures have eroded the expectation of privacy individuals have in public. Yet the Supreme Court has stressed in a number of cases that our public activities, movements and even our physical selves – when visible to the public – lack Fourth Amendment protection.[152]

There is also no requirement for a warrant when the use of technology merely enhances the officer's ability to gather information that he otherwise could have obtained through ordinary sensory perception. Thus, when new technology merely facilitates the use of ordinary human senses, the Court has typically held that the individual's subjective expectation of privacy has not been violated, since 'what a person knowingly exposes to the public, even in his own home or office, is not a subject of Fourth Amendment protection'.[153]

A helpful illustration is provided by *United States v. Knotts*,[154] which involved the use of an electronic tracking device to investigate individuals who were suspected of manufacturing illegal drugs. Police officers installed a radio transmitter – a 'beeper' – inside a five-gallon container of chloroform which is used to make methamphetamine. The drum was sold to an individual who kept it, along with the tracking device, inside his vehicle. Using visual electronic surveillance, police were able to monitor the drum as the vehicle was driven from Minnesota to Wisconsin. They then used the beeper to track the car to a cabin owned by Knotts. The police used this information to obtain a warrant to search the property where they discovered a secret drug laboratory.

Knotts challenged the warrantless use of the tracking device and Justice Rehnquist, who wrote the majority decision, found that there was no invasion of a reasonable expectation of privacy because a 'person traveling in an automobile on public thoroughfares has no reasonable expectation of privacy in his movements from one place to another'.[155] Justice Rehnquist observed that 'scientific enhancement of this sort raises no constitutional issues which visual surveillance would not also raise'.[156] In other words, the police could have obtained the same information using ordinary visual surveillance by merely following the vehicle at a distance, which would not have required a warrant. Since the vehicle was at all times visible to the naked eye, the warrantless surveillance did not violate Fourth Amendment guarantees.

152 Joh, *supra*, note 313 at 59.
153 *Katz, supra*, note 242 at 347.
154 460 U.S. 276 (1983).
155 *Ibid.* at 281.
156 *Ibid.* at 285.

However, this case can be contrasted with *United States v. Karo*, in which the government obtained a court order authorizing the installation and monitoring of a beeper inside a can of ether, which was to be used to extract cocaine from a fabric in which it was imported into the United States. Law enforcement officials watched Karo pick up the can and then used it to monitor the ether's location. They eventually tracked it to a house and used it to monitor the ether inside the house while they obtained a search warrant.

The facts are surprisingly similar to *Knotts*: in both cases, the police used a tracking device to locate a clandestine narcotics operation. However, in this case, the Supreme Court found that the use of the beeper invaded Karo's reasonable expectation of privacy because it sent a signal from a private residence, which is a 'location not open to visual surveillance'. Indeed, the case turned on the fact that the device was used to reveal information *inside the house*, which rests at the heart of Fourth Amendment protection.

Several U.S. Supreme Court Justices have recently indicated concerns about the big data surveillance capacities of the police. In *United States v. Jones*,[157] the police attached a GPS tracking device to the bottom of Jones's car and monitored his movements around the clock for 28 days. At trial, Jones was convicted and given a life sentence. That decision was eventually appealed to the Supreme Court, which found that a physical intrusion into a constitutionally-protected area, coupled with an attempt to acquire information, can create a violation of the Fourth Amendment.

Although *Katz* had previously shifted the focus of the Fourth Amendment away from property and physical trespass, the majority argued that this did not affect traditional spheres of Fourth Amendment protection, including a person's house, papers and effects. Here, the police invaded Jones's property (i.e. his car, which is an effect); thus, a Fourth Amendment search occurred when the police attached the GPS device to the undercarriage of his car. Justice Scalia explained, 'It is important to be clear about what occurred in this case: The Government physically occupied private property for the purpose of obtaining information.'[158]

Justice Scalia was careful to distinguish similar cases involving mere observation, with no accompanying trespass. For example, in both *Knotts* and *Karo*, law enforcement attached tracking devices to containers *before* they came into the defendant's possession. But in *Jones*, the police attached the GPS directly to Jones's vehicle, which was a trespass, and a 'search' within the meaning of the Fourth Amendment.

The troubling aspect of Scalia's decision rests with its inability to address the question of how advances in technologies might require a different Fourth Amendment framework to safeguard against modern intrusions such as ubiquitous tracking and data aggregation.[159] Instead, Scalia focused on the fact that

157 132 S. Ct. 945 (2012).

158 *Ibid.* at 949.

159 These possibilities were hinted at by Justice Sotomayor, who observed the Government's 'unrestrained power to assemble data' being 'subject to abuse.' *Jones, supra*, note 452 at 956.

the intrusion 'would have been considered a "search" within the meaning of the Fourth Amendment when it was adopted.' But the Bill of Rights came into effect in 1791.

Two hundred and twenty years later, focusing on the physical placement of the GPS device ignores the growing use of tracking technologies that make no contact with the individual.[160] These range from behaviour recognition, motion pattern learning and anomaly detection to object recognition and tracking.[161] This requires no suspicion of any individual; it functions as warrantless mass surveillance.[162] Yet Scalia deliberately left open the question of whether the extended monitoring would have violated the Fourth Amendment if no trespass occurred: '[i]t may be that achieving the same result through electronic means, without an accompanying trespass, is an unconstitutional invasion of privacy, but the present case does not require us to answer that question.'[163]

This is particularly unsettling because the Court has danced around this subject in the past. Indeed, in *Knotts* the respondent maintained that law enforcement's use of sophisticated surveillance technologies would allow for 'twenty-four-hour surveillance of any citizen of this country ... without judicial knowledge or supervision',[164] which is exactly what occurred in *Jones*. However, in *Knotts*, the Court declined to address that issue, reasoning that 'if such dragnet type law enforcement practices as the respondent envisions should eventually occur, there will be time enough then to determine whether different constitutional principles may be applicable'.[165] Again, though, Justice Scalia neglected to deal with such realities in *Jones*.

Justice Alito, in his concurring opinion in *Jones*, recognized this omission and observed, '...the Court's reasoning largely disregards what is really important (the use of a GPS for the purpose of long-term tracking) and instead attaches great significance to something that most would view as relatively minor (attaching to the bottom of a car a small, light object that does not interfere in any way with the car's operation)'.[166] Alito then argued that there are 'particularly vexing problems' with applying a trespass framework to cases involving technological surveillance that is carried out by making electronic, as opposed to physical, contact with the person or thing being tracked.[167]

However, in response, Scalia sidestepped the issue once again and quipped that '[s]ituations involving merely the transmission of electronic signals without

160 Donohue, *supra*, note 209 at 409.

161 *Ibid.* at 412.

162 *Ibid.* at 409.

163 Jones, *supra*, note 452 at 954.

164 Knotts, *supra*, note 449 at 283.

165 *Ibid.* at 284.

166 Jones, *supra* note 452.

167 *Ibid.* Justice Scalia notes that '[t]respass to chattels has traditionally required a physical touching of the property'.

trespass would *remain* subject to the *Katz* analysis'.[168] Yet Justice Alito further pointed out that the *Katz* test is inadequate for this purpose because:

> [it] rests on the assumption that this hypothetical reasonable person has a well-developed and stable set of privacy expectations. But technology can change those expectations. Dramatic technological change may lead to periods in which popular expectations are in flux and may ultimately produce significant changes in popular attitudes. New technology may provide increased convenience or security at the expense of privacy, and many people may find the tradeoff worthwhile. And even if the public does not welcome the diminution of privacy that new technology entails, they may eventually reconcile themselves to this development as inevitable.

In other words, once privacy-infringing innovations become commonplace, our expectations may be so skewed that we will be unwilling or unable to determine whether their use involves a degree of privacy intrusion that a reasonable person would not have anticipated prior to their widespread use. Surely, this is a low bar to set for Fourth Amendment privacy protections going forward.

Justice Sotomayor joined the majority in agreeing that trespass formed the underlying basis of Fourth Amendment jurisprudence; however, she too wrote separate concurring reasons in which she cautioned against electronic monitoring:

> GPS monitoring generates a precise, comprehensive record of a person's public movements that reflects a wealth of detail about her familial, political, professional, religious, and sexual associations … The Government can store such records and efficiently mine them for information years into the future … And because GPS monitoring is cheap in comparison to conventional surveillance techniques and, by design, proceeds surreptitiously, it evades the ordinary checks that constrain abusive law enforcement practices: "limited police resources and community hostility."[169]

Justice Sotomayor's comments point to the inherent risks in the use of new surveillance technologies to gather a substantial amount of intimate information about any person whom the government chooses to track. They also point to the threat of information being aggregated in a manner that allows the government to make observations that a reasonable person would not have anticipated. She also rightly observed that these futuristic developments may 'alter the relationship between citizen and government in a way that is inimical to democratic society'.[170]

168 *Ibid.* at 953.
169 *Ibid.*
170 *Ibid.*; quoting *United States v. Cuevas-Perez*, 640 F. 3d 272, 285 (CA7 2011).

The more sensible approach appears to come from Justice Alito, who suggests that Courts should ask 'whether the use of GPS tracking in a particular case involved a degree of intrusion that a reasonable person would not have anticipated'.[171] This enquiry seems to be well-suited to situations when governmental intrusions stand to fundamentally diminish individuals' expectations about the scope of their existing privacy rights. If a reasonable person would find that what the government is claiming an unfettered right to do is an unanticipated and intrusive violation of their privacy rights, then it is more likely that the Constitution can be used to curtail or halt them altogether *before* they become the norm.

For now, we can safely say that the monitoring of citizens through wearable GPS devices is only being used against convicted criminals in the United States. However, the surveillance capacities of the police today far exceed what armies of police officers could accomplish without access to big data.[172] What legal limits are there to prevent Orwellian abuses from occurring in the future?

The Supreme Court of Canada

The *Canadian Charter of Rights and Freedoms* (the *Charter*) is essentially an entrenched 'Bill of Rights' for Canadians. As with the *Bill of Rights*, there is no specific constitutional right to privacy in the *Charter*; however, section 8 provides that everyone 'has the right to be secure against unreasonable search or seizure', and the Supreme Court of Canada has recognized this provision as protecting the right to be secure against encroachment upon the citizens' reasonable expectation of privacy in a free and democratic society.[173]

Yet, as with other fundamental rights, the right to privacy is not absolute and the guarantee against unreasonable search and seizure only protects a 'reasonable expectation' of privacy, when balanced against the other societal interests, including law enforcement.[174] The balance between the need to protect an individual's privacy from unjustified state intrusion and the interest in overriding the right can shift, depending on the nature of the privacy interest at stake.

The Supreme Court of Canada has established that privacy arises in three domains: spatial and territorial; personal; and informational.[175] The protection of individual privacy is particularly important, with respect to all three zones of privacy, when the state seeks to monitor communications and conduct electronic surveillance. The Court has stressed its need to carefully scrutinize the state's use of new technologies and has required compliance with the requirements for a 'reasonable' search or seizure under s. 8, including the need to obtain judicial authorization, such as a valid search warrant.

171 *Ibid.* at 964.
172 Joh, *supra*, note 313 at 60.
173 *Hunter v. Southam*, [1984] 2 SCR 145 at para.24.
174 *Ibid.*
175 *R. v. Dyment*, [1988] 2 S.C.R. 417 at para.19.

The Court's insistence on legal authority for searches and seizures is consistent with its goal of preventing unjustified searches *before* they happen. In the words of Dickson J., in *Hunter v. Southam*, 'this can only be accomplished by a system of prior authorization, not one of subsequent validation'.[176] Generally speaking, the cases stand for the proposition that unauthorized electronic surveillance will violate s. 8 where the target has a 'reasonable expectation of privacy'. For example, in *R. v. Wong*, the Supreme Court found that unauthorized video surveillance of a hotel room offended the reasonable expectations of privacy of the occupants of the room and violated s. 8 of the *Charter*.[177]

The Supreme Court has also stated that as the information collected by the state nears a certain type of 'core' personal and 'biographical' information about the individual, the privacy interest becomes more important and the requirement for judicial authorization increases.[178] In *R. v. Plant*,[179] the Court found that information collected by a public utility company about its customers without a warrant, in the form of computerized records, could be freely shared with police without an infringement of s. 8 of the *Charter*. The Court distinguished the evidence disclosed on the basis that it did not fall within the protected 'biographical core of personal information' over which individuals in a free and democratic society would justifiably want to maintain and control.[180]

Similarly, in *R. v. Tessling*,[181] the police used a thermal imaging device to take a 'heat' picture of the respondent's home from an aeroplane. The camera used Forward Looking Infra-Red (FLIR) technology and recorded the relative distribution of heat over the surface of the house. The policed did not obtain a search warrant and Mr. Tessling argued that the FLIR technology constituted an unreasonable search of his home in violation of s. 8 of the *Charter*. The Supreme Court of Canada found that the taking of the FLIR image did not violate Tessling's reasonable expectation of privacy.

The judgment of the Court was delivered by Binnie J. who noted that a search will not violate s. 8 of the *Charter* if it is 'authorized by a reasonable law and carried out in a reasonable manner'.[182] He went on to observe that privacy is a 'protean concept, and the difficult issue is where the "reasonableness" line should be drawn'.[183] He relied on *Plant*, which establishes that not all information an individual may wish to keep private enjoys the protection of s. 8 of the *Charter*. Indeed, the purpose of s. 8 is 'to protect a biographical core of personal information which individuals in a free and democratic society would wish to maintain and control from dissemination to the state'.[184]

176 *Hunter, supra*, note 468 at para.27.
177 *R v Wong*, [1990] 3 S.C.R. 36.
178 *R. v. Plant*, [1993] 3 S.C.R. 281.
179 *Ibid.*
180 *Ibid.* at para.20.
181 [2004] 3 S.C.R. 432.
182 *Ibid.* at para.18.
183 *Ibid.* at para.25.
184 *Plant, supra*, note 472 at 293.

It follows that the potential for revealing private information is merely one factor to consider in determining whether a search attracts a reasonable expectation of privacy and is protected by s. 8 of the *Charter*. Before concluding that Mr. Tessling had no 'reasonable expectation of privacy' in the heat distribution information, Binnie J. observed that the protection is limited to the 'biographical core of personal information' and that which affects the 'dignity, integrity and autonomy' of the individual.[185]

Following these cases, on 8 December 2017, the Supreme Court of Canada released two landmark decisions establishing that Canadians may have a reasonable expectation of privacy in electronic communications they (may) have authored which are found on devices or networks over which they have no control. Both decisions focus on what is properly at the heart of the s. 8 inquiry: whether the accused has an objectively reasonable expectation of privacy in the information seized by the police.

The first case, *R. v. Jones*,[186] involved a man who was convicted of several firearms and drug trafficking offences. His convictions rested on records of text messages seized from his telecommunications service provider (Telus) that were obtained under a production order pursuant to s. 487.012 of the *Criminal Code* (now s. 487.014). The seized messages were from a Telus account possibly associated with Jones's co-accused. Some of the text messages were sent from a phone registered to Jones's wife but used by him. Jones sought to exclude the text messages on the basis that obtaining them by means of a production order contravened his s. 8 *Charter* right.

Justice Côté, who wrote the decision for the majority, found that Jones had a reasonable expectation of privacy in the text messages stored by the service provider. She noted that 'whether a claimant has a reasonable expectation of privacy must be answered with regard to the totality of the circumstances of a particular case'.[187] Claimants must establish: that they have a direct interest in the subject matter of the search; that they have a subjective expectation of privacy in that subject matter; and that their subjective expectation of privacy is objectively reasonable (para. 13). Côté J. explained that:

> it is objectively reasonable for the sender of a text message to expect a service provider to keep information private where its receipt and retention of such information is incidental to its role of delivering private communications to the intended recipient. That is intuitive. One would not reasonably expect the service provider to share the text messages with an unintended recipient, or post them publicly for the world to see (para.44).

Thus, on the totality of the circumstances, Jones had a reasonable expectation of privacy in the text messages. However, his s. 8 *Charter* right was not breached

185 *Ibid*. at para.63.
186 2017 SCC 60; [2017] 2 SCR 696.
187 Per *R. v. Spencer*, 2014 SCC 43, [2014] 2 S.C.R. 212 (para. 18).

because the records were lawfully seized from the service provider by means of a production order under s. 487.012 of the *Criminal Code*.

In the second case, *R. v. Marakah*,[188] the police obtained warrants to search Mr. Marakah's home, which he shared with his accomplice, Andrew Winchester, regarding illegal transactions in firearms. The police seized Marakah's BlackBerry and his accomplice's iPhone. Both contained a number of text messages exchanged between the two men pertaining to the illicit purchase and sale of firearms. At trial, Marakah successfully argued against the admission of the text message found on his phone. However, the application judge found that he had no standing to argue that the text messages found on his accomplice's iPhone should not be admitted; and he was convicted of multiple firearms offences. Writing for a majority of the Court of Appeal for Ontario, MacPherson J. A. agreed with the application judge.[189]

The issue before the Supreme Court was whether an accused 'can never claim s. 8 protection for text messages accessed through a recipient's phone because the sender has no privacy interest in the messages if they are not contained within his or her own device'. The majority found that Marakah had a reasonable expectation of privacy in the messages he sent to his accomplice's iPhone.

The then-Chief Justice McLachlin, who wrote the decision for the majority, held that, depending on the totality of the circumstances, an accused *can* have a reasonable expectation of privacy in sent and/or received messages. Importantly, however, the Court stressed that not 'every communication occurring through an electronic medium will attract a reasonable expectation of privacy and hence grant an accused standing to make arguments regarding s. 8 protection'. Whether an accused has a reasonable expectation of privacy in a sent text message (or other electronic communication) will depend on the particular facts and circumstances of the case.

The Court referred to *R. v. Wong*, and observed that 'the broad and general right to be secure from unreasonable search and seizure guaranteed by s. 8 is meant to keep pace with technological development'.[190] In this sense, '[t]echnical differences inherent in new technology should not determine the scope of protection afforded to private communications'.[191] For this reason, McLachlin CJ stated the following:

> Where data are physically or electronically located varies from phone to phone, from service provider to service provider, or, with text messaging more broadly, from technology to technology. The s. 8 analysis must be robust to these distinctions, in harmony with the need to take a broad, purposive approach to privacy protection under s. 8 of the Charter: *Spencer*, at para.15; *Hunter*, at pp. 156–157.[192]

188 2017 SCC 59, [2017] 2 S.C.R. 608.
189 2016 ONCA 542, 131 O.R. (3d) 561.
190 *Wong*, supra, note 472 at 44.
191 Per Abella J. in *R. v. TELUS Communications Co., 2013 SCC 16, [2013] 2 S.C.R. 3* at para.5.
192 *Marakah, supra*, note 483 at para.19.

McLachlin CJ went on to note that 'the claimant's subjective expectation of privacy in the subject matter of the alleged search must have been objectively reasonable in order to engage s. 8'. The Court placed the greatest emphasis on the private nature of the subject matter – in particular, whether the informational content of the electronic conversation revealed details of the claimant's lifestyle or information of a biographic nature – which is consistent with prior case law. The Court noted that people generally expect private electronic conversations to stay private, and as a result they often discuss personal matters. Indeed, McLachlin CJ observed that

> [o]ne can even text privately in plain sight. A wife has no way of knowing that, when her husband appears to be catching up on emails, he is in fact conversing by text message with a paramour. A father does not know whom or what his daughter is texting at the dinner table (para. 36).

Text messages, in other words, are inherently private. There is no need to take steps to shield one's self from the prying eyes of others; and thus, text messaging inevitably gives a heightened degree of privacy akin to the enclosed phone booth in *Katz*. McLachlin CJ also noted that an individual who sends a text message is often revealing a great deal of intimate and personal information that is central to one's biographical core: 'people ... communicate details about their activities, their relationships, and even their identities that they would never reveal to the world at large, and (expect) to enjoy portable privacy in doing so (para. 36)'. The Court went on to stress the following at para. 37:

> Electronic conversations, in sum, are capable of revealing a great deal of personal information. Preservation of a "zone of privacy" in which personal information is safe from state intrusion is the very purpose of s. 8 of the Charter ... As the foregoing examples illustrate, this zone of privacy extends beyond one's own mobile device; it can include the electronic conversations in which one shares private information with others. It is reasonable to expect these private interactions — and not just the contents of a particular cell phone at a particular point in time — to remain private.

Thus, the majority excluded the text messages under s. 24(2) of the *Charter* – as they were obtained by an unreasonable search – the convictions were set aside, and Marakah was acquitted.

These cases suggest that there is a strong connection between electronic evidence-gathering and the infringement of one's reasonable expectation of privacy. The Supreme Court of Canada has emphasized the need to restrict the government's ability to use sophisticated technologies to intercept private communications and gather evidence, stressing the requirement for prior judicial authorization. These decisions clearly have an impact on the admissibility of digital evidence seized by police. Yet they also have broader potential implications for privacy law.

It is now apparent that the decision to engage in a private electronic communication creates a situation where the individual can reasonably expect the messages to remain secure against the prying eyes of the state. Further, it is also important that participation in the online world leaves 'a trail of digital breadcrumbs' with various intermediaries (ISPs, social networking sites, private third-parties, etc.) and 'those breadcrumbs are capable of revealing a history of one's private activity on the Internet'.[193] It allows conclusions to be drawn concerning the private life of the person whose data has been retained, such as their habits of everyday life, permanent or temporary places of residence, daily and other movements, activities carried out, social relationships, and so on.

To date, these principles have only been applied to ISPs. The question of how s. 8 *Charter* principles will apply to the collection and use of biometric data is an important question that will generate controversy going forward. We have seen that the reasonable expectation of privacy test requires looking at the totality of circumstances in any given case. The reasonableness of an individual's expectation of privacy depends on the nature and strength of his or her connection to the subject matter; and this will vary depending on context. As such, an accused may have a reasonable expectation of privacy in one setting, but not in another. To illustrate, Muldover J. observed the following in *R. v. Marakah*, in dissent, at para.116:

> For instance, DNA is capable of revealing intimate details about people that are central to their biographical cores. Nonetheless, the reasonableness of an expectation of personal privacy in DNA may, and often will, vary depending on the context. While an accused may reasonably expect informational privacy in DNA when it is found on his body or stored at a hospital (*R. v. Dyment*, [1988] 2 S.C.R. 417), the same cannot be said when the same DNA is deposited on a complainant or a physical object at a crime scene in a public place: see *R. v. Stillman*, [1997] 1 S.C.R. 607, at para.62. Similarly, a person may have a reasonable expectation of personal privacy in his or her intimate thoughts about friends, hobbies and romantic interests when they are recorded in a diary, but not when these same thoughts are shared publicly on social media or reality television. Finally, a person may have a reasonable expectation of personal privacy in the informational contents of a garbage bag when it is inside his or her home, but not when that same garbage bag is placed on the curb outside the home for collection: see *Patrick*, at para. 64.

Thus, although the subject matter itself remains the same, the nature and strength of the person's privacy interest will vary greatly depending on the circumstances. Context is necessary for determining whether a person will be able to challenge a search involving biometric data under s. 8 of the *Charter*. A central question will probably be whether the individual loses his or her reasonable

193 Per Cote J. in *R. v. Jones, supra*, note 481 at para.42.

expectation of privacy in information once it's shared with others. After all, the basis of the reasonable expectation of privacy has always centred on the individual's right to exclude.

The European Court of Human Rights

The European Court of Human Rights (ECHR) is a judicial body established in 1959 that is charged with supervising the enforcement of the *Convention for the Protection of Human Rights and Fundamental Freedoms* (commonly known as the *European Convention on Human Rights*), which was drafted by the Council of Europe. The court hears applications alleging that a contracting state has breached one or more of the human rights provisions concerning civil and political rights set out in the Convention and its protocols.

S and Marper v United Kingdom[194] addresses the question of whether the storage and retention of biometric data violates the Convention. The first applicant, Mr. S., was arrested on 19 January 2001 at the age of eleven and charged with attempted robbery; however, he was acquitted on 14 June 2001. Michael Marper was arrested on 13 March 2001 and charged with harassment of his partner. Before a pre-trial review took place, he and his partner reconciled. In June 2001, the case was formally discontinued.

Fingerprints and DNA samples were taken by the police from both individuals. Both asked for their data samples to be destroyed, but the police refused. The applicants ultimately appealed to the ECHR, challenging the fact that even if an individual was never charged, or if criminal proceedings were discontinued, or if the person was later acquitted of a crime, their DNA profile could be kept permanently on record without their consent.

The applicants complained under Article 8 of the Convention about the retention of their fingerprints, cellular samples and DNA profiles pursuant to section 64 (1A) of the *Police and Criminal Evidence Act 1984*. Article 8 provides that:

1 Everyone has the right to respect for his private ... life...
2 There shall be no interference by a public authority with the exercise of this right except such as is in accordance with the law and is necessary in a democratic society ... for the prevention of disorder or crime...

In a unanimous verdict, the seventeen-judge bench of the ECHR held that there had been a violation of Article 8. Fingerprints, DNA profiles and cellular samples constitute personal data and their retention was capable of affecting the private life of an individual:

> 84. ...fingerprints objectively contain unique information about the individual concerned allowing his or her identification with precision in a wide

194 [2008] ECHR 1581.

> range of circumstances. They are thus capable of affecting his or her private life and retention of this information without the consent of the individual concerned cannot be regarded as neutral or insignificant.
>
> ...
>
> 125. In conclusion, the Court finds that the blanket and indiscriminate nature of the powers of retention of the fingerprints, cellular samples and DNA profiles of persons suspected but not convicted of offences, as applied in the case of the present applicants, fails to strike a fair balance between the competing public and private interests and that the respondent State has overstepped any acceptable margin of appreciation in this regard. Accordingly, the retention at issue constitutes a disproportionate interference with the applicants' right to respect for private life and cannot be regarded as necessary in a democratic society.

It is also significant that a para. 99, the ECHR also stated that:

> ...as in telephone tapping, secret surveillance and covert intelligence-gathering, [it is necessary] to have clear, detailed rules governing the scope and application of measures, as well as minimum safeguards concerning, *inter alia*, duration, storage, usage, access of third parties, procedures for preserving the integrity and confidentiality of data and procedures for its destruction, thus providing sufficient guarantees against the risk of abuse and arbitrariness.

Thus, the ECHR recognized that, since the protection of personal data is of fundamental importance to a person's enjoyment of his or her right to privacy, the domestic law must afford appropriate safeguards to prevent any misuse of that data.

Summary of the legal framework

What do these three different approaches to privacy, surveillance and data gathering have to say about the best framework for the protection of biometric data going forward? The Canadian approach strongly focuses on whether the data at issue falls within the protected 'biographical core of personal information' over which individuals in a free and democratic society would justifiably want to maintain control and protect from dissemination to the state.

The Supreme Court of Canada placed the most emphasis on the *private* nature of the subject matter – in particular, whether the information reveals details of the claimant's lifestyle or information of a biographic nature. The more the data reveals highly sensitive and intimate information about the individual, closer to the biographical core, the greater the need for protection from state interference.

The ECHR approach is similar in that it provides greater protection for information that is capable of affecting – or revealing – the private life of an individual. In both cases, it would appear that there is no more sensitive or personal data, which is capable of affecting a person's private life, than biometric data. Indeed, biometric data is capable of revealing the highest level of personal and private information – a person's biological make-up.

The American approach remains rooted in traditional liberal notions of privacy, particularly trespass and the individual's right to be let alone. However, in *US v. Jones*, the majority was deeply concerned about the broader effects of persistent monitoring by the state. Recall, for example, that Justice Alito remarked that there are 'particularly vexing problems' with applying a trespass framework to cases involving technological surveillance that is carried out by making electronic, as opposed to physical, contact with the person or thing being tracked. Similarly, Justice Sotomayor pointed to the inherent risks in the use of surveillance technologies to gather a substantial amount of intimate information about any person whom the government chooses to track. She also observed that these developments may 'alter the relationship between citizen and government in a way that is inimical to democratic society'.

Thus, both the Canadian and American approaches are concerned with whether or not the interference with the individual's expectation of privacy is reasonable and proportionate in a democratic society. However, the traditional 'trespass to property' approach to privacy is no longer appropriate to address modern concerns, including omnipresent surveillance, the automatic processing of personal data, and the aggregation of personal information for profiling purposes. Similarly, the requirement for judicial authorization (i.e. the search warrant) to safeguard against breaches *before they occur* may no longer be sufficient, by itself, in the modern age of big data. The reason is that even if the initial taking of the data is reasonable and lawful, there is great concern that such data will be communicated or made available to others far into the future, without the knowledge or consent of the individual, and used for all sorts of other potentially unjust purposes.

The approach taken by the ECHR focuses on the need to set national limits on the retention and use of such data, with a view to achieving a proper balance between the interests of the individual and the state. The ECHR considers that any state claiming a pioneering role in the development of new technologies bears special responsibility for striking the right balance in this regard. In other words, the domestic law should set reasonable limits on the collection, use and storage of personal data; and it must also afford adequate guarantees that retained personal data is protected from misuse and abuse. These concerns are especially important when it comes to the protection of highly sensitive data, like DNA information, within the framework of the criminal justice system.

Conclusion

The use of big data has already become a routine aspect of policing. These tools have clear benefits, including providing insights about how to direct police resources efficiently and effectively in ways that traditional policing methods have not been able to deliver. Digital policing helps reduce the criminal justice system's overall burden, creating economies of scale in law enforcement and allowing police departments to maximize their limited resources.[195] One consequence is that digital policing will usually require offenders to expend more resources to plan, execute and cover up their crimes; and this can lead to increased deterrence of some offenders as well as a greater number of crimes interrupted by the police before the offender can complete them.[196]

At the same time, the reliance upon artificial intelligence and the collection of vast amounts of information pose challenges for law enforcement and the courts. Digital policing creates a number of well-known concerns; and it can also increase the privacy and civil liberties intrusions borne by law-abiding citizens. It can lead the police to focus on detecting crimes committed by certain populations and in certain locations, giving rise to concerns about racial and class bias. Furthermore, without adequate legal safeguards, once biometric data is collected and stored in bulk, it can be shared amongst various entities, including state and local law enforcement, the federal government, private contractors, civilian agencies and the intelligence and military communities.[197]

Traditionally, law enforcement restraints have focused almost exclusively upon the acquisition of information. Yet once information is lawfully seized, its analysis is largely independent of any constitutional constraint. This system is no longer feasible in a world of big data and mass surveillance. The Court's treatment of other remote technologies, such as aerial surveillance and thermal imaging, proves similarly inadequate in addressing the challenges presented by modern biometric technologies.[198]

The solution appears to be, at least in part, to ensure that national governments put into place a robust regime for data protection. The creation of such a regime requires a careful balance between individual interests and legitimate state goals. The legitimate aims of the state include protecting national security and preventing and investigating crime. On the other hand, there is also a need for a structured regime for the protection of this data.

Bibliography

Louise Amoore, 'Biometric Borders: Governing Mobilities in the War on Terror', (2006) 25 *Political Geography* 336.

Julia Angwin, Jeff Larson, Surya Mattu & Lauren Kirchner, 'Machine Bias: There's Software Used Across the Country to Predict Future Criminals. And It's Biased Against Blacks', *ProPublica* (23 May 2016). Available online at: www.propublica.org/article/machine-bias-risk-assessments-in-criminal-sentencing.

Colin J. Bennett, Kevin D. Haggerty, David Lyon & Valerie M. Steeves (eds), *Transparent Lives: Surveillance in Canada (The New Transparency Project)* (Edmonton: Athabasca University Press, 2014).

195 Manuel A. Utset, 'Digital Surveillance and Preventive Policing', (2017) 49 *Connecticut Law Review* 1453 at 1456.

196 *Ibid.* at 1474.

197 Hu, *supra*, note 92 at 1444.

198 *Ibid.*

Thomas A. Bud, 'The Rise and Risks of Police Body-Worn Cameras in Canada', (2016) 14(1) *Surveillance & Society* 117.

Rene Chun, 'China's New Frontiers in Dystopian Tech', *The Atlantic*, April 2018.

Kate Crawford, 'Artificial Intelligence's White Guy Problem', *The New York Times*, 25 June 2016.

Chris Cubbage, 'Creating and Intelligent World', *Australian Security Magazine*, February/March, 2018, 20.

Deloitte, 'Public Sector Disrupted: How Disruptive Innovation Can Help Government Achieve More for Less', 2012. Available online at: www2.deloitte.com/content/dam/Deloitte/global/Documents/Public-Sector/dttl-ps-publicsectordisrupted-08082013.pdf.

Simon Denyer, 'China's Watchful Eye', *The Washington Post*, 7 January 2018.

Laura K. Donohue, 'Technological Leap, Statutory Gap', (2012) 97 *Minnesota Law Review* 407.

Editors, 'Briefs: Hand-Held Guide to "Most Wanted Terrorists" Revised', (2004) 15(7) *Military and Aerospace Electronics*.

Electronic Information Privacy Center, 'Algorithms in the Criminal Justice System'. Available online at: epic.org/algorithmic-transparency/crim-justice/.

Virginia Eubanks, *Automating Inequality: How High-Tech Tools Profile, Police, and Punish the Poor* (New York: St. Martin's Press, 2018).

Mary D. Fan, 'Justice Visualized: Courts and the Body Camera Revolution', (2017) 50 *U.C. Davis Law Review* 897.

Frank Farnham & David James, 'Dangerousness and Dangerous Law', (2001) 358 *The Lancet* 1926.

Megan Garber, 'When Algorithms Take the Stand', *The Atlantic*, 30 June 2016.

John Gramlich, 'America's Incarceration Rate is at a Two-Decade Low', *Pew Research Center*, 2 May 2018. Available online at: www.pewresearch.org/fact-tank/2018/05/02/americas-incarceration-rate-is-at-a-two-decade-low/.

Peter Griffiths, 'Britain Plans more 'Talking' Surveillance Cameras', *The Globe and Mail*, 4 April 2007. Andrew Guthrie Ferguson, 'Crime Mapping and the Fourth Amendment: Redrawing High-Crime Areas', (2011) 63 *Hastings Law Journal* 179.

Andrew Guthrie Ferguson, 'Beyond Big Data Policing', (2017) 105(6) *American Scientist* 377.

Home Office, *Terrorism: What you can do* (London: HMSO, 2005).

Jeremy Hsu, 'Face of the Future: How Facial-Recognition Tech Will Change Everything', *NBC News*, 11 June 2013.

Margaret Hu, 'Biometric Cyberintelligence and the Posse Comitatus Act', (2017) 66 *Emory Law Journal* 697.

Margaret Hu, 'From the National Surveillance State to the Cybersurveillance State', (2017) 13 *Annual Review of Law and Social Science* 161.

Margaret Hu, 'Bulk Biometric Metadata Collection', (2018) 96 *North Carolina Law Review* 1425.

Matthew Hutson, 'Even Bugs Will Be Bugged', *The Atlantic*, November, 2016.

Elizabeth E. Joh, 'Policing by Numbers: Big Data and the Fourth Amendment', (2014) 89 *Washington Law Review* 35.

Elizabeth E. Joh, 'Artificial Intelligence and Policing: First Questions', (2018) *Seattle University Law Review*. Available online at: papers.ssrn.com/sol3/papers.cfm?abstract_id=3168779.

Lyndon B. Johnson, 'Special Message to the Congress on Law Enforcement and the Administration of Justice', 8 March 1965.

Justin Jouvenal, 'To Find Alleged Golden State Killer, Investigators First Found his Great-Great-Great-Grandparents', *The Washington Post*, 30 April 2018.

Justin Jouvenal, Mark Berman, Drew Harwell & Tom Jackman, 'Data on a Genealogy Site Led Police to the "Golden State Killer" Suspect. Now Others Worry about a "Treasure Trove of Data",' *The Washington Post*, 27 April 2018.

Patrick Radden Keefe, 'The Detectives Who Never Forget a Face', *The New Yorker*, 22 August 2016.

Adam Liptak, 'Inmate Count in U.S. Dwarfs Other Nations', *New York Times*, 23 April 2008.

Jennifer Lynch, 'From Fingerprints to DNA: Biometric Data Collection in U.S. Immigrant Communities and Beyond', 22 May 2012.

Shoshanna Amielle Magnet, *When Biometrics Fail: Gender, Race and the Technologies of Identity* (Durham, NC: Duke University Press, 2011).

Mark Maguire, 'Vanishing Borders and Biometric Citizens', in Gabriella Lazaridis (ed.), *Security, Insecurity and Migration in Europe* (London: Routledge, 2011).

Bernadette McSherry & Patrick Keyzer, *Sex Offenders and Preventive Detention: Politics, Policy and Practice* (Leichhardt, NSW: The Federation Press, 2009).

Alex Perala, 'UK Police to Use Mobile Fingerprint Scanning System in the Field', *Find-Biometrics*, 12 February 2018.

The Pew Charitable Trusts, 'Collateral Costs: Incarceration's Effects on Economic Mobility', 2010. Available online at: ezto-cf-media.mheducation.com/Media/Connect_Production/hssl/english/integrated/connectirw/Excerpt_from_Collateral_Costs_Incarcerations_Effect_on_Economic_Mobility.pdf.

President's Commission on Law Enforcement and Administration of Justice, 'The Challenge of Crime in a Free Society' (Washington, DC: 1967).

Matt Reynolds, 'UK Police are Now Using Fingerprint Scanners on the Streets to Identify People in Less than a Minute', *Wired*, 10 February 2018.

Andrew D. Selbst, 'Disparate Impact in Big Data Policing', (2017) 52 *Georgia Law Review* 109.

Marcus Smith, Monique Mann & Gregor Urbas, *Biometrics, Crime and Security* (New York: Routledge, 2018).

Emily Steel & J. Angwin, 'Device Raises Fear of Facial Profiling'. *The Wall Street Journal*, 13 July 2011.

Malcom Thorburn, 'Identification, Surveillance and Profiling: On the Uses and Abuses of Citizen Data', in I. Dennis & G. R. Sullivan (eds), *Seeking Security: Pre-Empting the Commission of Criminal Harms* (Oxford: Hart Publishing, 2011) 15.

Manuel A. Utset, 'Digital Surveillance and Preventive Policing', (2017) 49 *Connecticut Law Review* 1453.

Graeme Wood, 'Prison Without Walls', in Peter P. Swire & Kenesa Ahmad (eds), *Privacy and Surveillance with New Technologies* (New York: International Debate Education Association, 2012) 290–312.

Elia Zureik & Karen Hindle, 'Governance, Security and Technology: The Case of Biometrics', (2004) 73(1) *Studies in Political Economy* 113.

Case Law

Floyd v. City of New York, 959 F. Supp. 2d 540.

Gardner v. Florida, 430 U.S. 349, 351 (1977).

Hunter v. Southam, [1984] 2 SCR 145.

Katz v. United States, 389 U.S. 347 (1967).
Pennsylvania v. Dunlap, 129 S. Ct. 448, 448 (2008).
R. v. Dyment, [1988] 2 S.C.R. 417.
R. v. Jones, [2017] 2 SCR 696.
R. v. Marakah, [2017] 2 S.C.R. 608.
R. v. Plant, [1993] 3 S.C.R. 281.
R. v. Spencer, [2014] 2 S.C.R. 212.
R. v. TELUS Communications Co., [2013] 2 S.C.R. 3.
R. v. Tessling, [2004] 3 S.C.R. 432.
R. v Wong, [1990] 3 S.C.R. 36.
S and Marper v. United Kingdom, [2008] ECHR 1581.
United States v. Jones, 132 S. Ct. 945 (2012).
United States v. Knotts, 460 U.S. 276 (1983).

5 Biometrics and national identification

Introduction

Of the digital biometric identity systems in existence today, the most noteworthy is that of the Republic of India. This system, which is known as Aadhaar, was deployed rapidly over the past decade or so; and it currently has more than one billion members.[1] Remarkably, the Indian government neglected to enact a comprehensive data protection and privacy law regime alongside the implementation of this biometric data-gathering system. Aadhaar therefore presents an interesting case study for the inherent risks and benefits of this sort of administrative regime.

Various questions and choices emerge about the role of biometric identity as an identifier and these choices are socially shaped by powerful interests.[2] For what purposeswill the system be developed – for single or multiple uses? Will the technology permit further functions and uses to be added down the road? Will membership be voluntary or compulsory? Will citizens lose benefits and entitlements as a result? What legal restrictions will control the circumstances under which the data might be used, and the agents who might use it? What are the systems of data storage and how will the data be secured from malicious attack, technical error and human fallibility? What personal identifiers will be used and how will these be assigned or obtained? What are the costs in terms of human resources, financial expenditures, security risks, as well as social relations?

Aadhaar, which is operated by the Unique Identification Authority of India (UIDAI), is the world's largest biometric database. The word '*Aadhaar*' means 'foundation' or 'base' in Hindi; and it was chosen for its power to communicate the need for all residents to be included in the political and economic development of the country.[3] It was thought that Aadhaar would act as a universal foundation for the transparent, reliable and efficient delivery of public services and benefits.[4]

1 Dixon, *supra*, note 8.
2 Bennett et al., *supra*, note 27 at 4.
3 Gursharan Singh Kainth, *Aadhaar India: Brand for a Billion* (Saarbrucken: LAP Lambert Academic Publishing, 2011) at 7.
4 *Ibid.* at 10.

As the second most populous nation in the world, India faces an enormous challenge in dealing with poverty. India is a developing country plagued by poverty and one of the lowest literacy rates in the world.[5] Recent economic growth has led to the implementation of new social programs and safety nets to tackle poverty, health and educational challenges.[6] From a policy perspective, the development of a compulsory national identification system seems to provide a means to extend social services and benefits to the poorest and most remote sectors of the population, while reducing fraud and bureaucratic waste.

Problems around lack of identification afflict millions of people in the remote interior areas and lowest income groups of India. Rural women, for example, have difficulties in accessing social benefits and employment; and the lack of access to one service, like a bank account, typically cuts off access to other services and benefits, employment or ration services.[7] Indeed, a 2008 Planning Commission report demonstrated that more than one third, or 36.7 per cent, of grain intended for poor households was sold to non-poor households and that 58 per cent of subsidized grains did not reach the intended recipients owing to various errors in delivery and identification.[8]

When you're poor, proving who you are can be a stressful and maddening process. This has always been the case, but with Aadhaar, it has become an unavoidable part of life.[9] If you're a migrant trying to earn a living selling goods on the roadside, you're asked to prove who you are before you can set up shop; if you're disabled, you need to prove your disability to collect benefits.[10] Opening a bank account requires proof of an address, like a utility bill, and people living in the slums of India often have no fixed address, much less access to water, electricity or sewage facilities.

Today, something as simple as a missing document or a defective fingerprint reader can mean that a person is deprived of food rations, or a pension, or a child is denied an education. The weight of this stark truth is born by hundreds of millions of unregistered children living in poverty throughout India,[11] many of whom have no fixed residence other than 'Under Moolchand Flyover' and who

5 Chethan Kumar, 'Literacy Rate Up, But So is Illiteracy', *Times of India*, 28 January 2016. The overall literacy rate in the country may have gone up to 74.4 per cent, but the drop in the illiteracy rate has not matched the increase in population.

6 Kainth, *supra*, note 499 at 2.

7 Kainth, *supra*, note 499 at 2.

8 Zelazny, *supra*, note 100 at 6.

9 Devjyot Ghoshal, 'The World's Largest Biometric ID Programme is a Privacy Nightmare Waiting to Happen', *Quartz India*, 28 March 2017.

10 *Ibid.*

11 Casey Dunning, Alan Gelb & Sneha Raghavan, 'Birth Registration, Legal Identity, and the Post-2015 Agenda', Center for Global Development, September, 2014 at 11. With some 71 million unregistered Indian children in the age range 0–5 and about three times this number in the range 0–15, it is thought that a centralized identification programme could help to complement the often-decentralized birth registration processes and 'reverse-engineer an identity' for many children.

spend their days wandering through the streets in rags, begging or scavenging for scrap metal to resell.[12] As one woman, who has been a teacher in Delhi for 18 years, put it:

> Why do you need an Aadhaar for education for the least privileged? Imagine a daily wage labourer who has moved here from Bihar with his family. He has nothing and probably lives in a shack. He has no papers. He can barely fend for himself and his family. Whatever he earns in one day lights the cookstove for dinner at night. If he has to spend three to four days running around getting an Aadhaar card, it will mean that he probably doesn't eat on those days. Would you do it?[13]

Human Rights Watch maintains that Aadhaar has led to millions of people being denied access to essential services and benefits in violation of their human rights. According to activists in Rajasthan state, for example, between September 2016 and June 2017, after Aadhaar was made mandatory, at least 2.5 million families were unable to get food rations.[14] In October 2017, the government instructed states not to deny subsidized food grains to eligible families merely because they did not have an Aadhaar number or had not linked their ration cards to it; however, reports of denied benefits continue.[15]

Hospitals in Haryana state are insisting on newborn babies being enrolled in Aadhaar before giving them birth certificates; and Aadhaar IDs are also required in some places for the issue of death certificates.[16] In some cases, people living with HIV/AIDS have decided to stop getting medical treatment or medicines when forced to submit Aadhaar numbers because they fear their identities being exposed. And some people with disabilities have been denied benefits because they were unable to obtain Aadhaar numbers.[17]

In January 2018, as a cold front gripped the nation's capital and moved through North India, homeless persons were denied access to shelters owing to their lack of Aadhaar registration.[18] During a hearing on the lack of shelters for homeless people, the Supreme Court's Social Justice Bench asked the Uttar Pradesh state government if a permanent address was mandatory for Aadhaar enrolment, to benefit from welfare services. The Uttar Pradesh government responded that the homeless were required to have documents, Aadhaar included, if they wanted to use night shelters.[19] According to the 2011 Census, there are

12 Goshal, *supra*, note 505.

13 *Ibid.*

14 Human Rights Watch, 'India: Identification Project Threatens Rights', 10 January 2018.

15 *Ibid.*

16 *Ibid.*

17 *Ibid.*

18 Rituparna Chatterjee, 'The Supreme Court of India Raised an Important Humanitarian Question about Aadhaar', *The Huffington Post*, 11 January 2018.

19 *Ibid.*

1.77 million homeless people in India, with an estimated 150,000–200,000 residing in New Delhi alone.[20] Justice Lokur stated:

> So, how do homeless people get Aadhaar if they have no home or a permanent address...Does this mean that they do not exist for the Government of India?
>
> We are talking about human beings who have no place to stay. Those who have no place to stay have to be given a place to live...what about the people who are homeless and destitute. How will they make Aadhaar if they don't have an address?[21]

We should think of the intensification of existing inequalities, such as this, as system failures.[22]

Introduction to national identity and identification

Hundreds of millions of people worldwide have absolutely no legal identification, which keeps them in the shadows of the global economy. According to UNICEF, 98 per cent of people in rich countries have birth certificates, whereas 40 per cent of children in the developing world are not registered at birth – and the proportion grows even higher in poorer parts of the world.[23] As of 2012, the world failed to account for the births of roughly 230 million children under the age of five; and an additional 70 million registered children had not received a birth certificate.[24]

In the year 2000, South Asia had the highest proportion (63 per cent) of children not registered at birth, even higher than Sub-Saharan Africa.[25] The poor in rural areas are the most likely to be under-registered. In India, for example, roughly 26 million births take place each year, with only 14 million registered; and a non-registration figure as high as 45 per cent exists in rural areas.[26]

Since birth registration, and correspondingly, the birth certificate, constitutes the first and most direct way for an individual to obtain a legal identity and access the state, the lack of registration in childhood often results in their never gaining access to basic public services or registering to vote – condemning them to a lifetime of marginalization and vulnerability.[27] As the European Parliament observed in its Public Policy Issue Paper, *Birth Registration and Children*,

20 *Ibid.*
21 *Ibid.*
22 Magnet, *supra*, note 57 at 150.
23 Gleb & Kenny, *supra*, note 1.
24 Dunning et al., *supra*, note 507 at 2.
25 Govind Kelkar, Dev Nathan, E. Revathi & Swati Sain Gupta, *Aadhaar: Gender, Identity and Development* (New Delhi: Academic Foundation, 2014) at 21.
26 *Ibid.*
27 *Ibid.* at 22.

> the right to identity consists in the legal and social acknowledgement of a person as a holder of rights and responsibilities, as well as the acknowledgement of his or her belonging to a country, a territory, a society and a family.[28]

As the *Universal Declaration of Human Rights* (UDHR (United Nations 1948)) makes clear, everyone has a right to a nationality[29] based on where they're born. Citizenship, on the other hand, is a legal status, signifying that the individual has been registered with the government in some country. States have considerable power in drawing distinctions between persons on the basis of their citizenship status.

Article 1 of the *Convention on Certain Questions relating to the Conflict of Nationality Law* states that 'it is for each State to determine under its own laws who are its nationals'. While it is the right of a state to determine who its citizens are, this decision must accord with the relevant provisions of international law. Certain human rights principles and the existence of a link between the individual and the state act as a basis for citizenship under international law. And the principle of equality and non-discrimination generally prohibits discrimination based on the lack of nationality status.

For instance, the *International Covenant on Economic, Social and Cultural Rights* (ICESCR) establishes that states must, in general, protect the rights of all individuals – regardless of citizenship – to work; just and favourable working conditions; an adequate standard of living; good health; education; and other economic, social and cultural rights. Other international instruments also mention the right to citizenship. The 1965 *International Convention on the Elimination of All Forms of Racial Discrimination* states that citizenship is a civil right (Article 5). The 1989 *Convention on the Rights of the Child* provides that children of non-citizens shall have the right to a name and to acquire a nationality and should not be excluded from schools – even if they lack legal status.

While these examples underscore the general consensus that everyone should be able to acquire, and change citizenship, and convey it to one's offspring, the international legal system also respects the sovereign right of states to create their own nationality laws and does not permit any other entity to impose citizenship requirements upon, or make citizenship decisions for, states.[30] Most countries with a common law heritage – such as India – have a domestic citizenship act which determines citizenship status. What constitutes acceptable legal identity can differ across countries; and there is considerable ambiguity and lack of consistency attached to citizenship status among the various states.

28 European Parliament, 'Birth Registration and the Rights of the Child', May, 2007. Available online at: https://docplayer.net/43800420-Birth-registration-and-the-rights-of-the-child.html.

29 UNHCR, *Handbook on Protection of Stateless Persons Under the 1954 Convention Relating to the Status of Stateless Persons* (Geneva, 2014) at 1.

30 Kristy A. Belton, 'The Neglected Non-Citizen: Statelessness and Liberal Political Theory', (2011) 7(1) *Journal of Global Ethics* 59 at 61.

In some states, like India, the range of citizenship rights, and the vast array of individuals excluded from them, is extensive. Examples of such political, social, economic and cultural rights include property rights, the right of association, the right to gainful employment, welfare rights (including rationing, housing, public education, public relief/access to the courts, labour rights and social security) and administrative measures (including freedom of movement, identity papers, travel documents and naturalization). Thus, a tension exists between the lofty goal of universal human rights, and the right of sovereign states to control who is a citizen, particularly as the enjoyment of rights is still mostly linked to citizenship status.[31]

While India has recently undertaken extraordinary efforts to provide legal identity to all residents through Aadhaar, the fact remains that, owing to its complex political history, it has a patchwork of laws and regulations relating to citizenship status. And, in August of 2016, the Calcutta High Court ruled that the Aadhaar card is not valid proof of Indian citizenship.[32] The Court held that 'it is clear that the said Aadhaar Card by itself shall not confer any right of or be proof of, citizenship or domicile in respect of the holder thereto'.[33]

Nevertheless, we shouldn't underestimate the importance of identity recognition by the state. This makes it possible to access formal institutions which consider the individual's unique needs, goals and circumstances. This is particularly important for women, as they can obtain documentation of identity that is both individual – i.e. independent from the stereotypical woman's role as wife or mother within the traditional male-dominated household – and portable. It can thus provide increased gender equality, social inclusion, and autonomy, as well as economic and geographic mobility.[34]

Ultimately, this tool can empower residents as they are given opportunities to access services and benefits and interact with a responsive and accessible government – surely this lies at the very heart of the democratic process itself. Identity is also linked to autonomy, mobility, income generation, status, inclusion and equal treatment.[35] For a country like India, such systems are essential to empower millions of people and provide them with the necessary tools to rise above poverty.

History and background of Aadhaar India

Recent connections between terrorism and illegal migrants, especially following high-profile attacks, have only exacerbated antimigrant sentiments, particularly directed at Muslims. This has put increasing pressure on nation states to identify and 'categorize' residents on the basis of perceived risks, particularly considering

31 *Ibid.*

32 The Hitavada, 'Aadhaar Not a Proof of Citizenship: Dist. Court'. Available online at: www.pressreader.com/india/the-hitavada/20180726/281728385314630.

33 *Ibid.*

34 Kelkar et al., *supra*, note 521 at 10.

35 *Ibid.* at 19.

whether or not they're likely to pose a threat to 'national security' interests. Of course, similar sentiments have been expressed in other jurisdictions, like the US and the UK, where we have witnessed the push towards 'walled states' and the fortification of geographic boundaries.

In India, reform has been urged by multiple reviews and enquiries since the 1990s, including those initiated after the Kargil war in 1999 and the Mumbai terrorist attacks in 2008. From May to July 1999, India and Pakistan engaged in a violent conflict over the Kargil district on the border between the two states. This conflict is said to have triggered the need to ensure that 'terrorists' are not allowed to enter the Indian territory.[36]

The Kargil Review Committee (KRC) was asked to '...review the events leading up to the Pakistani aggression in the Kargil District of Ladakh in Jammu and Kashmir; and, to recommend such measures as are considered necessary to safeguard national security against such armed intrusions'.[37] Though it was given a relatively narrow mandate, the committee looked generally at the threats and challenges facing India and conducted an in-depth examination of its national security.[38] The KRG Report, which was tabled in Parliament on 23 February 2000, brought to light many deficiencies in India's security management, particularly in the areas of intelligence, border management, and defence.

The committee was of the view that the 'political, bureaucratic, military and intelligence establishments appear to have developed a vested interest in the status quo'.[39] One of the key observations was that the Kargil episode highlighted 'gross inadequacies in the nation's surveillance capability...' It recommended that '...steps...be taken to issue ID Cards to border villagers in certain vulnerable areas on a priority basis, pending its extension to other or all parts of the State'.[40]

The Cabinet Committee on Security (CCS) set up a Group of Ministers (GoM) to study the Kargil Review Committee report and recommend measures for implementation. The GoM submitted a report in 2001 on 'Reforming the National Security System', in which it recommended sweeping reforms to the national security system.[41] It also recommended that a multi-purpose National Identity Card (MNIC) should be issued: '[t]here should be compulsory registration of citizens and non-citizens living in India'.[42] The GoM further observed that

> [i]llegal migration from across our borders has continued unabated for over five decades. We have yet to fully wake up to the implications of the

36 Sahana Basavapatna, 'The UID Project in India: Should Non-citizen Residents be Concerned?' Presented at 'The Biopolitics of Development: Life, Welfare, and Unruly Populations', on 9–10 September 2010 at 2.

37 Gurmeet Kanwal, 'Big Chinks in Our Security Armour', *Times of India*, 24 July 2011.

38 *Ibid.*

39 *Ibid.*

40 Basavapatna, *supra*, note 532 at 3.

41 Group of Ministers Report, 'Reforming the National Security System', 23 May 2011.

42 *Ibid.*

> unchecked immigration for the national security...[s]uch large-scale migration has obvious social, economic, political and security implications. There is an all-round failure in India to come to grips with the problem of illegal immigration...The massive illegal immigration poses a grave danger to our security, social harmony and economic well being.[43]

Together, these reports recognized that the problem of illegal migration had assumed serious proportions in India, as illegal migrants were able to seamlessly enter the country and, in some cases, acquire multiple documents reserved for citizens.

In 2003, a Parliamentary Committee under the Chairmanship of then-deputy Prime Minister Advani approved the creation of a Multipurpose National Identity Card with a note that there should be compulsory registration of Indian citizens and non-citizens.[44] In that same year, the *Citizenship Act*, 1955 was amended to allow the central government to compulsorily register every citizen and issue them all with identity cards.

On 3 March 2006, approval was given by the Department of Information Technology, Ministry of Communications and Information Technology for the project entitled 'Unique Identification for BPL Families' to be implemented by the National Informatics Centre (NIC) over a period of 12 months. As a result, a Processes Committee was set up on 3 July 2006 to suggest the process for a database to be created under the Unique Identification for BPL Families project. This Committee, on 26 November 2006, prepared a paper known as 'Strategic Vision Unique Identification of Residents'.

The Empowered Group of Ministers (EGoM) was set up on 4 December 2006, to collate the National Population Register under the *Citizenship Act* and the Unique Identification Number project of the Department of Information Technology. Various meetings on the Unique Identification project were held from time to time. It was ultimately decided that: The Unique Identification Authority of India (UIDAI) would be formed as an executive authority (statutory authority to be constituted later); a numbering format of 12 digits would be used; and the project would be rolled out through the Planning Commission over the next five years.

There was also a critical need to create an institutional mechanism that would 'own' the database and be responsible for its maintenance and updating. In 2009, the Planning Commission formed the Unique ID Authority of India (UIDAI) and appointed its first Chairman, Mr. Nandan Nilekani; and in February the then-Finance Minister allocated funds towards the initiative. In 2010, the then-Chairman of UIDAI unveiled the brand strategy and logo for the project. The goal was to create a universal proof of identity, allowing residents to prove their identities anywhere in the country. The project would

43 Dutta Choudhury, 'Centre Yet to Take Effective Steps', *The Assam Tribune*, 3 October 2017.

44 Kainth, *supra*, note 499 at 64.

also give the Government a clear view of India's population, enabling it to target and deliver services effectively, achieve greater returns on social investments and monitor money and resource flows across the country.[45]

The first Aadhaar number was launched in the village of Tembi, Maharashtra in 2009.[46] By September 2010, the project had been initiated nationwide. By October 2017, India had issued 1.18 billion identity cards. With nearly 1.2 billion participants, the Aadhaar programme is currently the largest national database of people in the world.[47] Its use is spreading like wildfire, which is the result of robust and aggressive campaigning by the government, administrative agencies and other bodies.

Every resident of India is entitled to enrol and obtain a unique, randomly selected 12-digit Aadhaar number. Each number is unique and cannot be re-assigned to another individual. In return, every person must provide her demographic information along with biometric details for future identification. Demographic information includes information relating to the name, date of birth, address and 'other relevant information' of an individual.[48] Photograph, fingerprint, iris scan 'or such other biological attribute of an individual as may be specified by regulations' are treated as biometric information.[49]

The 12-digit individual identification (ID) is stored in a centralized database and linked to the basic demographic and biometric information about the individual. This serves the purpose of safeguarding against duplicate or fake identifications, which were a major problem in the past, with respect to both the public and private sectors. Now, whenever an Aadhaar ID holder wants to prove his identity, he simply submits his Aadhaar number and then has his fingerprint or iris scanned. This data is then matched against the data housed in the centralized server.

All the system provides is a 'Yes' or 'No' confirmation for the vendor – the school, bank, hospital, or government agent – to verify that the individual is, or is not, who he claims to be.[50] An obvious advantage of this system is that it uses the individual's personal data – her fingerprint, iris scan, and so on – as the sole source of authentication; and thus it doesn't rely on a card or document, which could easily be lost, stolen or duplicated.[51] On confirming the identity of a person, the individual is entitled to receive subsidy, benefit or service.

The Aadhaar database can be accessed by a range of individuals and entities, from employers, to banks, to law enforcement.[52] Yet, while the number of Aadhaar-Enabled Payments System transactions have been steadily rising, many

45 Writ Petition (Civil) No. 494 of 2012 & Connected matters (26 September 2018) at 14.

46 Kainth, *supra*, note 499 at 65.

47 *Ibid.* By comparison, the second largest human biometric database is one-tenth the size, with 1.2 million in the United States.

48 *The Aadhaar (Targeted Delivery of Financial and Other Subsidies, Benefits and Services) Act*, section 3.

49 *Ibid.*

50 Kainth, *supra*, note 499 at 11.

51 *Ibid.* at 12.

52 Dixon, *supra*, note 8.

rural areas still suffer from poor infrastructure. For example, while 250 million people in India have smartphones and can use apps to pay digitally; as many as 350 million have no mobile phones.[53] And as many as a third of adults in India still lack bank accounts.[54] Indeed, those who belong to the poorest and most marginalized social groups – women, children, senior citizens, persons with disabilities, migrant unskilled and non-organized workers, and nomadic tribes – are the most likely to be left behind.[55]

A system that relies on a number only – and no card – must also be able to support online authentication at all times.[56] Yet the failure rate of a 2015 government pilot project testing new Aadhaar-enabled biometric machines in Delhi was more than 50 per cent; and, of the 42 shops where the machines were tested, only 18 remained until the end of the project, with many citing technical glitches and the lack of mobile phone network coverage. Complaints about the unreliable machines eclipse a bigger problem – people who get excluded owing to biometric failures or mismatch.

While the speed of Aadhaar's rollout has been exemplary, coverage is not distributed universally throughout all states.[57] The state of Jharkhand had a 49 per cent failure to match rate, and Rajasthan had a 37 per cent failure to match rate, according to the Indian government.[58] Even with sufficient technical equipment, registration problems can sometimes interfere. For example, reports have emerged that portable biometric scanners were unable to read the fingerprints of rural residents whose hands were calloused or worn from years of manual labour.

Both the NFSA – which provides subsidized rations to poor households – and the NREGA – which guarantees employment to rural households for at least 100 days a year – were affected by Aadhaar failure rates, with millions of people were being excluded from these and other schemes.[59] Indeed, problems have emerged with the government deleting 'fake' job cards – which belonged to real people[60] – and the denial of job cards to remote villagers who don't have Aadhaar, although they are eligible for the scheme.[61] Thus, Aadhaar is being criticized for enabling social exclusion, rather than easing it, particularly for vulnerable populations; and for enhancing the weakness of existing welfare

53 Government of India, 'Economic Survey 2016–17', January, 2017. Available online at: www.indiabudget.gov.in/es2016-17/echapter.pdf at 64.

54 *Ibid.* at 194.

55 *Ibid.*

56 Zelazny, *supra*, note 100 at 28.

57 Government of India, *supra*, note 549 at 194.

58 *Ibid.*

59 Niha Masih, 'Lost in Transition: Has Linking Aadhaar to Government Welfare Schemes made it Difficult for Beneficiaries to Avail of Aid?' *Hindustan Times*, 8 October 2017.

60 In April 2017, it was reported that the Indian government had deleted 94,09,448 'fake' NREGA job cards after verifying Aadhaar IDs. An RTI filed by economist Jean Dreze, however, revealed that only 4 per cent of the job cards that were deleted were fake.

61 Masih, *supra*, note 555.

schemes, which were already riddled with misallocation, fraud, theft and exclusions of the poor.

Government supporters argue that the primary benefit behind this scheme is efficiency. The delivery of benefits through Aadhaar is vastly more effective than via alternative systems, particularly given that India has an extensive rural population, with many in remote villages, some without plumbing in their homes, in extreme poverty without access to modern technology. It also has large numbers of people who live on the streets and are unaccounted for in the census.

Of particular concern, though, is the profound mission creep associated with the Aadhaar system. A voluntary identity card can rapidly become a *de facto* universal ID card if it is well-integrated with finance, health, and other functions. Citizens without it then experience difficulty gaining access to public services or even basic goods. Such is the case in India, where Aadhaar enrolment is legally required for authentication if residents want to access many services and programmes. Initially, it was only used for subsidies, but now it is used for an ever-growing range of activities and services, including bank accounts, medical records, pension payments, and more.[62]

These problems are exacerbated by the fact that until mid-2017, India had virtually no privacy law protections whatsoever. The *National Identification Authority of India Bill 2010* was introduced to address the unanswered privacy issues in the Aadhaar system. The Bill sought to prevent the collection of information related to race, religion, caste, language, income or health. It also mandated that the information collected be stored in the Central Identities Data Repository; and it stipulated that the sharing of data was prohibited except by: the consent of the resident; a court order; or for national security, if directed by an authorized official of the rank of Joint Secretary or above. The Bill also established an Identity Review Committee to monitor the usage patterns of Aadhaar numbers.

However, the Parliamentary Standing Committee on Finance rejected the 2010 bill. *The Privacy Bill of 2011* was put forward again in 2012 to provide data protection for the Aadhaar system, but it was not passed. In the year 2012, enrolment in the Aadhaar programme continued, despite the lack of privacy protections. Another Privacy Bill was put forward in 2014, which also failed. The result was that throughout that time period, the Aadhaar scheme did not have any statutory backing; yet it continued to operate in exercise of executive power of the Government. The Government also set up enrolment centres run by private third parties, which continued to enrol people under the UID scheme.

Meanwhile, as the mission behind Aadhaar expanded, the rising tide of criticism culminated in public-interest litigation before the Supreme Court of India in mid-2013, when eight petitioners, most of them NGOs, asked the court to suspend the Aadhaar programme. Their opposition was centred on three fundamental concerns. First, although advertised as a voluntary programme by the

62 Dixon, *supra*, note 8.

central government, several state governments had made Aadhaar the required ID for those receiving such services as subsidized liquefied petroleum gas (LPG) cylinders used in homes for cooking; and unfortunately, some residents were denied this benefit because they had not enrolled in Aadhaar, even though it was supposed to be a voluntary scheme.[63]

The second concern was that Aadhaar was unconstitutional because it was being rolled out under executive rather than legislative authority, without any statutory basis. Indeed, there was no public discussion or debate about the desirability or feasibility of this project and no debate in Parliament.[64] Moreover, from the start, the project has been run like an institutional start-up inside a government programme.[65] The UID programme was first spearheaded by a government-appointed entrepreneur – Nandan Nilekani, the co-founder of tech giant InfoSys – who was unilaterally granted a Cabinet post by the Prime Minister.[66] Thus, fears were raised about the non-transparency of this process and the fact that decisions were made and influenced by vested private and corporate interests.

The third concern was data privacy. Since there was no national law to protect private information, there was no way to ensure that the data collected for the Aadhaar ID (name, date of birth, fingerprints, etc.) would not be misused. Of particular concern was the perceived violation of the right to privacy, because the technology had the ability to track a person through their use of online authentication, which was seen as equivalent to every resident of India's being continuously watched.

Other concerns included possible errors in the collection of information, the recording of inaccurate data, corruption of the data from anonymous sources, like hackers, and related cases of unauthorized access to or disclosure of personal information.[67] And, given that India has no generally established data protection laws, unlike the United States, Canada and Europe, it may be ill-equipped to deal with such problems. Meanwhile, other countries such as Canada, Australia, and the United States, have found similar schemes unworkable because of the serious threat of misuse and strong public opposition.[68]

On 11 March 2016 the government passed *The Aadhaar Act (Targeted Delivery of Financial and Other Subsidies, Benefits and Services).*[69] It allowed for expanded uses of the Aadhaar programme and made it mandatory for some government schemes and services. The Bill was introduced as a money bill in the

63 Vijay Sathe, 'Managing Massive Change India's Aadhaar, the World's Most Ambitious ID Project', (2014) 87 *Innovations: Technology, Governance, Globalization* 85 at 87.

64 Kainth, *supra*, note 499 at 36.

65 Vanita Yadav, 'Unique Identification Project for 1.2 Billion People in India: Can It Fill Institutional Voids and Enable Inclusive Innovation', (2014) 6 *Contemporary Readings Law and Social Justice* 38 at 39.

66 *Ibid.*

67 *Ibid.* at 38.

68 *Ibid.*

69 *The Aadhar (Targeted Delivery of Financial and Other Subsidies, Benefits and Services) Act* (2016).

Lok Sabha, India's lower house of Parliament. Money bills can be passed by the Lok Sabha alone, without need for approval by the upper house.[70] This led to complaints that the bill passed as part of a much larger budget act, without its own debate and vote in Parliament; and thus became law without full democratic scrutiny and approval.[71] Parliamentarian Jairam Ramesh challenged its introduction as a money bill as 'malafide and brazen'.[72]

Since the passing of the *Aadhaar Act* in 2016, there has been rapid mission creep associated with its mandate. The government has made Aadhaar compulsory for at least 87 welfare schemes – from pensions and scholarships to fertilizer, farming subsidies and health care.[73] Individuals must also have an Aadhaar number to book rail tickets, for religious worship in some private temples and for children's school lunches.[74] It's becoming increasingly difficult to conduct just about any routine task in India without an Aadhaar ID. For these reasons, Aadhaar has been referred to as the 'many-headed Hydra'[75] and questions are being raised about the implementation and aims of this scheme.

An overview of the legal issues around Aadhaar

The expansion of Aadhaar over the years has opened a Pandora's box of litigation. There have been a multitude of petitions filed about the Aadhaar scheme and its usage by various federal and state agencies across the country. Another question before the Indian Supreme Court related to the manner in which the *Aadhaar Act* was passed by Parliament. These cases highlight how discourses surrounding government benefits and services can be shaped by actors outside state institutions, using legal recourse to frame the issues.

The Court continued to endorse its use for access to everything, from paying taxes to procuring a driving licence. But Aadhaar wasn't supposed to be mandatory for residents to avail themselves of *any* government benefit or service, which is something the Supreme Court of India made clear in 2013. The court reiterated the voluntary nature of Aadhaar in 2014 and 2015 and stated that no one can be denied benefits to which they're already entitled just because they don't have an Aadhaar ID.

The first successful case challenging Aadhaar brought to the Indian Supreme Court was *Justice K.S. Puttaswamy & Ors. v. Union of India & Ors. (W.P.(C)*

70 Jacqueline Bhabha & Amiya Bhatia, 'India's Aadhaar Program: A Legitimate Trade-off Between Social Protection and Privacy?' *HarvardFXB – Center for Health and Human Rights*, 28 March 2016. Available online at: https://fxb.harvard.edu/2016/03/28/indias-aadhaar-program-a-legitimate-trade-off-between-social-protection-and-privacy/.

71 Dixon, *supra*, note 8.

72 Krishnadas Rajagopal, 'Right to Privacy Verdict: A Timeline of SC Hearings', *The Hindu*, 24 August 2017.

73 Masih, *supra*, note 555.

74 Dixon, *supra*, note 8.

75 S. Meghnad, 'Aadhaar Act: It's a Web of Regulations Out There', *NewsLaundry*, 2 May 2017.

494/2012).[76] The matter goes to back to 2012, when former justice K. S. Puttaswamy filed a writ petition arguing that it violated a citizen's right to privacy, which flows from the fundamental right to life under Article 21 of the Indian Constitution. Before long, more petitioners came forward to oppose Aadhaar, and the court linked those petitions to this case. The petitioners also objected to the system on grounds ranging from exclusion and denial of benefits to national security on account of the indiscriminate enrolment of illegal immigrants.

On 23 September 2013, the Supreme Court passed an interim order that Aadhaar could not be made compulsory for the provision of government services. The court also said that Aadhaar should not be issued to illegal immigrants as it would legitimize their stay in the country. The relevant extract from the Order is as follows:

> [N]o person should suffer for not getting the Aadhaar card in spite of the fact that some authority had issued a circular making it mandatory and when any person applies to get the Aadhaar card voluntarily, it may be checked whether that person is entitled for it under the law and it should not be given to any illegal immigrant.[77]

The order dealt a swift blow to the government's plans to extend Aadhaar and also created confusion among citizens, especially because many state agencies were insisting that citizens enrol themselves for the UID number to gain access to services and subsidies.

Over the next several years, India's Supreme Court repeatedly reiterated that its ruling stood, leading to an ongoing game of cat and mouse between the executive and judicial branches of government – with the country's poorest and most disadvantaged citizens caught in the middle. And, in a country rife with illiteracy and a broad range of languages, mixed messages about whether Aadhaar was mandatory or not led to widespread confusion.

In August 2015, the Attorney General of India argued that the Constitution does not grant a fundamental right to privacy, and that since this right did not exist, the Aadhaar scheme could not violate it. A three-judge bench of the Supreme Court referred the matter to a larger five – and subsequently nine – judge bench to decide 'whether there is any "right to privacy" guaranteed under our Constitution'. In addition, the Court ordered that 'obtaining an Aadhaar Card is not mandatory and the benefits due to a citizen under any scheme are not to be denied in the absence of Aadhaar Card'.[78]

Yet, paradoxically, the Supreme Court progressively *endorsed* the government's expansion of the Aadhaar programme into a wide range of programmes

76 *Puttaswamy, supra*, note 234.

77 *K. S. Puttaswamy v. Union of India*, Writ Petition (Civil) No. 494 of 2012 (Sup. Ct. India 23 September 2013).

78 *K. S. Puttaswamy v. Union of India*, Writ Petition (Civil) No. 494 of 2012 (Sup. Ct. India 11 August 2015).

and services. On 11 August 2015, the Court held that the unique identification number could be used for the rationed distribution of basic food items (i.e. rice, wheat, sugar, edible oils) and non-food items (i.e. kerosene, coal, cloth). Then, on 15 October 2015, the Supreme Court stated:

> ...if we add... Schemes like The Mahatma Gandhi National Rural Employment Guarantee Scheme 12 (MGNREGS),[79] National Social Assistance Programme (Old Age Pensions, Widow Pensions, Disability Pensions) Prime Minister's Jan Dhan Yojana (PMJDY) and Employees' Provident Fund Organisation (EPFO) for the present, it would not dilute earlier order passed by this Court. Therefore, we now include the aforesaid Schemes apart from the other two Schemes that this Court has permitted in its earlier order dated August 11, 2015.
>
> We impress upon the Union of India that it shall strictly follow all the earlier orders passed by this Court commencing from September 23, 2013. We will also make it clear that the Aadhaar card Scheme is purely voluntary and it cannot be made mandatory till the matter is finally decided by this Court one way or the other.[80]

Thus, the Court permitted the government to use Aadhaar for the provision of additional important welfare schemes throughout the country. At the same time, though, the Court reiterated the position that the scheme is purely voluntary and is not to be made mandatory by the government.

Since then, both the central and state governments have continued to mandate the unique identification for various services, schemes and subsidies. And, even though the interim ruling regarding voluntariness was still in place, in March 2016, the government passed *The Aadhaar Act*. The passage of this Act called into question the status of the various interim Supreme Court orders directing that Aadhaar must remain voluntary until the petitions challenging the constitutionality of the scheme were decided.[81]

In *Dr. Kalyan Menon Sen v. Union of India and Others*,[82] where the constitutional validity of linking bank accounts and mobile phones with Aadhaar was challenged, an interim order was passed on 3 November 2017 extending the last dates of linking to 31 December 2017 and 6 February 2018, respectively.

79 The MGNREGA was a flagship programme launched by the government in 2006 under the Mahatma Gandhi National Rural Employment Guarantee Act, whereby any adult who applies for employment in rural areas has to be given work on local public works within 15 days. If employment is not given, an unemployment allowance has to be paid. Civil society activists have alleged that the drive to link Aadhaar to the MGNREGA had led to many being excluded from the job-security scheme.

80 *K. S. Puttaswamy v. Union of India*, Writ Petition (Civil) No. 494 of 2012 (Sup. Ct. India 15 October 2015).

81 Barry Lerner, 'India: Supreme Court Upholds Mandatory Use of Biometric Identification for Filing Taxes and Tax Account Applications', *Library of Congress*, 21 July 2017.

82 Writ Petition (Civil) No. 1002 of 2017.

Subsequently, on 15 December 2017, the Supreme Court ordered that the completion date for linking Aadhaar with bank accounts would be extended to 31 March 2018; and that persons opening new accounts would be required to provide proof to the bank of an application having been submitted for obtaining an Aadhaar card, together with the application number.[83]

In June 2017, the Supreme Court stated that the government could make Aadhaar mandatory for children's school lunches. By 30 June, children (and cooks) had to be enrolled in the Aadhaar scheme, or they would be denied the right to eat free hot meals at school. In an attempt to defend its decision, the government reasoned that Aadhaar cards were necessary since it made the process of delivery of services easier and more transparent. Again, the government's decision flies in the face of the Supreme Court ruling in 2013 that no person shall be deprived of any service for want of an Aadhaar number to which he or she is otherwise eligible/entitled.

On 9 June 2017, in *Binoy Viswam v. Union of India*,[84] the Court heard a challenge to the validity of Section 139AA of the *Income Tax Act*, which made the linking of Aadhaar with Permanent Account Numbers (PAN) cards mandatory for filing of income tax returns. The new provision stated that if a person failed to link their PAN with the Aadhaar number by 1 July 2017, their PAN would be invalidated. The Court upheld section 139AA of the *Income Tax Act*, stating that the new provision that makes Aadhaar mandatory for income tax is not in violation of the fundamental right to equality, nor the fundamental right to practise one's profession or trade.[85]

As the government continued to make Aadhaar mandatory for an increasingly wide array of benefits and services, banks, telecom companies, airports, schools, hospitals, insurance companies, mutual funds and workplaces were all asking citizens for Aadhaar.[86] No one knew when it would stop and how Aadhaar would continue to grow, or what other purposes it would be deployed for.

Decisions of the Supreme Court of India (Constitution Bench)

Recall that in August 2015, the Attorney General of India argued that the Constitution does not grant a fundamental right to privacy, and that since this right did not exist, the Aadhaar scheme could not violate it. A three-judge bench of the Supreme Court referred the matter to a larger Constitutional bench. Nine judges of the Court assembled in July 2017 to determine whether privacy is a constitutionally protected value.

83 *K. S. Puttaswamy v. Union of India*, Writ Petition (Civil) No. 494 of 2012 (Sup. Ct. India 15 December 2017).

84 Writ Petition (Civil) No. 247 of 2017.

85 *Ibid.* at para.128.

86 Times of India Edit, 'Limit Aadhaar: Linking It to Everything Paints a Bull's Eye on India for Cyber Warfare', *The Times of India*, 11 January 2018.

On 24 August 2017, the court delivered its landmark ruling, *Justice K. S. Puttaswamy (Retd.) and Anr. vs Union Of India And Ors.*[87] The Court unanimously held that the right to privacy is a fundamental constitutional right under Articles 14, 19 and 21 of the Constitution. The judgment of the nine-judge bench contains six concurring opinions affirming the right to privacy. The judgment explicitly overrules previous judgments of the Court in *M.P Sharma v Union of India*[88] and *Kharak Singh vs. State of Uttar Pradesh*,[89] which held that there is no fundamental right to privacy under the Indian Constitution.

The decision in *Kharak Singh* is noteworthy because while invalidating Regulation 236(b) of the Police Regulations which provided for nightly domiciliary visits, the majority construed this to be an unauthorized intrusion into a person's home and a violation of liberty. Justice Subba Rao observed that

> the right to personal liberty takes away not only a right to be devoid of restraints on his movements, but also devoid of intrusions on his private life. It is a fact that our Constitution does not explicitly possess a right to privacy as a fundamental right but the said right is a necessary constituent of individual liberty. Every democratic country seeks to secure domestic life of its individuals; it should give him rest, bodily contentment, harmony of mind and safety. In the last recourse, a person's home, where he stays with his family, is his 'castle', it is his barricade against intrusion on his individual liberty.[90]

Thus, Justice Subba Rao's dissenting view in *Kharak* can be seen as the first judicial declaration that privacy is a subset of individual liberty, which paved the way for the recognition of a right to privacy in India.

In August 2017, the nine-judge Supreme Court bench in *K.S. Puttaswamy*[91] ruled that the right to privacy is a fundamental right which is inherently protected under the various rights enshrined in the Constitution – in particular, Articles 14, 19 and 21. The judgment also discusses in detail the scope and ambit of right to privacy.

The Court stressed that certain human rights cannot be confined within the bounds of geographical location of a nation, but have universal application.[92] The international law provides a framework for the right to privacy, protected in article 12 of the *Universal Declaration of Human Rights* and article 17 of the *International Covenant on Civil and Political Rights*. The Court stated that 'the recognition of privacy as a fundamental constitutional value is part of India's

87 *Puttaswamy, supra*, note 234.
88 1954 AIR 300, 1954 SCR 1077.
89 1963 AIR 1295, 1964 SCR (1) 332.
90 *Ibid.*
91 *K. S. Puttaswamy v. Union of India*, Writ Petition (Civil) No. 494 of 2012 (Sup. Ct. India 24 Aug 2017).
92 *Ibid.* at para. 66.

commitment to a global human rights regime'.[93] The Court also drew attention to Article 51 of the Constitution, which requires the State to 'foster respect for international law and treaty obligations in the dealings of organised peoples with one another'.[94] In other words, it must adhere to the practice of developing and protecting the rights that other countries have embraced.

The Court said that the right to privacy, like life and personal liberty, is an 'inalienable right' that cannot be separated from the right to 'a dignified existence'.[95] Indeed, the Court tied this to 'the right of the individual to exercise control over his or her personality', which is a natural right that 'finds an origin in the notion that there are certain rights which are natural or inherent in a human being'.[96]

At its core, this right protects personal dignity: 'personal intimacies, the sanctity of life, marriage, procreation, the home and sexual orientation'.[97] Privacy is intrinsic to freedom, liberty and dignity – it protects 'the inner sphere of the individual from interference...'[98] allowing individuals to make 'autonomous life choices'.[99] Thus, it protects the right to be left alone as well as 'choices governing a way of life'.[100]

Aadhaar has prompted fears of increased surveillance, with the merging of databases making it easier for the government to track individuals and target dissent. These fears are heightened by the absence of privacy and data protection laws. And certain provisions of the *Aadhaar Act* intensify concerns regarding transparency and accountability. For example, the law prevents anyone other than the UIDAI from approaching the courts in case of a breach or violation of the law; there is no effective grievance redress system; Aadhaar does not allow anyone enrolled under it to opt out or withdraw; and the regulations do not require the authorities to inform an individual if their information has been shared or used without their knowledge or consent.[101]

It's significant that the Constitutional bench pushed Parliament to pass a data privacy law:

> We commend to the Union Government the need to examine and put into place a robust regime for data protection. The creation of such a regime requires a careful and sensitive balance between individual interests and legitimate concerns of the state. The legitimate aims of the state would include for instance protecting national security, preventing and investigating crime, encouraging innovation and the spread of knowledge, and preventing the dissipation of social welfare benefits. These are matters of

93 *Ibid.* at para. 29.
94 *Ibid.*
95 *Ibid.* at Part T; para. 3(A).
96 *Ibid.* at para. 40.
97 *Ibid.* at para. 124.
98 *Ibid.* at para. 77.
99 *Ibid.*
100 *Ibid.* at Part T; para. 3(F).
101 Human Rights Watch, *supra*, note 510.

policy to be considered by the Union government while designing a carefully structured regime for the protection of the data.[102]

Yet, in the wake of this epic decision, the Aadhaar programme continued to expand. In the meantime, the retired judge's 2012 petition swelled into heated national debate centred on privacy, security and denials of welfare entitlements owing to authentication problems.[103] More than two dozen petitioners raised problems with Aadhaar and their petitions were linked together and referred back to the Supreme Court.

The petitioners contended that Aadhaar violates right to privacy of citizens – upheld as a fundamental right by the Constitution bench – by requiring individuals to part with demographic and biometric information to private enrolling agencies. Compelling the citizen to part with this information violates individual autonomy and dignity.[104] Also, an individual has the right to control the dissemination of personal information; thus, compelling him to establish his identity by planting his biometrics at multiple points of service violates the right to informational privacy.[105]

The petitioners stressed that at its core, Aadhaar alters the relationship between the citizen and the state.[106] According to them, it violates democratic principles and the rule of law – the very foundation of the Indian Constitution. The threat lies in the potential for the misuse of the programme by various public and private bodies. For example, according to the petitioners, it has the potential to cause the 'civil death' of an individual by simply erasing the Aadhaar records of that person.[107]

They also argued that Aadhaar's architecture would pave the way for a surveillance state, whereby the state could converge the data, profile citizens, track their movements, assess their habits and silently influence their behaviour.[108] Over time, the profiling would enable the state to stifle dissent and influence political decision-making: 'instead of the State being transparent to the citizen, it is the citizen who is rendered transparent to the State'.[109] The petitioners therefore demanded that the entire project be demolished.

In response, government lawyers continued to dispute that privacy was at stake. They stressed that there is minimal biometric information recorded about the applicant; and no data in respect of "religion, caste, tribe, language of records of entitlement, income or medical history of the applicant" at the time of

102 *Puttaswamy, supra*, note 587 at Part T; para.5.

103 Vidhi Doshi, 'India's Top Court Upholds World's Largest Biometric ID Program, Within Limits', *Washington Post*, 26 September 2018.

104 *K. S. Puttaswamy v. Union of India*, Writ Petition (Civil) No. 494 of 2012 & Connected matters (26 September 2018) at 92.

105 *Ibid.* at 91.

106 *Ibid.* at 54.

107 *Ibid.* at 87.

108 *Ibid.* at 5 and 53.

109 *Ibid.* at 94.

Aadhaar enrolment. While undertaking the authentication process, the authority simply matches the biometrics and no other information is received or stored in respect of purpose, location or nature of transaction – making it difficult for profiling to occur. They also stressed that the data is encrypted and stored safely and securely.[110]

The government further claimed that the Aadhaar project was ushering in good governance, advancing socioeconomic rights and promoting economic prosperity.[111] They filed reports demonstrating how fraud — double-dipping, ghost beneficiaries and counterfeit identities — added enormous strain to the country's already overburdened welfare system. Trillions of rupees were allocated by the government for social benefits, yet more than half the money never reached the intended beneficiaries.[112]

This was the heart of the dilemma facing the five-judge panel: the state's duty to provide welfare services to India's enormous and largely underprivileged population versus citizens' right to privacy. In a 4 to 1 decision,[113] the panel upheld the constitutional validity of the Aadhaar programme, noting that it pursues a legitimate state aim: 'Aadhaar empower[s] marginalised sections of the society, particularly those who are illiterate and living in abject poverty or without any shelter etc. It gives identity to such persons also'.[114] Moreover, with the aid of the Aadhaar card, they can claim various privileges and benefits, which are actually meant for them.

The petitioners raised concerns about the privacy and protection of data. The question was whether the safeguards provided for the protection of data in the *Aadhaar Act* and Rules were sufficient.[115] The Court found that the *Act* simply uses demographic information which is not sensitive and where no reasonable expectation of privacy exists, such as name, date of birth, address, gender, mobile number and email address. Section 2(k) specifically provides that the data must not include race, religion, caste, tribe, ethnicity, language, records of entitlement, income or medical history.[116] Thus, the collection of sensitive information about the individual was said to be 'expressly prohibited'.

Also, the Court found that the architecture of Aadhaar, as well as the provisions of the *Aadhaar Act*, does not create a surveillance state. This is ensured by the manner in which the Aadhaar project operates.[117] Section 32 (3) of the *Aadhaar Act*, in particular, prohibits the authority from collecting, storing or

110 *Ibid.* at 51.
111 *Ibid.* at 6.
112 *Doshi, supra*, note 599.
113 *Puttaswamy, supra*, note 600.
114 *Ibid.* at 85.
115 *Ibid.* at para.190.
116 *Ibid.* at 273
117 *Ibid.* at 541.

maintaining, either directly or indirectly, any information about the purpose of authentication.[118]

The Court found that there are sufficient authentication security measures taken, as well. While seeking authentication, for example, neither the location of the person whose identity is to be verified, nor the purpose for which authentication of such identity is needed, comes to the knowledge of the Authority.[119] Therefore, the threat of real-time surveillance and profiling was said to be 'far-fetched'.

Yet several reports have already shown that the Aadhaar system is vulnerable to data breaches and leaks.[120] In January 2018, the Tribune newspaper reported that unrestricted access to the personal details of people enrolled in Aadhaar could be purchased for less than US$10 from racketeers.[121] The UIDAI responded by filing a criminal complaint against the journalists, which brought criticism from civil society groups and even exiled American whistle-blower Edward Snowden, who tweeted:

> The journalists exposing the Aadhaar breach deserve an award, not an investigation. If the government were truly concerned for justice, they would be reforming the policies that destroyed the privacy of a billion Indians. Want to arrest those responsible? They are called UIDAI.[122]

In 2017, millions of Aadhaar numbers, along with people's personal information, including bank account details, were published by government websites.[123] The government has repeatedly dismissed reports of such leaks, saying 'mere display of demographic information cannot be misused without biometrics', emphasizing that the biometric data is secure.[124] Still, the UIDAI filed another criminal complaint in February 2017 against three companies for alleged illegal transactions using the stored biometric data.

The Court insisted that it could 'assuage' the concerns of the petitioners about data security and safety by striking down, reading down, or clarifying some of the provisions of the *Aadhaar Act*.[125] Amongst other things, the Court stated that authentication records are not to be kept beyond a period of six months; an individual 'whose information is sought to be released, shall be afforded an

118 *Ibid.* at para. 194.
119 *Ibid.* at para. 197.
120 Human Rights Watch, *supra*, note 510.
121 Rachna Khaira, 'Rs 500, 10 Minutes, and you Have Access to Billion Aadhaar Details', *The Tribune*, 4 January 2018.
122 TNN, 'Probe UIDAI, Not Scribe, for Aadhaar Breach: Edward Snowden', *The Times of India*, 10 January 2018.
123 Human Rights Watch, *supra*, note 510.
124 *Ibid.*
125 *Puttaswamy, supra*, note 600 at 545.

opportunity of hearing'; and it 'impressed upon' the government to develop a robust data protection regime.[126]

The Court further stated that the proper means by which to assess whether the Aadhaar scheme violates that reasonable expectation of privacy is through a proportionality test which asks: (1), does the measure restricting the right serve a legitimate goal? (legitimate goal stage); (2), is it a suitable means of furthering this goal? (suitability or rational connection stage); (3), are there any less restrictive but equally effective alternatives? (necessity stage); and (4), does the measure have a disproportionate impact on the right-holder(s)? (balancing stage)[127]

This approach is adopted from Canadian law. In *R. v. Oakes,*[128] the Supreme Court of Canada set out the analytical framework for determining whether the violation of a *Charter* right can be justified. Once a breach of a *Charter* right is found, the onus falls on the government to establish, on a balance of probabilities, that the infringement 'can be demonstrably justified in a free and democratic society'.[129]

The Indian Supreme Court explained its findings on proportionality as follows:[130]

1 **Legitimate goal stage:** The Aadhaar scheme is backed by the statute, i.e. the *Aadhaar Act.* It serves a legitimate state aim, which is to ensure that social benefit schemes reach the deserving community. That has become an aspect of the social justice and fundamental rights (i.e. human dignity) stipulated in the Constitution.
2 **Suitability or rational connection stage:** The failure to establish the identity of an individual is a major hindrance to the successful implementation of those programmes, as it was difficult to ensure that subsidies, benefits and services reached the intended beneficiaries in the absence of a credible system to authenticate identity.
3 **Necessity stage:** The Aadhaar system is aimed at ensuring 'good governance' by bringing accountability and transparency to the distribution system with the aim of ensuring that benefits actually reach those who deserve them.
4 **Balancing stage:** The information collected at the time of enrolment, as well as authentication, is minimal. Also, there is a balancing of two competing fundamental rights: dignity in the form of autonomy and informational privacy; and dignity in the form of the right to food, shelter and better living standards. Aadhaar gives individuals their unique identities and it also enables the underprivileged to avail themselves of the welfare scheme, so it is not so invasive that it creates an imbalance.

126 *Ibid.* at 546.
127 *Puttaswamy, supra*, note 600 at 210.
128 [1986] 1 SCR 103.
129 *Ibid.*
130 *Puttaswamy, supra*, note 600 at 252–256.

However, the Court placed limits on how the data can be used and stored; and who must comply with its terms. For example, children who are enrolled in Aadhaar with the consent of their parents, shall be given the option to opt out of the programme once they reach adulthood, if they no longer need the benefits of the scheme.[131] It can no longer be made compulsory for the admission of children to school; and no child can be denied benefit of any welfare scheme, service or subsidy if she is not able to produce an Aadhaar number.

Also, it can't be used for establishing the identity of an individual 'for any purpose'; rather, the stated 'purpose' has to be backed by law – and any such law is subject to judicial scrutiny.[132] Thus, it can no longer be used by private entities such as banks or mobile phone operators for authentication purposes, curbing the programme's ambitious scope as a universal ID system. Moreover, the linking of Aadhaar with opening a bank account and obtaining a mobile phone number was said to be unconstitutional.[133]

Finally, the Court upheld the passing of the *Aadhaar Act* as a Money Bill. The whole purpose of the Act is to ensure the receipt of a subsidy or benefit by those categories of persons for whom it is actually meant. It is also very clear that the expenditure incurred in respect of such a subsidy, benefit or service would be from the Consolidated Fund of India.

There was a strong and lengthy dissent from Justice Dhananjaya Y. Chandrachud. He stated that the *Aadhaar Act* should not have been passed as a Money Bill because it falls outside the scope of that framework. Furthermore, the decision of the Speaker of the lower house to certify it as a Money Bill violates 'constitutional norms and values, as it damages the essence of federal bicameralism, which is a part of the basic structure of the Constitution'.[134] Thus, he declared that 'the *Aadhaar Act* is unconstitutional for having been passed as a Money Bill'.[135]

Justice Chandrachud further stated that '[t]he entire Aadhaar programme, since 2009, suffers from constitutional infirmities and violations of fundamental rights. The enactment of the *Aadhaar Act* does not save the Aadhaar project'.[136] To clarify, he observed:

> The absence of a legislative framework for the Aadhaar project between 2009 and 2016 left the biometric data of millions of Indian citizens bereft of the kind of protection which must be provided to comprehensively protect and enforce the right to privacy. Section 59 therefore fails to meet the test of a validating law since the complete absence of a regulatory framework

131 *Ibid*. at 556.
132 *Ibid*. at 560.
133 *Ibid*. at 566–567.
134 *Ibid*. at 463.
135 *Ibid*. at 466.
136 *Ibid*. at 480.

> and safeguards cannot be cured merely by validating what was done under the notifications of 2009 and 2016.[137]

He also found that Aadhaar violates the 'privacy norm' because by allowing private entities to use Aadhaar numbers, it would 'lead to commercial exploitation of the personal data of individuals without consent and could also lead to individual profiling'.[138] This means that the data could be used to predict the future choices and preferences of individuals, including voters.

Furthermore, the scope of the Act suffers from 'overbreadth since the broad definitions of the expressions "services" and "benefits" enable the government to regulate almost every facet of its engagement with citizens under the Aadhaar platform. If the requirement of Aadhaar is made mandatory for every benefit or service which the government provides, it is impossible to live in contemporary India without Aadhaar'.[139] He stressed that the government's objective could be achieved by adopting less intrusive measures than biometric identification. The scheme therefore fails the proportionality test relied on by the majority, and must be considered unconstitutional.[140]

Effective remedies for violations of privacy can come in a variety of judicial, legislative or administrative forms; however, effective remedies typically share specific characteristics.[141] First, those remedies must be known and accessible to *anyone* with an arguable claim that their rights have been violated. Second, effective remedies will involve prompt, thorough and impartial investigation, for instance by providing an 'independent oversight body...governed by sufficient due process guarantees and judicial oversight, within the limitations permissible in a democratic society'.[142] Third, for such remedies to be effective, they must be capable of ending ongoing violations. Fourth, where human rights violations rise to the level of gross violations, non-judicial remedies will not be adequate and criminal prosecution will be required.[143] At a minimum, these requirements should have been met before Aadhaar was rolled out nationwide.

137 *Ibid.* at 477.

138 *Ibid.* at 474.

139 *Ibid.* at 475.

140 *Ibid.* at 477.

141 Office of the United Nations High Commissioner for Human Rights, 'The Right to Privacy in the Digital Age', 30 June 2014 at para. 40.

142 Special Rapporteur on the promotion and protection of the right to freedom of opinion and expression and the Special Rapporteur for Freedom of Expression of the Inter-American Commission on Human Rights, 'Joint Declaration on Surveillance Programs and their Impact on Freedom of Expression', June 2013. Available online at: www.oas.org/en/iachr/expression/showarticle.asp?artID=927&lID=1 at para. 9.

143 General Assembly Resolution, "Basic Principles and Guidelines on the Right to a Remedy and Reparation for Victims of Gross Violations of International Human Rights Law and Serious Violations of International Humanitarian Law," adopted and proclaimed by General Assembly resolution 60/147 of 16 December 2005.

Questions remain about whether Aadhaar will provide opportunities for disadvantaged groups in a large and diverse society with rapidly increasing mobility.[144] Will it strengthen the position of individuals in relation to social services and programmes, or will it displace and further alienate various subsets of individuals? Can it be used to identify the poor correctly to deliver rations to those who need them and increase employment opportunities? Or will it continue to be used to exclude individuals and groups from the rights and services they're entitled to?

Identification projects in other countries

India's plunge into national biometric identification comes as the drive towards secure identity is happening all over the world. Indeed, many countries are seeking to improve their identity infrastructures, owing largely to rising global fears about terrorism. It is clear that 9/11 was a tipping point that motivated many countries to look seriously at establishing national ID systems.[145] The other major imperative came from the need for administrative efficiency and the drive towards 'e-Government' within most modern states; as well as the need for reliable identification in commercial spheres, particularly banking and credit.[146]

To date, more than 50 countries around the world, including most of continental Europe, China, Hong Kong, Japan, Malaysia, South Africa, Brazil, Iran, Israel and Indonesia, have some form of national identity card. The international experience clearly indicates that identity cards, biometric passports, and population registers operate within many liberal democratic nations throughout the world. However, very few countries have such a comprehensive national biometric identity system as that which has been implemented in India.

Successful operation of national identity programs requires sustained popular and political support as well as intergovernmental cooperation. Many countries are phasing in these systems slowly, for example by starting to bring in passports with computer chips linked to digital photographs, or fingerprints, or both.[147] Unlike India, many other nations are adopting data protection laws along with their ID programmes to address privacy concerns relating to widespread and easy access to personal information across government agencies. Conversely, some countries with existing privacy and data-protection laws are rejecting or reconsidering the implementation of these schemes. Each approach finds expression through different laws, standards, technologies and practices, which in turn are contingent upon domestic cultures and institutions.[148]

While the effort in India might be noteworthy for trying to move the farthest the fastest, it can also be criticized for overlooking a number of privacy

144 Kelkar et al., *supra*, note 521 at 10.
145 Bennett et al., *supra*, note 27 at 11.
146 *Ibid.* at 10.
147 Rama Lakshmi, 'Biometric Identity Project in India Aims to Provide for Poor, End Corruption', *Washington Post*, 28 March 2010.
148 Bennett et al., *supra*, note 27 at 18.

and human rights questions that should have been asked – but weren't. Unlike other common law countries, India never had a broad national debate about the implications of its mammoth national ID project; and we have seen that public support for this system has been widely called into question as flaws in the system have been revealed over time. Not surprisingly, India is not alone in facing problems and push-back from concerned citizens. This is perhaps best exemplified by the United Kingdom (UK), which ultimately rejected the desirability and financial viability of a comprehensive national identity programme.

The now-defunct UK *Identity Cards Bill* – which was introduced on 29 November 2004 – was put forward in the interest of 'national security' for the purpose of combatting terrorism, detecting and preventing crime, enforcing immigration controls and preventing unauthorized working or employment (Clause 1(4)). Following an initial roll-out in Greater Manchester in 2009, the entire project was scrapped in 2010 on account of public criticism, along with the corresponding national identity register, notwithstanding the fact that wasted public expenditure on the project was said to be as high as £5 billion.[149]

The project raised a wide range of concerns, which were documented by the London School of Economics and Political Science Identity Project Report.[150] The central concerns were that the proposals were then untested and not known to be safe and reliable on such a large scale; and that they were likely to be too complex and technically dangerous, and that they lacked a foundation of public trust and confidence.[151] The prospect of mission creep – similar to what occurred with respect to India's Aadhaar – was also raised.

The authors of the report concluded that many of the public interests that the Bill was aimed to serve could be satisfied by other means. Concerns about identity theft, for example, could be resolved by giving people more control over their personal information; and threats about terrorism could be addressed by enhanced border security.[152] Indeed, the claim that the scheme would be necessary to counter terrorism was subject to vociferous criticism, including that expressed in a 2004 Privacy International report, which stated that:

> the presence of an identity card is not recognized by analysts as a meaningful or successful component in anti-terrorism strategies.
>
> The detailed analysis of information in the public domain in this study has produced no evidence to establish a connection between identity cards and successful anti-terrorism measures. Terrorists have traditionally moved

149 MoneyLife Digital Team, 'UK Scraps National ID Project; Will India's UID Face the Same Fate?' 31 May 2010. Available online at: www.moneylife.in/article/uk-scraps-national-id-project-will-indias-uid-face-the-same-fate/5684.html.

150 London School of Economics and Political Science (LSE), 'The Identity Project, An Assessment of the UK Identity Cards Bill and its Implications', (London: London School of Economics and Political Science, 2005).

151 *Ibid.* at 20.

152 *Ibid.*

> across borders using tourist visas (such as those who were involved in the US terrorist attacks), or they are domicile [sic] and equipped with legitimate identification cards (such as those who carried out the Madrid bombings).

The draft Bill was also said to violate Article 8 (privacy) and Article 14 (discrimination) of the *European Convention on Human Rights*. It was thought that the right of individuals to freely move throughout the EU and the UK might be infringed if new biometrics were introduced. The scheme was also in conflict with the principles of the *Data Protection Act*, particularly since the national identity register would lead to the centralization of personal data, much of which is highly sensitive. Other concerns related to the large volume of information in the register, the broad purposes for which it could be used, and the number of private and public organizations that would have access to the data.[153] Not surprisingly, many of the problems raised in the report were subsequently shown to be true with respect to India's Aadhaar project.

Notably, however, the ID card debate in the UK has been largely 'surpassed by an e-borders system, multiple trusted traveler schemes, monitoring of credit card and urban transit card transactions, biometric visas and work permits'.[154] To institute a 'voluntary' national ID card system is ostensibly redundant, as this mode of identification already functions as but one element of a broader collection of practices of digital identification. Thus, where privacy cultures mitigate against a national ID card system in a particular place, we tend to find the same forms of identification by other means.

Another example is provided by Canada, which shares the world's longest land border with the United States. As the strategic reach of the United States and its claims over airspace and defence intensified after 9/11, Canada progressively adopted US rules for Canadian border interactions in return for easing restrictions that made it difficult for people and goods to cross into the United States.[155] In early 2011, then-Prime Minister Stephen Harper and President Barack Obama signed a formal declaration entitled: 'Beyond the Border: A Shared vision for Perimeter Security and Economic Competitiveness'. The two promised to 'work together to establish and verify the identities of travellers and conduct screening at the earliest possible opportunity' and to 'work toward common technical standards for the collection, transmission, and matching of biometrics that enable the sharing of information on travellers in real time'.[156]

Often, practical issues of cost and technical feasibility have been powerful deterrents to the national identification process. Political and social instability has affected the successful implementation of these systems in less developed parts of the world, such as Afghanistan and Ukraine, and both programmes are now

153 *Ibid.* at 27.
154 Amoore, *supra*, note 167 at 22.
155 Bennett et al., *supra*, note 276 at 118.
156 *Ibid.*

considered stalled.[157] We have also seen that national identification programmes can be used to identify, single out, and target ethnic minorities for discrimination, social exclusion – and even genocide.

The Government of Israel learned the hard way about the vulnerabilities that can come with having a national biometric database. In 2011, Israeli authorities announced that their entire databank had been hacked and all of its information stolen, including the names, dates of birth, social security numbers, family members, adoption details, immigration dates and medical records of nine million Israelis.[158] The information was sold to Crime, Inc. and was posted online in full in the digital underground – leading to widespread concerns about fraud, identity theft and other security issues.[159]

In other cases, the implementation of national identification systems has gone extremely well. The Republic of Estonia, a Baltic country with a population of only 1.3 million, has been transformed over the past four years or so into a digital society.[160] There, the national ID is integrated into a broad range of e-government services, albeit without biometrics.[161] In 2014, the government launched a digital 'residency' programme, which allows foreigners to take advantage of some Estonian services, such as banking, as if they were living in the country; and this has helped the tiny nation to attract investors and workers from overseas in the midst of falling national birth rates.[162]

It also launched an ambitious government project called e-Estonia, whereby virtually every government system, function or service — legislation, voting, education, justice, health care, banking, taxes, policing, and more —has been digitally linked across a single platform.[163] Through this system, which is associated with individual chip-I.D. cards, citizens can vote, challenge parking tickets, register a car, pay an electric bill, apply for loans, pay their taxes, and much more.[164] For both individuals and the government, the primary advantage of mass-digitization has been convenience, efficiency and the elimination of bureaucratic backlog; however, for the Estonian government it has also resulted in a substantial cost saving of as much as 2 per cent of its total G.D.P. per year.[165]

The ubiquitous nature of this system, and the vast amount of data it sustains, is astonishing; especially, given that in 2007, a Russian cyber-attack against Estonia's essential electronic infrastructure compromised all major commercial banks, telecommunications companies, media outlets and name servers, and this

157 International Telecommunication Union (ITU), *Review of National Identity Programs*, May, 2016.
158 Goodman, *supra*, note 121 at 274.
159 *Ibid.*
160 Nathan Heller, 'Estonia The Digital Republic', *The New Yorker*, 18 December 2017.
161 Zelazny, *supra*, note 100 at 3.
162 Heller, *supra*, note 656.
163 *Ibid.*
164 *Ibid.*
165 *Ibid.*

affected the majority of the Estonian population.[166] This was, in fact, the first time that a botnet had threatened the national security of an entire nation. For the Estonians, this breach, and their ongoing susceptibility to Russian aggression, made them sit up and take notice.

Today, within e-Estonia, the data isn't centrally held; instead, the government's data platform, X-Road, links individual servers through end-to-end encrypted pathways. In other words, the public and private entities hold their own information securely, and data is only shared when a particular user, or another entity, requests the information.[167] This has allowed major private firms, including those in neighbouring Finland, to access and share data too; and an important rule of thumb is that the individual owns all information recorded about him or her, such that any time someone accesses the data – a border guard, a police officer, a pharmacist or a banker – it's recorded and reported.[168] This provides a powerful tool to monitor and regulate against abuse. And to further secure the data, last year, the Estonian government created a backup of its entire system in Luxembourg.[169]

Conclusion

Over the past few years, the Government of India has pushed to compile the world's largest biometric database by sending officials out to remote villages to take iris scans and fingerprints of more than a billion of the country's residents. Those in favour of the programme say that Aadhaar is critical for more effective and efficient government and can save taxpayers – only 5 per cent of the Indian population before Aadhaar[170] – billions of dollars by reducing welfare and tax fraud, not to mention addressing the denial of benefits and services to the poorest, who need them most.

Critics counter that the new rules have actually deprived the poorest and most vulnerable members of society of benefits and services to which they are entitled, including subsidies for rice, fuel, and other necessary staples. The centralized system is also vulnerable to misuse and leaks, as well as compromising the privacy rights of more than a sixth of the world's population.[171] In a landmark ruling, India's Supreme Court stated in that the Aadhaar scheme is valid pursuant to the country's Constitution. Yet the true test of a decision is its application – and the ruling has yet to be applied.

The use of powerful technologies for data collection and state surveillance now exists worldwide. Reviewing the practices of other countries is essential because we can learn from their successes and failures. The defence against abuse is

166 Joshua Davis, 'Hackers Take Down the Most Wired Country in Europe', *Wired*, 21 August 2007.

167 Heller, *supra*, note 656.

168 *Ibid.*

169 *Ibid.*

170 Lakshmi, *supra*, note 643.

171 Doshi, *supra*, note 599.

not to avoid the use of these technologies altogether, but to look at the benefits they bring and the safeguards they require. We've seen that Estonia recently established a robust database on its citizens; but it also developed a number of rules and restrictions to protect them. A vigilant society will need to look for ways to counter the threats posed by the commercial and governmental use of biometric systems.

Bibliography

Sahana Basavapatna, 'The UID Project in India: Should Non-citizen Residents be Concerned?' Presented at 'The Biopolitics of Development: Life, Welfare, and Unruly Populations', on 9–10 September 2010.

Kristy A. Belton, 'The Neglected Non-Citizen: Statelessness and Liberal Political Theory', (2011) 7(1) *Journal of Global Ethics* 59.

Colin J. Bennett & David Lyon, 'Playing the ID Card – Understanding the Significance of Identity Card Systems', in Colin J. Bennett & David Lyon (eds), *Playing the Identity Card: Surveillance, Security and Identification in Global Perspective* (New York: Routledge, 2008) 3.

Jacqueline Bhabha & Amiya Bhatia, 'India's Aadhaar Program: A Legitimate Trade-off between Social Protection and Privacy?' *HarvardFXB – Center for Health and Human Rights*, 28 March 2016. Available online at: https://fxb.harvard.edu/2016/03/28/indias-aadhaar-program-a-legitimate-trade-off-between-social-protection-and-privacy/.

Robert Chambers et al., *To the Hands of the Poor: Water & Trees* (London: Intermediate Technology Publications, 1989).

Rituparna Chatterjee, 'The Supreme Court of India Raised an Important Humanitarian Question About Aadhaar', *The Huffington Post*, 11 January 2018.

Dutta Choudhury, 'Centre Yet to Take Effective Steps', *The Assam Tribune*, 3 October 2017.

Joshua Davis, 'Hackers Take Down the Most Wired Country in Europe', *Wired*, 21 August 2007.

Pam Dixon, 'A Failure to "Do No Harm" – India's Aadhaar Biometric ID Program and its Inability to Protect Privacy in Relation to Measures in Europe and the U.S.', (2017) 7(4) *Health & Technology* 539.

Vidhi Doshi, 'India's Top Court Upholds World's Largest Biometric ID Program, Within Limits', *Washington Post*, 26 September 2018.

Casey Dunning, Alan Gelb & Sneha Raghavan, 'Birth Registration, Legal Identity, and the Post-2015 Agenda', *Center for Global Development*, September, 2014.

European Parliament, 'Birth Registration and the Rights of the Child', May, 2007. Available online at: https://docplayer.net/43800420-Birth-registration-and-the-rights-of-the-child.html.

General Assembly Resolution, 'Basic Principles and Guidelines on the Right to a Remedy and Reparation for Victims of Gross Violations of International Human Rights Law and Serious Violations of International Humanitarian Law', adopted and proclaimed by General Assembly resolution 60/147 of 16 December 2005.

Devjyot Ghoshal, 'The World's Largest Biometric ID Programme is a Privacy Nightmare Waiting to Happen', *Quartz India*, 28 March 2017.

Alan Gleb & Charles Kenny, 'The Case for Big Brother (Foreign Policy)', *CGD in the News*, 4 March 2013.

Marc Goodman, *Future Crimes* (New York: Doubleday, 2015).
Government of India, 'Economic Survey 2016–17', January, 2017. Available online at: www.indiabudget.gov.in/es2016-17/echapter.pdf.
Group of Ministers Report, 'Reforming the National Security System', 23 May 2011. Available online at: http://pibarchive.nic.in/archive/releases98/lyr2001/rmay2001/23052001/r2305200110.htm.
Nathan Heller, 'Estonia The Digital Republic', *The New Yorker*, 18 December 2017.
Human Rights Watch, 'India: Identification Project Threatens Rights', 10 January 2018.
International Telecommunication Union (ITU), *Review of National Identity Programs*, May, 2016.
Gursharan Singh Kainth, *Aadhaar India: Brand for a Billion* (Saarbrucken: LAP Lambert Academic Publishing, 2011).
Gurmeet Kanwal, 'Big Chinks in Our Security Armour', *Times of India*, 24 July 2011.
Govind Kelkar, Dev Nathan, E. Revathi & Swati Sain Gupta, *Aadhaar: Gender, Identity and Development* (New Delhi: Academic Foundation, 2014).
Rachna Khaira, 'Rs 500, 10 Minutes, and You Have Access to Billion Aadhaar Details', *The Tribune*, 4 January 2018.
Chethan Kumar, 'Literacy Rate Up, But So is Illiteracy', *Times of India*, 28 January 2016.
Rama Lakshmi, 'Biometric Identity Project in India Aims to Provide for Poor, End Corruption', *Washington Post*, 28 March 2010.
Barry Lerner, 'India: Supreme Court Upholds Mandatory Use of Biometric Identification for Filing Taxes and Tax Account Applications', *Library of Congress*, 21 July 2017.
London School of Economics and Political Science (LSE), 'The Identity Project, An Assessment of the UK Identity Cards Bill and its Implications', (London: London School of Economics and Political Science, 2005).
Shoshanna Amielle Magnet, *When Biometrics Fail: Gender, Race and the Technologies of Identity* (Durham, NC: Duke University Press, 2011).
Niha Masih, 'Lost in Transition: Has Linking Aadhaar to Government Welfare Schemes Made It Difficult for Beneficiaries to Avail of Aid?' *Hindustan Times*, 8 October 2017.
S. Meghnad, 'Aadhaar Act: It's a Web of Regulations Out There', *NewsLaundry*, 2 May 2017.
MoneyLife Digital Team, 'UK Scraps National ID project; Will India's UID Face the Same Fate?' 31 May 2010. Available online at: www.moneylife.in/article/uk-scraps-national-id-project-will-indias-uid-face-the-same-fate/5684.html.
Office of the United Nations High Commissioner for Human Rights, 'The Right to Privacy in the Digital Age', 30 June 2014.
Krishnadas Rajagopal, 'Right to Privacy Verdict: A Timeline of SC Hearings', *The Hindu*, 24 August 2017.
Vijay Sathe, 'Managing Massive Change India's Aadhaar, the World's Most Ambitious ID Project', (2014) 87 *Innovations: Technology, Governance, Globalization* 85.
Special Rapporteur on the promotion and protection of the right to freedom of opinion and expression and the Special Rapporteur for Freedom of Expression of the Inter-American Commission on Human Rights, 'Joint Declaration on Surveillance Programs and their Impact on Freedom of Expression', June 2013. Available online at: www.oas.org/en/iachr/expression/showarticle.asp?artID=927&lID=1.
TNN, 'Probe UIDAI, Not Scribe, For Aadhaar Breach: Edward Snowden', *The Times of India*, 10 January 2018.
The Hitavada, 'Aadhaar Not a Proof of Citizenship: Dist. Court', Available online at: www.pressreader.com/india/the-hitavada/20180726/281728385314630.

Times of India Edit, 'Limit Aadhaar: Linking It to Everything Paints a Bull's Eye on India for Cyber Warfare', *The Times of India*, 11 January 2018.

UNHCR, *Handbook on Protection of Stateless Persons Under the 1954 Convention Relating to the Status of Stateless Persons* (Geneva, 2014).

Vanita Yadav, 'Unique Identification Project for 1.2 Billion People in India: Can It Fill Institutional Voids and Enable Inclusive Innovation', (2014) 6 *Contemporary Readings Law and Social Justice* 38.

Frances Zelazny, 'The Evolution of India's UID Program', *Center for Global Development*, 8 August 2012.

Case Law

K. S. Puttaswamy v. Union of India, Writ Petition (Civil) No. 494 of 2012 (Sup. Ct. India 23 September 2013).

K. S. Puttaswamy v. Union of India, Writ Petition (Civil) No. 494 of 2012 (Sup. Ct. India 11 August 2015).

K. S. Puttaswamy v. Union of India, Writ Petition (Civil) No. 494 of 2012 (Sup. Ct. India 15 October 2015).*K. S. Puttaswamy v. Union of India*, Writ Petition (Civil) No. 494 of 2012 (Sup. Ct. India 24 Aug. 2017).

K. S. Puttaswamy v. Union of India, Writ Petition (Civil) No. 494 of 2012 (Sup. Ct. India 15 December 2017).

K. S. Puttaswamy v. Union of India, Writ Petition (Civil) No. 494 of 2012 & Connected matters (Sup. Ct. India 26 September 2018).

R. v. Oakes, [1986] 1 SCR 103.

Dr. Kalyan Menon Sen v. Union of India and Others Writ Petition (Civil) No. 1002 of 2017.

M.P Sharma v Union of India 1954 AIR 300, 1954 SCR 1077.

Kharak Singh vs. State of Uttar Pradesh 1963 AIR 1295, 1964 SCR (1) 332.

Binoy Viswam v. Union of India Writ Petition (Civil) No. 247 of 2017.

6 Biometrics and border security

Introduction

Is there a 'right' to leave a country and relocate elsewhere? Many people would not consider the right to leave very important among basic human rights; and some would not deem it to be a right at all.[1] Yet for centuries, countless people have – given their unique history and experience – found the need to relocate. In recent years, unprecedented numbers of refugees have arrived on Europe's shores, while countries in the Middle East, South East Asia and Africa continue to host the majority of the world's displaced people.[2]

At the same time, there has been a tightening of border and immigration controls in most western liberal democracies.[3] Present-day national politics of migration has fashioned the 'illegal immigrant' as a negative identity that has widely come to be regarded as the *enemy*, the *other* or the *infiltrator*; and, as a conceptual category that is *de facto* accepted as the single way of framing migration policy – from post 9/11 Islamophobia to the systematic detention and deportation of refugees and asylum-seekers.[4] The criminalization of 'unauthorized' border crossing has become a vital control strategy worldwide.[5]

So-called 'legitimate' travellers are offered high-tech initiatives to facilitate the appearance of freedom of movement for all citizens.[6] Yet, behind the scenes, government agencies across the West are producing risk profiles for all

1 Alan Dershowitz, *Rights from Wrongs* (New York: Basic Books, 2004) 187.
2 Amnesty International, '2015 Has Seen the Worst Refugee Crisis Since WWII', *Human Rights Now Blog*, 28 December 2015. Available online at: https://blog.amnestyusa.org/refugees/2015-has-seen-the-worst-refugee-crisis-since-wwii/.
3 Wilson, *supra*, note 60 at 94.
4 Archit Guha, 'The Illegal Immigrant Identity and Its Fragments – From Enemy Foreigner to Bangladeshi Illegal Immigrant in (Post) Colonial India', (2016) 12 *Socio-Legal Review* 108 at 110.
5 Sharon Pickering & Leanne Weber, 'Borders, Mobility and Technologies of Control', in Sharon Pickering and Leanne Weber (eds), *Borders, Mobility and Technologies of Control* (Dordrecht: Springer, 2006) 1 at 2.
6 Huub Dijstelbloem, Albert Meijer & Michiel Besters, 'The Migration Machine', in H. Dijstelbloem et al. (eds), *Migration and the New Technological Borders of Europe* (London: Palgrave Macmillan, 2011) 1 at 1.

sorts of aliens. If migrants risk crossing the Mediterranean to Europe illegally, there are boats, helicopters, drones and satellites on the hunt for them.[7] Similarly, in various harbours and at land borders, containers and other cargo spaces are searched using heat sensors and carbon dioxide detectors to check for the presence of human beings.[8] As borders are increasingly transformed into spaces for the testing of new 'smart' technologies of surveillance and control, there is a constant state of emergency that goes beyond the normal politics and the rule of law, threatening the values that rest at the heart of the liberal democratic state.[9]

Article 13(2) of the *Universal Declaration of Human Rights* recognizes that 'everyone has the right to leave any country, including his own and to return to his country'.[10] The international community has declared this right necessary in order to protect other human rights. The right to travel is also a necessary feature of the modern liberal democratic state. Immigration and migration play vital roles in the complex and violent turmoil ongoing in many parts of the world.[11] Yet this international legal framework must be balanced against the state's sovereign right to protect its borders; confer nationality; admit and expel foreigners; combat crime; and safeguard national and regional security.[12]

The 2011 'Arab Spring' crisis in the Middle East and North Africa sparked migration from the region and governments throughout the West have since been examining how they can respond to the pressure this has been putting on their borders.[13] Following popular uprisings against dictatorships in several Arab countries, many Syrians poured into the streets to protest the Bashar al-Assad government. These street protests evolved into a civil war that has caused an enormous refugee incursion over time.[14]

In Africa, rising politically motivated tension and violence in Burundi in recent years led to thousands of people fleeing to neighbouring Tanzania, Rwanda, Democratic Republic of the Congo and Uganda. Thousands of Bangladeshis and persecuted Rohingya from Myanmar have also been displaced. The UN's refugee agency states that the number of displaced people is now at its highest

7 *Ibid.*

8 *Ibid.*

9 Panagiotis Loukinas, 'Surveillance and Drones at Greek Borderzones: Challenging Human Rights and Democracy', (2017) 15(3/4) *Surveillance & Society* 439 at 441.

10 Universal Declaration of Human Rights, G/A/RES 217A, at 13(2), U.N. GAOR, 3d Sess., 1st plen. mtg., U.N. Doc. A/810 (12 Dec 1948).

11 Vanessa Diaz, 'Legal Challenges of Biometric Immigration Control Systems', (2014) 7(1) *Mexican Law Review* 3 at 13.

12 *Ibid.* at 13.

13 Wesley Dockery, 'The Syrian Conflict and its Impact on Migration', *InfoMigrants*, 14 March 2018. Available online at: www.infomigrants.net/en/post/8077/the-syrian-conflict-and-its-impact-on-migration.

14 Pinar Yazgan, Deniz Eroglu Utku & Ibrahim Sirkeci, 'Syrian Crisis and Migration', (2015) 12(3) *Migration Letters* 181 at 185.

ever – surpassing even post-World War Two numbers.[15] More than half of all refugees are children.

Around the world, some 68.5 million people have been forcibly displaced. Most people remain displaced within their home countries, but about 25.4 million have fled to other countries as refugees.[16] The reasons are primarily that long-term conflicts, which inevitably cause enormous refugee outflows, are occurring with greater frequency and lasting longer; and the rate at which solutions are found for these displaced people has been declining since the end of the Cold War.[17]

The ongoing conflict in Syria continues to account for the largest forcibly displaced population globally. As of the end of 2017, there were 12.6 million forcibly displaced Syrians, comprising around 6.3 million refugees, 146,700 asylum-seekers and 6.2 million internally displaced persons.[18] Hundreds of thousands are struggling in makeshift tents and tin shelters in neighbouring countries, like Lebanon, Jordan, Turkey, Iraq and Egypt. Many Syrians have left those nations and sought refuge elsewhere, particularly in Europe.[19]

The Schengen Agreement abolished many of the EU's internal borders, enabling passport-free movement across most of Europe.[20] However, in 2015, the influx of more than a million migrants – many of them Syrian refugees – greatly increased pressure on politicians throughout the EU. For most countries of the European Union, 2015 marked a discussion about the so-called 'migration crisis'.[21] Schengen was roundly criticized by nationalists and Euro-sceptics who claim it is an open door for migrants and criminals.

The rhetoric of security and terrorist threats on the part of refugees featured prominently in the statements of leading politicians. They framed migrants as threats for the security of the EU, not only as potential criminals, but also as the ones to blame for increasing rates of unemployment and economic hardship. This blaming of migrants and refugees justified the call for the increase of surveillance measures aimed at monitoring and intercepting them.

15 The UN Refugee Agency (UNHCR), 'Global Trends: Forced Displacement in 2017', United Nations High Commissioner for Refugees, 2018. Available online at: www.unhcr.org/5b27be547.pdf.

16 *Ibid.* at 61. The UNHCR defines refugees as: 'individuals recognized under the 1951 Convention relating to the Status of Refugees, its 1967 Protocol, the 1969 Organization of African Unity (OAU) Convention Governing the Specific Aspects of Refugee Problems in Africa, those recognized in accordance with the UNHCR Statute, individuals granted complementary forms of protection, and those enjoying temporary protection'.

17 Euan McKirdy, 'UNHCR Report: More Displaced Now Than After WWII', *CNN*, 20 June 2016.

18 UNHCR, *supra*, note 683.

19 Dockery, *supra*, note 681.

20 BBC, 'Schengen: Controversial EU Free Movement Deal Explained', 24 April 2016. Available online at: www.bbc.com/news/world-europe-13194723.

21 Witold Klaus, 'Security First: New Right-Wing Government in Poland and its Policy Towards Immigrants and Refugees', (2017) 15(3/4) *Surveillance & Society* 523 at 523.

Consequently, a series of EU states reimposed temporary border controls. Push-backs and deportations, and the absence of safe and legal routes to countries in the European Union – including the militarization of the Greek-Turkish borders and the closure of the Western-Balkan route – have left thousands stranded. The crusade towards biometric border controls throughout the EU is only likely to intensify the desperate situation these people face.

The refugee crisis also turned UK politics on its head. The number of asylum-seekers in Europe has soared over the past ten years, unleashing a populist backlash. However, the UK was never a full member of the EU's Schengen agreement, as it retained control of its own borders and passports.[22] Nevertheless, the horrific attacks of September 11, 2001, as well as subsequent terrorist incidents in Madrid and London, exacerbated public anxiety towards migrants throughout Europe.

Immigrants and asylum seekers are now frequently seen as a threat to public order and stability in the UK.[23] They are also believed to be exploiting national welfare provisions and economic opportunities at the expense of citizens. Yet these exaggerated concerns about migration lowering wages, causing unemployment or harming the welfare system, are largely unfounded.[24]

The UK's position on smart borders is most clearly articulated in the 2005 Home Office publication, *Controlling our Borders: Making Migration Work for Britain.*[25] Then-Prime Minister Tony Blair's preface remains with the reader:

> [T]his traditional tolerance is under threat. It is under threat from those who come and live here illegally by breaking our rules and abusing our hospitality. And, unless we act to tackle abuses, it could be increasingly exploited by extremists to promote their perverted view of race.
>
> ...
>
> There will be a new drive to prevent illegal entry, to crack down on illegal working and a tough policy of removals for those who should not be here. There will be on-the-spot fines for employers who collude with illegal immigration. We will fingerprint visitors who need visas, and those planning longer stays, before they arrive ... And over time, we will move towards the point where it becomes the norm that those who fail can be detained, as asylum intake falls and removals become easier as we negotiate ever more effective returns agreements.[26]

22 David Wills, "The United Kingdom Identity Card Scheme: Shifting Motivations, Static Technologies," in Colin J. Bennett and David Lyon (eds), *Playing the Identity Card: Surveillance, Security and Identification in Global Perspective* (New York: Routledge, 2008) 163 at 173.

23 Georgios Karyotis, "The Fallacy of Securitizing Migration: Elite Rationality and Unintended Consequences," in Gabriella Lazaridis (ed.), *Security, Insecurity and Migration in Europe* (Oxon: Routledge, 2016) 13 at 13.

24 *Ibid.* at 21.

25 UK Home Office, "Controlling our Borders: Making Migration Work for Britain," February 2005. Available online at: https://assets.publishing.service.gov.uk/government/uploads/system/uploads/attachment_data/file/251091/6472.pdf.

26 *Ibid.* at 6.

The underlying problem is presented here as one of unstable, unfixed identities. The existing model of identity is deemed insufficient because terrorists and criminals are able to leach off society and even kill the innocent.[27] The presumption is that a single identifier is needed to prove who you are, or that you are who you say you are; and that identifiers can be used to keep out the undesirable before they arrive and ferret out those who should be required to leave.

One of the arguments of many Brexit leaders was that exiting the EU and getting control of Britain's borders would allow for a drastic reduction in numbers and enable the government to meet its stated aim of capping immigration at 'tens of thousands'.[28] In the 2016 referendum over the UK's membership of the EU, immigration was a key driver of Britons' vote to leave.[29] Those leading the campaign promised lower levels of immigration and the introduction of an 'Australian type points based system' to regulate future inflows of EU nationals to the country, and to let in only the skilled and the educated.[30]

On the other side of the Atlantic, few adversaries loomed larger in the narrative of Donald Trump's presidential campaign than the illegal immigrant who threatens Americans — the 'rapists' and 'killers' from Mexico, as Mr. Trump famously stated. Today, TV, social media and newspapers are full of people vilifying migrants. They argue that they push down wages, increase pressures on health and education, and make it harder for the young to afford housing. Yet, far from stealing jobs, migrants take the work that locals spurn. Most are productive, law-abiding members of society, rooted in communities, working hard, living peacefully, paying taxes and raising families.

Yet underlying the general unwillingness to welcome and resettle migrants is the notion that they are problems, or even parasites, rather than potential contributors, regardless of race, skin colour, language, ethnic or social background, or religion. The focus on national security is also occurring in a broader context than it was in the recent past. With the rise of Islamic extremism, asymmetrical struggles are taking place between state and non-state actors, like terrorist groups. Correspondingly, if a country is overrun by a mass migration of people fleeing their homes, its borders are no longer secure. These developments call on us to rethink our definition of what it means to be a citizen or resident of a nation state in the modern age. They also remind us that these definitions are not neatly defined categories, but reflect the inherent flux of law, politics and society.

It's remarkable that the United States, Canada, Australia and the UK are largely comprised of individuals whose ancestors sought this very same right in the face of famine, poverty, discrimination and tyranny. Had so many refugees not been able to escape torment and terror in Europe during the early part of

27 Wills, *supra*, note 690 at 176.

28 The Economist, 'Raising the Drawbridge', 27 August 2016. Available online at: www.economist.com/britain/2016/08/27/raising-the-drawbridge.

29 The Economist, 'Let Them Not Come', 2 April 2016. Available online at: www.economist.com/britain/2016/04/02/let-them-not-come.

30 The Economist, *supra*, note 698.

the twentieth century, and resettle in those countries, many more would have lost their lives to the Holocaust.[31] As members of nations comprised of immigrants who are largely better off as a result of their chance to relocate, one might assume that we inherently recognize the importance of people's freedom to leave their place of residence and move elsewhere, particularly if they have been grossly mistreated by their home countries, and that we have a duty to act with compassion when other people's fates rest in our hands. Sadly, though, this is not the case.

Since 9/11, the world's attitude has hardened against refugees. Elite-driven claims that there is a direct threat posed to society – our 'way of life' – by allowing people from war-torn regions to enter and live peacefully within other more stable and prosperous parts of the world exemplify such attitudes. Yet the fear of being overrun by a tide of desperate people surging across continents has persisted for centuries and has been incited by generations of leaders on all sides of the political spectrum. The consequences are an increased urgency to deal with the issue with additional resources and extraordinary measures outside the formal legal system and established procedures of politics.

Affluent states in the global north have assessed the threat of migration as a risk to their sovereignty and opted for a 'tough on crime' stance that sees would-be border crossers as fraudulent and criminal, justifying their exclusion from services and mobility. The 'criminal migrant' is based on the demonization of the 'other' and the creation of a false continuum between migration, crime and terrorism.[32] The assumption is that *our* security justifies limitations to *their* rights.[33] The urgency for securitization of borders legitimizes repressive measures against migrants, particularly those who match an ethnic, religious or political profile.[34]

Bureaucracy and registration have long been associated with the darker side of state control. Both fiction (e.g. Orwell's omniscient Big Brother) and history (e.g. the bureaucratic engine of the Third Reich) have provided chilling images of the power of surveillance when it is not morally or legally restrained.[35] Today, technology plays an expanding role in determining the nature and 'place' of the border. Within these systems, we see the linking of physical identifiers with databases, and the capturing of patterns of behaviour and their associated identities, to facilitate or restrict movement across territorial boundaries.

In some cases, surveillance is used to categorize people and select groups for opportunities or preferential treatment. The use of air miles databases, for example, is coupled with the biometric submission of an iris scan to produce the

31 Dershowitz, *supra*, note 669 at 188.
32 Karyotis, *supra*, note 691 at 20.
33 *Ibid.* at 16.
34 *Ibid.*
35 Dennis Broeders, 'A European "Border" Surveillance System Under Construction', in H. Dijstelbloem et al. (eds), *Migration and the New Technological Borders of Europe* (London: Palgrave Macmillan, 2011) 40 at 42.

identity of a 'trusted traveller'.[36] Thus, policies, legislation and technologies are also being used to enhance the mobility and degree of access for 'high value' travellers – a securitized elite.[37] Indeed, the position of elites demands particular attention, not just as beneficiaries of securitization but also as an important grouping driving these processes. Yet the deployment of these systems is also used to promote increasingly punitive measures against an immobilized 'global underclass', who are not considered worthy of admission.[38]

Massive migration databases have been deployed at national and European levels, which are capable of logging, storing and monitoring the details and movements of passengers.[39] Migration technology does not only consist of the computers that occupy virtually every government office these days, but also of various scientific techniques that involve the human body, such as DNA tests (saliva, hair), age testing (X-rays) and biometric data (fingerprints and iris scans).[40] For the unfortunate few, this leads to electronic segregation and hidden populations continually trailed by their digital selves.[41]

The pervasive reliance upon such technologies for border security means that the crossing of a physical border is merely one example of how people are now classified in all sorts of ways as 'safe vs dangerous'; 'legitimate vs illegitimate'; or 'illegal migrant vs innocent traveller'.[42] The border is now a means of identifying and distinguishing the safe from the unsafe at multiple points of daily life. This speaks to the importance of borders as a societal phenomenon and the significance of individual experience in defining and negotiating them.

They are part of the process by which normative behaviours are defined and by which citizens are 'distinguished from others as strangers, outsiders, non-status people and the rest'.[43] Much has been written about the dangers of becoming a surveillance society in which passing through public spaces is akin to the experience of airport security. And we have seen how this threat comes not only from the state itself, but from ordinary citizens seeking to enhance their status or regulate mobility through activities that facilitate the monitoring and reporting of 'suspicious' individuals and behaviour. Biometric security is both marking and (dis)enabling traditional relationships in favour of the kinds of graduated access to spaces and privileges afforded by the securitization of identity.[44]

The new technologies of risk management, which pervade the governance of modern states, have pushed border controls to the extreme, both legally

36 Amoore, *supra*, note 363 at 342.
37 Maguire, *supra*, note 81 at 44.
38 Pickering & Weber, *supra*, note 673 at 8.
39 Broeders, *supra*, note 703 at 41.
40 Dijstelbloem et al., *supra*, note 647 at 6.
41 Maguire, *supra*, note 81 at 44.
42 Amoore, *supra*, note 363 at 338.
43 Corey Johnson, Reece Jones, Anssi Paasi, Louise Amoore, Alison Mountz, Mark Salter & Chris Rumford, 'Interventions on Rethinking "The Border" in Border Studies', (2011) 61 *Political Geography* 30 at 68.
44 Maguire, *supra*, note 81 at 41.

and technologically, through complex visa procedures, biometric data, detention centres, and transnational information exchange networks – all aimed at pre-empting and preventing unwanted arrivals. Much of this happens far from the political border itself through data monitoring, immigration raids, offshore detention facilities, and exclusionary narratives in the media and popular culture.[45] Yet these efforts have been backed by strong institutional and public support for strengthening state power in the face of increasingly permeable borders.

The climate of fear that characterizes life since 9/11 inclines many of us to agree to more surveillance measures, without question. The notion that refugees and asylum-seekers are potential terrorist suspects who need to be restrained from movement and/or sent back to their home countries has been used to justify the continuing mistreatment of people who have done nothing worse than flee hardship and oppression in search of a safe place to live. But securitization does not create a safer society – only one that lives in permanent fear from real or perceived threats.[46]

There has been a recent tendency to rely on biometrics as an absolute or indisputable human measurement. The idea that a bright-line can be drawn between those with legitimate claims to mobility and those who are potentially dangerous is equally fallacious. One can point to the immigration policy of Donald Trump, especially his plans to build a wall and to increase surveillance along the border between Mexico and the USA. This far-right rhetoric has also been used to justify increasing levels of surveillance within Greece, including the building of a wall along land borders with Turkey and the targeting of migrants and refugees either by the police or by far-right groups acting in a paramilitary fashion, including the deployment of drones in the region.[47]

In what is perhaps the most punitive of such cases, asylum-seekers who arrive in Australia's waters by boat have been transported to offshore detention centres in the Pacific islands – Manus Island in Papua New Guinea, and the Pacific island nation of Nauru – instead of being allowed to land on the Australian mainland. This 'offshore' solution has been heavily criticized, including for abuses of international human rights standards; and in 2015, the UN Special Rapporteur on Torture found Australia to be in violation of the Convention Against Torture owing to the conditions on Manus Island.[48] Weak legal rights to privacy in Australia underpin the secrecy with which the Australian government operates its offshore detention centres.[49]

45 Johnson et al., *supra*, note 711.

46 Karyotis, *supra*, note 691 at 23.

47 Loukinas, *supra*, note 677 at 440.

48 Luke Heemsbergen & Angela Daly, 'Leaking Boats and Borders: The Virtu of Surveilling Australia's Refugee Population', (2017) 15(3/4) *Surveillance & Society* 389 at 389.

49 *Ibid.* Note that Australia is the only Western-style liberal democracy that does not have a comprehensive set of civil rights in its Constitution (like Canada and the US) or a separately legislated Bill of Rights (like New Zealand) at the federal level.

Paradoxically, the effect of excessive surveillance and 'pushback' at the borders only means that would-be migrants resort to even more precarious means that cannot be easily detected, such as smaller dinghies and more dangerous routes. The failures of Europe's search-and-rescue operations has exposed tragedy after tragedy at sea, as hundreds of people, including infants, have died seeking refuge. Desperate people have suffocated in trucks, been blown up in minefields between Greece and Turkey, been crushed to death in the undercarriages of trains and frozen in the wheel compartments of planes.[50] They have sewn their lips shut and taken their own lives in Australian detention centres, and have died at the hands of border guards, police, people smugglers, security guards and vigilantes. By allowing this to continue, we in the West seem to have forgotten that asylum-seekers and refugees are human beings and that their rights matter just as much as ours do.

What are biometric borders?

With an ever-increasing number of travellers seeking to move freely across borders, various governments are working to ensure that their border control procedures meet the growing demand for better security and more efficient processing.[51] Secure and resourceful border control is an economic requirement because our borders play an essential role in keeping the wheels of the global economy functioning.[52] Post 9/11, social and economic problems are progressively interpreted through the lens of security; and biometric technologies project the sovereignty of the nation state and the assurance of both internal and external security.[53] The biometric border can thus be viewed as the hallmark of a 'strong' state, with robust institutions and resources.[54]

Biometric technology installed at national border points is a key component in regulating the transnational flow of bodies in a global economy.[55] The deployment of biometric systems for immigration control has generally helped increase efficiency at border control checkpoints via enhanced security and innovative methods to collect and record travellers' identities.[56] The spread of biometric technologies is now most evident at the borders between nation states, where the use of biometric passports along with surveillance systems, such as face and iris recognition, is being deployed at airports and other land and sea entry points.[57]

50 Pickering & Weber, *supra*, note 673 at 10.

51 Georg Hasse, 'Document Quality Issues Jeopardise Border Biometrics', *Biometric Technology Today*, January 2012 at 7.

52 *Ibid.*

53 Wilson, *supra*, note 60.

54 Bennett et al., *supra*, note 27 at 15.

55 Heather Murray, "Monstrous Play in Negative Spaces: Illegible Bodies and the Cultural Construction of Biometric Technology," (2007) 10(4) *The Communication Review* 347 at 348.

56 Diaz, *supra*, note 679 at 5.

57 Wilson, *supra*, note 60 at 88.

However, while biometric technologies have typically been introduced with respect to specific categories of people – such as travellers, welfare recipients and asylum-seekers – the scope and reach of these systems is now expanding to encompass whole national populations. Earlier in this book, we saw that although these systems appear to be neutral and unbiased, they are used within particular political contexts to increase securitization and discrimination. Biometric technologies are thus deeply rooted within new modalities of power and control.

In the context of border security, this involves the collection, filing and coding of biometric identifiers in order to categorize and monitor individuals between and within nation states.[58] E-passports, for example, have a contactless integrated circuit imbedded in the back page which holds a biometric identifier that can be read off the chip along with the issuer's name, user's identifying information, and digital signature.[59] The information on the passport bio page can be matched to the information read from the chip, significantly reducing fraud and counterfeiting.[60] Countries such as Germany have added two fingerprints to the biometric on the chip, adding additional security.

On the surface, it seems that many countries have introduced e-Passports for the relatively simple purpose of increased efficiency and reduced cost. And we have already seen that the rationale underpinning governmental efforts to secure and sort identities is frequently embedded within arguments for administrative utility.[61] Biometric solutions are now faster, cheaper and more accurate.[62] As well, the biometric community has matured greatly in its ability to implement large projects successfully, even in countries relatively unfamiliar with identity management.[63]

A number of biometric modalities lend themselves to use at the border but the most commonly used are face and fingerprint, as that is what is used by police forces worldwide for watch-listing.[64] Moreover, if governments include all organizations that will use the biometric-enabled document in the decision-making process, the same tools can be used for e-Passports, e-IDs or e-Visas, thus achieving regulatory efficiencies and economies of scale. These systems also have symbolic import in that they facilitate the movement of capital and global elites while, at the same time, protecting against unwanted intrusions from potentially problematic outsiders.

The need for biometric data incorporated into travel documents is most often cited as a 'national security issue' – meaning that protection is needed against 'illegal' migrants and terrorists.[65] There is evidence that the level of acceptance

58 Wilson, *supra*, note 60 at 89.

59 Tracey Caldwell, 'Market Report: Border Biometrics', *Biometric Technology Today*, May 2015 at 5.

60 *Ibid.*

61 Wilson, *supra*, note 60 at 102.

62 Caldwell, *supra*, note 727 at 5.

63 *Ibid.*

64 *Ibid.*

65 Wilson, *supra*, note 60 at 101.

of biometric technology at borders is generally high because people understand the need for security.[66] We have already seen that there has been a global market boom in databases, biometric readers, data mining programs and other new technologies of control, with multinational corporations poised to make huge profits. The 9/11 attacks were essential to the implementation of heightened security measures in airports, and in spreading the idea that airports are critical spheres of risk.[67]

Mark B. Salter has observed that the airport has been transformed into a city unto itself – 'with all the attendant institutions, social forces, politics, and anxieties' of modern life.[68] In Foucauldian terms, airports have become a giant 'surveillance machine for automated bodies', reinforcing the dominant modes of social sorting, coercion and authorization.[69] This process has been augmented by biometrics that enable the tracking of bodies through airports using scanning devices for fingers, hands, eyes, faces and whole bodies.[70] Yet, according to Foucauldian analysis, the airport is essentially a series of enclosures – a dispersed system of dominance – within contemporary societies of control.[71]

With the help of sophisticated new technologies, airports have become extremely complex and powerful sites of surveillance and policing. Moreover, the state has increasingly appropriated this space for regulating mobility and the 'legitimate means of movement' through the control of identity documents, as well as accelerated lanes for the elite, and holding cells – or interrogation rooms – for the suspicious. We have also seen this role shifting from governments to private companies, or public–private partnerships, and an increased emphasis on profit-making[72] at the expense of government accountability and due process.

Biometric border security post-9/11

Following the 9/11 attacks, the US government began to use biometric technologies as a major weapon in the War on Terror. Within days of the attacks, security technology companies were aggressively marketing their products to airport officials; and within a fortnight, the International Biometrics Industry Association (IBIA), an advocacy organization representing major biometric companies in the United States, issued a press release stressing the importance of biometrics in the fight against terrorism.[73] Prior to this, biometric technologies

66 Caldwell, *supra*, note 727 at 5.
67 Wilson, *supra*, note 60 at 94.
68 Mark B. Salter, 'Airport Assemblage', in Mark B. Salter (ed.), *Politics at the Airport* (Minneapolis: University of Minnesota Press, 2008) i at ix.
69 *Ibid.* at x.
70 Lyon, *supra*, note 41 at 35.
71 Salter, *supra*, note 736 at xiii.
72 Salter, *supra*, note 195 at 2.
73 Wilson, *supra*, note 60 at 93.

were a fringe industry widely regarded as being of limited application and subject to considerable error. Yet, in the age of global terror, they were quickly made indispensable to homeland security efforts.

One of the key players peddling this profiling tool in the wake of 9/11 was Frank Asher, a drug dealer turned technology entrepreneur.[74] His private data-services company, Seisint, had already amassed data on 450 million people. After giving each person a risk-based score according to name, religion, travel history and other personal characteristics, Asher came up with a list of 1200 'suspicious' individuals, which he then gave to the FBI. Unknown to him, five of the terrorist hijackers were on the list; and the FBI was suitably impressed.[75]

Asher's company was subsequently rebranded 'the Multistate Anti-Terrorism Information Exchange', or 'Matrix', and taken over by the FBI to predict who might – one day in the future – commit a terrorist act. A new version, known as 'the System to Assess Risk' – or 'STAR' – was subsequently launched using information from both private and public databases. Since much of the information was already public, there was no requirement for the state to obtain a search warrant to carry out profiling – based on airline tickets, job records, car rentals and the like – in trying to pre-empt future attacks.

Congress and the 9/11 Commission also called for increased use of biometrics, and the White House created a cabinet-level subcommittee to coordinate policy to deploy biometric technologies across many federal agencies.[76] At a United States House subcommittee hearing in February 2002, a panel of commercial information technology experts and management consultants were asked for advice on how the War on Terror might be fought using risk-profiling techniques. The hearing concluded that technologies designed to classify people according to their degree of risk should be deployed for border security.

Since then, we have witnessed the amalgamation of individual physical characteristics with information systems and the growing reliance on biometric data as a means of risk management and identification at borders around the world. Similarly, anti-terrorist measures have turned the airport into an electronically controlled environment rivalled by only the maximum-security prison; and it's no surprise that the architects behind many of the heavily fortified terminals previously designed penitentiaries.[77] For example, as terrorist threats have increased at airports over time, security screening has moved farther away from the gates towards massive, technologically driven, secluded holding points.[78]

74 The Economist, *supra*, note 37 at 26.

75 *Ibid.*

76 US Department of Homeland Security, 'Enhancing Security Through Biometric Identification', Washington, DC, 2008. Available online at: www.dhs.gov/xlibrary/assets/usvisit/usvisit_edu_biometrics_brochure_english.pdf.

77 Salter, *supra*, note 195 at 6.

78 *Ibid.* at 13.

In the *Enhanced Border Security and Visa Entry Reform Act* of 2002, the US Congress mandated the use of biometrics in US visas.[79] This law requires that US embassies and consulates abroad must issue to international visitors 'only machine-readable, tamper-resistant visas and other travel and entry documents that use biometric identifiers'. In addition, the Homeland Security Council decided that the US standard for biometric screening is ten fingerprint scans collected at all US embassies and consulates for visa applicants seeking to travel to the United States.

In 2004, Congress required the US Department of Homeland Security (DHS) to develop a biometric entry and exit system.[80] That year, the DHS announced the Smart Border Alliance, led by Accenture – the prime contractors for the United States Visitor and Immigration Status Indicator Technology (US-VISIT) – a $US10-billion project to overhaul and manage all aspects of US air, land and sea ports of entry. In September 2013, Accenture was awarded a nine-month contract by DHS for $30 million, to create the U.S. Office of Biometric Identity Management (OBIM), replacing US-VISIT and streamlining operations. Accenture also worked with the EU Commission on the EU-VIS project, the visa program of the EU, in addition to its Schengen Information System (SIS).[81] Accenture similarly has national border agency clients, including the UK Border Force and the Ministry of Internal Affairs in the Netherlands; and it has overseen the deployment of such solutions at Heathrow Airport in London and Schiphol Airport in Amsterdam.[82]

In the United States, OBIM is the leading entity within the DHS responsible for biometric identity management services. OBIM provides a powerful example of the proliferation of risk-management tools as a means of enabling the DHS to assess the security risks of all US-bound travellers and prevent potential threats from ever reaching US soil. It checks a person's biometrics against a watch list of known or suspected terrorists, criminals and immigration violators.[83] It is also used to determine if a person is using an alias and/or attempting to use fraudulent identification.

It further helps many federal, state and local agencies with their investigations into crimes, including terrorist investigations. OBIM also monitors and records the status of people who apply for immigration benefits in the United States, as well as extensions of stay, or changes from one non-immigrant visa category to another. It matches the entry and exit records of people to identify those who

79 US Department of State – Bureau of Consular Affairs, 'Safety & Security of U.S. Borders: Biometrics'. Available online at: https://travel.state.gov/content/travel/en/us-visas/visa-information-resources/border-biometrics.html.

80 *2002 Enhanced Border Security and Visa Entry Reform Act, the Intelligence Reform and Terrorism Prevention Act of 2004, and the Implementing Recommendations of the 9/11 Commission Act of 2007:* Establishment of a nationwide biometric entry-exit system. Executive Order 13780, 'Protecting the Nation from Foreign Terrorist Entry into the United States' 9 March 2017: DHS requirement to 'expedite the completion and implementation of a biometric entry-exit tracking system for in-scope travelers to the United States'.

81 Caldwell, *supra*, note 727 at 5.

82 *Ibid.*

83 US Department of Homeland Security, *supra*, note 744.

may have overstayed the terms of their admission and provides this information to US Immigration & Customs Enforcement.

OBIM's most visible service is the collection of biometrics – digital fingerprints and a photograph – from international visitors at US visa-issuing posts and ports of entry. In 2017, OBIM processed over 100 million people; identified 175,000 known or suspected terrorists; added more than 15 million new unique identities to its biometric databank; and performed 3.8 million latent print comparisons.[84] It has also greatly improved data-sharing procedures, in terms of time and cost, between Five Eyes partners – the US, the UK, New Zealand, Canada and Australia. For example, in 2009, a Five Country Conference on biometric information-sharing was established between the Five-Eyes countries and a protocol has since allowed for the exchange of biometric fingerprint records to detect identity fraud and enhance security screening.[85]

OBIM brings together more than 20 databases, from police authorities to health, financial and travel records. Among the most noteworthy are the Automated Biometric Identification System (IDENT), a biometric database that stores and identifies electronic fingerprints from all foreign visitors, immigrants and asylum-seekers; the Arrival and Departure Information System (ADIS), storing visitors' entry and exit data; CBP Advance Passenger Information System (APIS), containing passenger manifest information; the US Immigration and Customs Enforcement (ICE) Student and Exchange Visitor Information System (SEVIS), containing data on all foreign and exchange students in the US; the INTERPOL Ballistic Information System (IBIS), a watch list linked with Interpol and national crime data; the Computer Linked Application Management System 3 (CLAIMS 3), comprising information on foreign nationals claiming benefits; as well as links to finance and banking, education, and health databases.[86]

OBIM uses these databases to profile and classify people according to degrees of riskiness, checking 'hits' against passenger manifests and visa applications. The risk-based identity of the person who attempts to cross an international border is in this way determined well in advance of their reaching the physical border; and, of course, the underlying assumption is that such risk profiles can be used as a basis to predict and prevent future criminal acts.[87] The diverse and decentralized networked information environment has thus created a vast and elusive system of surveillance networks, within and outside government, collecting information about identity and behaviour.[88]

84 Gemalto, 'DHS's Automated Biometric Identification System IDENT – the Heart of Biometric Visitor Identification in the USA', 22 May 2018. Available online at: www.gemalto.com/govt/customer-cases/ident-automated-biometric-identification-system.

85 Smith et al., *supra*, note 68 at 30.

86 Amoore, *supra*, note 363 at 340.

87 Amoore, *supra*, note 363 at 340.

88 Colin J. Bennett, 'Unsafe at Any Altitude: The Comparative Politics of No-Fly Lists in the United States and Canada', in Mark B. Salter (ed.) *Politics at the Airport* (Minneapolis: University of Minnesota Press, 2008) 51 at 68.

Those caught up in terrorist-profiling systems, like the Automated Targeting System used by the airline industry, are not allowed to know their scores or challenge the findings.[89] Yet their risk profiles may be secretly shared with federal, state and foreign governments and agencies, in addition to consultants, contractors, grantees, and others.[90] This can have far-reaching implications in that they might be denied access to a government job, a student visa or even the ability to fly ever again.[91] At the same time, Bruce Schneier reminds us what the no-fly list is: 'It's a list of people who are so dangerous that they can't be allowed to board an airplane under any circumstances, yet so innocent that they can't be arrested – even under the provisions of the Patriot Act'.[92] What, then, explains the persistence of this approach?

In early 2018, Northrop Grumman Corporation was awarded a $95-million contract by OBIM to develop the Homeland Advanced Recognition Technology (HART) system.[93] Northrop Grumman will serve as systems developer and integrator for this 42-month effort to expand the nation's biometric surveillance program.[94] It will replace the IDENT system – one of the largest biometric databases in the world – which currently contains information on 220 million unique individuals and processes 350,000 fingerprint transactions every day.[95] This is a startling increase from 20 years ago, when IDENT only contained information on 1.8 million people. Between IDENT and other DHS-managed databases, the agency manages over 10 billion biographic records and adds 10–15 million more each week. The new HART system will grow even larger to encompass biometrics for some 500 million people, including hundreds of millions of Americans.[96]

HART will support at least seven types of biometric identifiers, including face and voice data, DNA, scars and tattoos and a blanket category for 'other modalities'. It will also include biographic information, like name, date of birth,

89 The Economist, *supra*, note 37 at 27.

90 Bennett, *supra*, note 758 at 59.

91 The Economist, *supra*, note 37 at 27.

92 Bruce Schnier, 'Schnier on Security: Definition of No-Fly', 26 September 2005.

93 Northrop Grumman, 'Northrop Grumman Wins $95 Million Award from Department of Homeland Security to Develop Next-Generation Biometric Identification Services System', 26 February 2018. Available online at: https://news.northropgrumman.com/news/releases/northrop-grumman-wins-95-million-award-from-department-of-homeland-security-to-develop-next-generation-biometric-identification-services-system.

94 Medium, 'US Border Cops Set to Use Biometrics to Build a Line Up of the World', 25 October 2017. Available online at: https://medium.com/@privacyint/us-border-cops-set-to-use-biometrics-to-build-a-line-up-of-the-world-c1e864d31995.

95 Jennifer Lynch, 'HART: Homeland Security's Massive New Database Will Include Face Recognition, DNA, and People's 'Non-Obvious Relationships'," *Electronic Frontier Foundation*, 7 June 2018. Available online at:www.eff.org/deeplinks/2018/06/hart-homeland-securitys-massive-new-database-will-include-face-recognition-dna-and.

96 Chesbro on Security, 'Homeland Advanced Recognition Technology (HART)', 9 June 2018. Available online at: https://chesbro-on-security.blogspot.com/2018/06/homeland-advanced-recognition.html.

physical descriptors, country of origin and government ID numbers. And it will include highly subjective data, including information collected from officer 'encounters' with the public and information about people's 'relationship patterns'.[97] At this point, it is not known where DHS or its external partners will be getting these 'relationship pattern' records, but they could come from social media profiles and posts, which the US State Department recently proposed they collect – in addition to social media handles (i.e. those from Facebook, Twitter, Instagram, Pinterest and Snapchat), phone numbers, and email addresses used in the last five years – from those seeking both immigrant and non-immigrant visas to the United States.[98]

President Trump's recent travel ban, issued in September 2017, singled out countries that the DHS deemed were not making efforts to share information with the US, including Iran, Libya, Syria, Yemen, Somalia, Chad, North Korea and Venezuela.[99] The assessment explicitly considered whether these national groups were providing enough data to the DHS, including whether they are '[p]roactively shar[ing] biographic and biometric information about known and suspected terrorists'.[100] If the system expands as planned, the DHS, other agencies, and other countries will be widely collecting and sharing sensitive biometric data across systems and borders at unprecedented levels at a time when biometric data will be used for an increasing number of purposes by governments and industry.

In view of migratory pressures and terrorist attacks suffered by Europe over the last few years, border management has also become a priority for the European Commission. Criminal activities such as human trafficking, migrant smuggling and trafficking of goods are made possible by illegal border crossings. These crimes have long been facilitated by the absence of *any* uniform system for recording entry/exit movements across Europe.[101]

The European Union Visa Information System (VIS) – a database containing information, including biometrics, on visa applications by third-country nationals – has been operational since 2015.[102] The VIS is intended to serve a number of purposes, including improving the way that joint visa policy is implemented and enabling cooperation between consulates by sharing data on visa

97 Lynch, *supra*, note 763.

98 David Ruiz, 'EFF and Other Groups Fight State Department Collection of Social Media Information...Again', *Electronic Frontier Foundation*, 30 May 2018. Available online at: www.eff.org/deeplinks/2018/05/eff-and-other-groups-fight-state-department-collection-social-media-information.

99 Michael D. Shear, 'New Order Indefinitely Bars Almost All Travel from Seven Countries', *The New York Times*, 24 September 2017.

100 Privacy International, 'US Border Cops Set to Use Biometrics to Build a Line Up of the World', 25 October 2017. Available online at: https://privacyinternational.org/blog/648/us-border-cops-set-use-biometrics-build-line-world.

101 Gemalto, 'The Schengen Entry/Exit System: Biometrics to Facilitate Smart Borders', 2 April 2018. Available online at: www.gemalto.com/govt/coesys/eborder/entry-exit-system.

102 *Ibid.*

applications and decisions, combating 'visa shopping' and visa fraud.[103] The system has a role to play in 're-identifying' illegal migrants (i.e. those who overstay their visas). After all, such migrants do not only enter illegally or via the asylum process; a large portion enter the European Union with a tourist visa and then overstay their welcome when their visa expires.[104]

Prior to this, EURODAC was established pursuant to the Dublin Convention in 2000.[105] It's the EU's common fingerprinting and data comparison system, which has been described by the European Commission as 'essential in ensuring the efficiency of the European Asylum System'.[106] It contains a vast database, operated by a central unit in the Commission, to store fingerprints submitted by the member states.[107]

EURODAC was launched with the aim of identifying asylum-seekers who have entered the territory of member states unlawfully or have previously lodged asylum applications in more than a single member state (i.e. to prevent 'asylum shopping' and to ensure that each asylum applicant's case is processed by only one member state).[108] It is an EU-wide data system designed to record all asylum applications in the European Union and enable comparison based on fingerprints. It is binding upon all member states, except Denmark, and it has been made applicable through agreement in Iceland and Norway.[109] The directive establishing EURODAC requires member states to collect and 'promptly transmit' fingerprints of persons seeking asylum aged at least fourteen years, but it leaves the methods by which the fingerprints are gathered to domestic

103 Broeders, *supra*, note 703 at 56.

104 *Ibid.* at 55.

105 Council Regulation 2725/2000, Concerning the Establishment of 'Eurodac' for the Comparison of Fingerprints for the Effective Application of the Dublin Convention, 2000 O.J. (L 316) 1. Available online at: http://eur-lex.europa.eu/LexUriServ/ LexUriServ.do?uri=OJ:L:2000:316:0001:0010:EN:PDF.

106 Commission Communication to the Council and the European Parliament on Improved Effectiveness, Enhanced Interoperability and Synergies among European Databases in the Area of Justice and Home Affairs, at 4, COM (2005) 597 final (November 24, 2005). In 2006, the Commission reviewed the performance of the Central Unit of Eurodac and found it "very satisfactory . . . in terms of speed, output, security and cost-effectiveness."

107 The Eurodac Regulation also applies in Switzerland. Council Decision 2008/147/EC, On the Conclusion on Behalf of the European Community of the Agreement between the European Community and the Swiss Confederation Concerning the Criteria and Mechanisms for Establishing the State Responsible for Examining a Request for Asylum Lodged in a Member State or in Switzerland, 2008 O.J. (L 53) 1.

108 Council Regulation 2725/2000, Concerning the Establishment of 'Eurodac' for the Comparison of Fingerprints for the Effective Application of the Dublin Convention, 2000 O.J. (L 316) 1, http://eur-lex.europa.eu/LexUriServ/ LexUriServ.do?uri=OJ:L:2000:316:0001:0010:EN:PDF.

109 European Council on Refugees and Exiles, Report on the Application of the Dublin II Regulation in Europe, AD3/3/2006/EXT/MH, 2006, at 10, Available at www.ecre.org/wp-content/uploads/2016/07/ECRE-ELENA-Report-on-the-Application-of-the-Dublin-II-Regulation-in-Europe-_March-2006.pdf [hereinafter ECRE Report].

law, unless otherwise provided in other international and regional law.[110] The fingerprints are automatically matched against the database and are retained for ten years from the date on which they were taken, unless an applicant acquires citizenship, receives a residence permit or leaves the EU at an earlier date.

In February 2013, the 'Smart Borders' Package was first proposed by the Commission. At the time, the European Parliament and the EU member states dismissed the proposal owing to its technical complexity, cost, and negative civil liberties implications. On 6 April 2016, the Commission adopted a revised proposal for Smart Borders. This ambitious package of legislative measures, drawn up in consultation with the European Parliament, will establish a new system for recording the border crossings of all non-EU nationals – except the UK, but including Norway and Iceland. The system, called the Entry, Exit System (EES), will replace manual stamping of passports and will apply both to travellers requiring a visa and to visa-exempt travellers admitted to the Schengen area for 90 days or less. It will establish a database of fingerprints and other biometric data. The system will be gradually implemented at land, sea and air borders of all EU member countries.

The new automatic data system will register name, travel document, fingerprints, facial image, exit and enter information as well as refused-entry register, today available in the so-called SIS. This data will be stored for up to four years and will be accessible to law enforcement, border control and visa authorities. In addition to EU nationals, citizens of countries in the Schengen Zone of visa-free travel will be exempt from the new system.

The system will also be interconnected with the VIS database and used by the same authorities to safeguard against overstays. Moreover, it will allow member states' law-enforcement authorities and INTERPOL to perform restricted queries relating to an individual's cross-border movements and travel history for criminal identification and intelligence-gathering purposes. It will also be used in conjunction with the European Passenger Name Record (PNR) Directive which, from 25 May 2018, collects data on air passengers. The EES is expected to become fully operational by 2020 at the latest.

It is hoped that it will act as a powerful means of preventing and detecting terrorist activities or other serious criminal offences throughout the EU. It will also make border crossing faster whilst making checks and controls more robust. Unlike the US biometric database discussed above, EES data cannot be transferred or made available to any third country, international organization or private entity established in or outside the European Union. Of course, in the case of law-enforcement investigations to identify a third-country national, and the prevention or detection of terrorist offences, exceptions may be made. Still, the EES is quite robust with regard to the right to protection of personal data; in fact, the data collected and stored, and its period of retention, are strictly limited to what is necessary for the system to function and meet its objectives.

110 Council Regulation ('Eurodac Regulation'), *supra*, note 771 at 3.

Clearly, a major concern surrounding the implementation of biometric border management schemes relates to the security of the data that is collected, and that goes to ensuring that it will not be hacked, leaked, or otherwise distributed to the wrong individual(s) and misused. One of the major criticisms of these systems is the fact that data could easily fall into the wrong hands if leaked or hacked into by cyber attackers. Given the highly intimate nature of the data being collected on people – not just criminal suspects, but everybody transiting through the borders between nation states – if this material were to fall into the wrong hands, it could lead to widespread identity theft, or any number of other offences involving the misappropriation of a person's identity.

There is also the risk that it will be misused by a public or private organization for purposes that are either not permitted, or perhaps not even contemplated, at the present time. This relates to the problem of ethnic and racial profiling/segregation, which has reared its ugly head in the past and threatens to do so again. Indeed, it was mentioned earlier that the Trump administration has imposed restrictions upon individuals from certain 'illegitimate' countries that are either not sharing any biographic data or not providing enough information about their citizens. Not surprisingly, this includes a cluster of national groups that have become 'suspect' since 9/11.[111]

This affords a blanket allowance to exclude entire populations based on fears around Islamophobia, and other such knee-jerk reactions. We may see increasing cooperation between the liberal democratic nations of the global north in sharing information to keep suspected criminals, particularly terrorists, at bay. In turn, this may result in the segregation – or 'balkanization' – of those from impoverished and war-torn regions within Asia, Africa and the Middle East. They may no longer be able to flee poverty, hardship, famine and war in their own countries in search of a better life in the West.

To some extent, this has already been happening for some time. Throughout the West, but particularly in the United States, new technologies of control have led to visitors from some countries being subject to increased surveillance, while visitors from other (predominantly Caucasian and affluent) countries are treated as 'tourists' rather than as terrorist threats.[112] Moreover, if these systems develop as planned, we will see the sharing and use of sensitive biometric data across all sorts of systems and borders at unprecedented levels by governments and industry. The potential for data mining, profiling, segregation and misuse is astounding and likely to deeply trouble privacy advocates.

Migration policy and border surveillance are not limited to geographical borders. Border management is also performed within a country's territory via activities that legislate and maintain the separation between those who are entitled to be there and those who are not. The modern state is erecting a wall

111 Lyon, *supra*, note 41 at 42.

112 Nancy A. Wonders, 'Global Flows, Semi-Permeable Borders and New Channels of Inequality', in Sharon Pickering and Leanne Weber (eds), *Borders, Mobility and Technologies of Control* (Dordrecht: Springer, 2006) 63 at 79.

of documents and legal rules around its social institutions, such as the formal labour market, education, the housing market and the provisions of the welfare state. For example, in Britain, after being granted refugee status, people stop receiving the support they have been getting as asylum-seekers and must apply to receive benefits, and have 28 days to leave the accommodation provided to them by the Home Office. Owing to the difficulties involved in applying for benefits, very few refugees are able to register in this period, forcing them to go to food banks; and many find themselves homeless.[113]

DNA testing has also recently been embraced by US refugee and immigration agencies to determine whether people within a family are indeed genetically related, with the aim of stymying fraud and child trafficking.[114] DNA tests for refugees and other immigrants are controversial because they can reveal family secrets about parentage – for example, if a child is the product of infidelity or rape. Critics also say they impose a narrow, 'nuclear' conception of family that is blind to the reality of refugee life, where people often care for unrelated children whose parents may be dead or missing.[115]

The UN has said DNA testing should be used as a last resort for refugees. In Canada, a similar approach has been taken by the courts. A 2003 Federal Court decision noted that because DNA testing intrudes into an individual's privacy, it is 'a tool that must be carefully and selectively utilized'.[116] A 2008 Immigration Appeal Division decision noted that '...DNA testing should be limited to those relatively rare cases where viable alternatives to such testing do not exist'.[117]

There is great faith in technology and new possibilities are widely embraced with interest. Yet history clearly shows that data collected for one purpose can easily be made available for other purposes. The availability of large quantities of digital information provides a tempting invitation to use them more widely, such as for profiling individuals and groups. Indeed, the whole concept of digital border surveillance is already based on profiling and sorting – so why wouldn't this happen?

Legal issues with biometric border control systems

The demonization and criminalization of asylum-seekers has been accompanied by coercive measures such as indefinite detention and forced deportation. These measures are part of a continuous process whereby the act of seeking asylum is

113 Kate Lyons, Eva Thöne, Stephanie Kirchgaessner, Marilyne Baumard & Naiara Galarraga, 'Britain is One of Worst Places in Western Europe for Asylum Seekers', *The Guardian*, 2 March 2017.

114 Katie Worth, 'Can Biometrics Solve the Refugee Debate?' *Frontline*, 2 December 2015.

115 *Ibid.*

116 *MAO v Canada (Minister of Citizenship and Immigration)*, 2003 FC 1406 at paras 84 and 91, [2003] F.C.J. No. 1799 [MAO].

117 *Mohamad-Jabir v Canada (Minister of Citizenship and Immigration)*, [2008] IADD 44 at para. 33.

itself construed as a 'crime of arrival'.[118] Such discriminatory measures violate multiple international human rights conventions, including the *Convention on the Rights of the Child*, the *Convention Against Torture*, the *Universal Declaration Against Human Rights*, and the *International Covenant on Civil and Political Rights*. They also expose refugees and asylum-seekers to illegal smugglers, criminal gangs and other forms of serious danger.

Article 27 of the *Refugee Convention* requires that Contracting States issue identity papers to any refugee in their territory who does not possess a valid travel document.[119] Article 28 provides that Contracting States 'shall issue to refugees lawfully staying in their territory travel documents for the purpose of travel outside their territory, unless compelling reasons of national security or public order otherwise require'. The Schedule, however, makes no mention of biometrics, and aside from a recommendation that it be printed in a manner that would allow detection of erasure or alteration, it lacks anti-fraud protections.[120]

UNHCR has successfully used biometrics in refugee camps to assist in the registration of refugees and to prevent errors and fraud. UNHCR is expanding its capacity to use biometrics, and the refugees under its protection will most probably benefit as a result. Fraud inflates the population of refugee camps, strains their resources and contributes to an inequitable distribution of goods and services. The use of biometrics has proven to be an effective counter-measure. For example, their use in the registration of refugees in the Ali Addeh refugee camp in Djibouti helped reveal that the population had been overestimated by some four thousand.[121]

Domestically, the establishment of biometric databases raises privacy challenges and ethical concerns about who can access immigration data; data integrity contained in centralized databases; immigration data protection for third parties; the classification of individuals upon arrival (and corresponding discrimination issues); data storage restrictions; and the subsequent use of data for crime-control purposes and its impact on privacy.[122] Internationally, these challenges are magnified because of the broader range of people affected, compared with those listed in national databases. This is particularly true given the demands posed by globalization and the significant increase in trans-border biometric information flows for purposes of immigration control.

Article 13 of the *Convention on International Civil Aviation* further deals with the use of biometric technology by states: 'The laws and regulations of a contracting State as to the admission to or departure from its territory of

118 Wilson, *supra*, note 60 at 98.

119 Refugee Convention, art. 27. See United Nations Treaty Collection. Available at: http://treaties.un.org/Pages/ViewDetailsII.aspx?&src=TREATY&mtdsg_no=V~2&chapter=5&Temp=mtdsg2& lang=en dead and not in bibliography.

120 Achraf Farraj, 'Refugees and the Biometric Future: The Impact of Biometrics on Refugees and Asylum Seekers', (2011) 42 *Columbia Human Rights Law Review* 891 at 914.

121 *Ibid.* at 915.

122 Diaz, *supra*, note 679 at 7.

passengers, crew or cargo of aircraft, such as regulations relating to entry, clearance, immigration, passports, customs and quarantine shall be complied with by or on behalf of such passengers, crew or cargo upon entrance into or departure from, or while within the territory of that State'.[123] The global interoperability of biometric systems depends on uniform enrolment, data processing, identification, issuance and storage; as well as image quality, reading and verification.[124]

The *International Civil Aviation Organization* ('ICAO') is a specialized agency of the United Nations formed under the Treaty of Chicago (1944) to formalize shared national civil-aviation standards in pursuit of safety, security and efficiency.[125] The ICAO is also in charge of biometric passports and visa specifications – it has been investigating biometrics and its use for travel-document identification since 1995.[126]

On 28 May 2003, the ICAO announced the adoption of a 'global, harmonized blueprint for the integration of biometric identification information into passports and other Machine Readable Travel Documents (MRTDs)'.[127] The ICAO decided that these travel documents, dubbed 'e-Passports', will use facial recognition as their primary means of biometric identification, but it allowed states the option of using secondary biometrics to supplement facial recognition. The information, along with biographical information and a digital photograph, would be stored in contactless RFID chips embedded within the MRTDs.

By 2007, these requirements helped spur 'some 40 States', including Germany, South Africa, Australia and Poland, to incorporate biometrics into travel documents.[128] Biometric passports issued in compliance with ICAO specifications contain biometric data with controlled access, contactless microchips and a minimum 32kb data-storage capacity.[129] The biometric characteristics used by the ICAO in passports are: (a) facial recognition (mandatory); and (b) fingerprint or iris recognition (optional). Face photographs can be used by either personnel or automated systems to: (a) confirm identities via database search (recognition); or (b) authenticate images (verification).[130] Biometric fingerprint and/or iris characteristics may also be used for recognition purposes when agencies have access to information needed for verification.

123 *International Civil Aviation Organization, Convention on International Civil Aviation*, art. 13, 7 Dec 1944, Doc 730019.

124 Diaz, *supra*, note 679 at 17.

125 Magnet, *supra*, note 57 at 138.

126 Diaz, *supra*, note 679 at 3.

127 ICAO, 'Biometric Identification to Provide Enhanced Security and Speedier Border Clearance for Traveling Public', *PIO 09/03* (28 May 2003). http://www.asiatraveltips.com/travelnews03/285Biometric.shtml [hereinafter ICAO, Biometrics Announcement].

128 Farraj, *supra*, note 788 at 909.

129 International Civil Aviation Organization [I.C.A.O.], Machine Readable Travel Documents, DOC 9303 (Pt 1, 6th edn 2006).

130 Face photographs are used in passports, visas, driving licences and other sorts of identification documents. International Civil Aviation Organization [I.C.A.O.].

The *International Organization for Migration* ('IOM') is another international organization focused on immigration issues. IOM works with national governments to assess and improve the integrity of their travel and identity documents. Working with ICAO and the company IBM, IOM helps oversee an 'Identity Management' program that covers travel documents and related issuance systems, as well as travel document inspection.[131] As part of this Identity Management program, IOM manages a Personal Identification and Registration System (PIRS) which facilitates the collection, processing and storage of traveller information, including biometric data. The PIRS can also be linked to Interpol's Lost Travel Documents Database via the service's I-24/7 Global Communication System.

The legitimacy of biometric immigration control systems also largely depends on their basis in domestic law, particularly when it comes to individual privacy, civil liberties and data protection rights. In a fully functioning democracy, citizens may *demand* transparency and accountability, particularly with respect to (a) how biometric data is handled for immigration purposes; and (b) how it is exchanged by nations and organizations.[132] This includes the right to identify the national and international entities involved in processing biometric data and cross-border exchanges.[133]

Even between the various nation states that use biometric passports and visas, there are differences with respect to the types of biographical data collected (e.g., name, date, country of birth; medical information; and facial image; fingerprints, iris patterns, and so on.) The obvious reason is that countries differ in their approach to managing their borders; and this applies not only to the collection of biometric data, but also to the use of databases to manage that data (e.g. the use of criminal biometric databases) as well as various border-control procedures and immigration/crime control strategies. Thus, it is extremely difficult to tackle this topic from a reliable and uniform international perspective.

Many other countries around the world have now realized the importance of implementing biometric identification management technology for more effective and secure border control. For island nations such as Britain or Australia, checks at the border have long been the preferred method of immigration control, and – as we have seen in Chapter 4 – other sorts of measures involving identity cards have been strongly resisted.[134] More recently, the expansion of internal checks and pre-emptive measures has been justified in the name of fighting both international and domestic terrorist threats.[135]

In 2015, Australia's then-Minister for Immigration and Border Protection, Peter Dutton, introduced *The Migration Amendment (Strengthening*

131 Diaz, *supra*, note 679 at 13.

132 *Ibid.* at 8.

133 *Ibid.*

134 Leanne Weber, 'The Shifting Frontiers of Migration Control', in Sharon Pickering and Leanne Weber (eds), *Borders, Mobility and Technologies of Control* (Dordrecht: Springer, 2006) 21 at 24.

135 *Ibid.*

Biometrics Integrity) Bill.[136] Minister Dutton said the bill would address gaps in in Australia's biometric legislative framework.[137] Overall, the process continues to operate at multiple sites and involves sophisticated and extensive networks of public and private agencies to prevent and deter unauthorized arrival, particularly through the application of advanced border technologies (e.g. biometric passports and passenger processing systems); and punitive responses, such as detention and forcible deportation, directed at those who enter or remain without authorization.[138]

The Department of Immigration and Border Protection first implemented Australia's biometric program in 2006. The 2015 bill amended the *Migration Act 1958* to implement a number of reforms to consolidate and simplify the provisions relating to the collection of personal identifiers and addressed gaps in the legislative framework.[139] Previously, the Act contained eight different provisions authorizing the collection of personal identifiers. The bill streamlined the personal identifier collection powers into one discretionary power. Specifically, it gives the Immigration and Border Protection Minister the power to authorize the collection of new types of identifiers, including iris scans, without the need for new legislation. The bill further expanded biometric data to include fingerprints and iris scans, which was largely aimed at tackling the threat of Australians seeking to travel overseas to fight with terrorist organizations such as ISIS.[140]

The bill also provides greater flexibility with respect to the ways in which personal identifiers may be collected.[141] Thus, mobile fingerprint checks at airports can be implemented in order to detect foreign fighters with fake passports.[142] Immigration does not plan to collect fingerprints from all those entering and leaving Australia; rather, it merely wants to have the ability to do so when required.[143] The fingerprint data will also not be retained after the scan, only used to check against existing data to confirm the identity of the person.

The Bill further gives customs authorities the ability to collect biometric identifiers from minors and incapable persons without the consent of a parent or guardian. Australia 'faces the return of potentially radicalised minors', Minister Dutton told the Australian Parliament in March 2015.[144] This new capability

136 M2sys, 'Biometric Border Control in 2015: Is it Making Our World More Secure?' Available online at: www.m2sys.com/blog/border-control-2/biometric-border-control-in-2015-is-it-making-our-world-more-secure/.

137 Allie Coyne, 'Govt Pushes to Collect More Biometric Data at Aussie Airports', *Itnews*, 17 March 2015. Available online at: www.itnews.com.au/news/govt-pushes-to-collect-more-biometric-data-at-aussie-airports-401738.

138 Weber, *supra*, note 802 at 2.5.

139 TimeBase, 'Migration Amendment (Strengthening Biometrics Integrity) Bill 2015', 6 March 2015. Available online at: www.timebase.com.au/news/2015/AT082-article.html.

140 Coyne, *supra*, note 805.

141 TimeBase, *supra*, note 807.

142 Coyne, *supra*, note 805.

143 *Ibid.*

144 *Ibid.*

would 'further contribute to the protection of children who have been, or who are at risk of, being trafficked', according to the Bill.[145]

Critics have argued that the Bill provides for a protracted period of data retention which is longer than necessary to identify people who are traversing the country's borders.[146] Also, the collection of data from children without parents and without any kind of oversight or protection for vulnerable individuals may run contrary to the United Nations *Convention on the Rights of the Child*.[147] Yet the federal government insists the capability entails 'strong privacy safeguards'; but it does not provide detail beyond noting that facial recognition records will not be stored in a centralized database.[148] Instead, the records will be held by participating agencies, which will be able to reach in to one another's records.

In the United States, the fingerprinting of refugees and asylum-seekers is unlikely to be considered an illegal search under the Fourth Amendment. Since the founding of the United States, Congress has granted broad authority to customs officials to conduct searches and seizures at the border based on reasonable suspicion, without obtaining a warrant or establishing probable cause.[149] In fact, the First Congress of the United States, which proposed the *Bill of Rights*, including the Fourth Amendment, passed a far-reaching customs statute in 1789 exempting border searches from the requirement of probable cause.[150]

The government's interest in preventing the entry of unwanted persons and items has been said to be 'at its zenith'[151] at the international border and the Supreme Court has stated that border searches are reasonable by virtue of the fact they occur at the border.[152] Routine searches of persons or effects are not subject to reasonable suspicion, probable cause or warrant because they intrude very little on a person's privacy.[153] Against this background, a court would most likely find fingerprinting to be routine. Fingerprinting has been used in the United States since 1902, and it is commonly used today, with millions of individuals fingerprinted at the US border and ports of entry each year.[154]

145 *Ibid.*

146 The Greens. Available online at: https://scott-ludlam.greensmps.org.au/articles/scott-speaks-migration-amendment-strengthening-biometrics-integrity-bill-2015.

147 *Ibid.*

148 The Conversation, 'Your face is Part of Australia's "National Security Weapon": Should You be Concerned?' 14 September 2015. Available online at: https://theconversation.com/your-face-is-part-of-australias-national-security-weapon-should-you-be-concerned-47364.

149 *United States v. Montoya de Hernandez*, 473 U.S. 531, 537 (1985).

150 Act of July 31, 1789, c. 5, 1 Stat. 29. Section 24 of this statute granted customs officials 'full power and authority' to enter and search 'any ship or vessel, in which they shall have reason to suspect any goods, wares or merchandise subject to duty shall be concealed …'. See *United States v. Ramsey*, 431 U.S. 606, 619 (1977) at 616–17.

151 *United States v. Flores-Montano, 541 U.S. 149 (2004) at 152.*

152 *Ibid.*: Justice Rehnquist, for the Court, stated that '…searches of belongings at the border are reasonable simply by virtue of the fact that they occur at the border'.

153 *Montoya de Hernandez, supra*, note 817 at 538.

154 Farraj, *supra*, note 788 at 928.

The Supreme Court has also suggested that the collection of biometrics, namely fingerprinting, does not constitute a search under the Fourth Amendment. In *Davis v. Mississippi*, the Supreme Court distinguished fingerprinting from standard searches in that fingerprinting (1) 'involves none of the probing into an individual's private life and thoughts that marks an interrogation or search', (2) cannot be repeatedly collected 'to harass any individual, since the police need only one set of each person's prints', and (3) 'is an inherently more reliable and effective crime-solving tool than eyewitness identifications or confessions and is not subject to such abuses as the improper line-up and the "third degree"'.[155]

DHS reports that 'US-VISIT shares information with federal, state, local, tribal, foreign, and international agencies for national security, law enforcement, criminal justice, immigration and border management, and intelligence purposes...'[156] Data-sharing restrictions, with respect to the access and handling of data by external users, outside of DHS, is governed by formal written data-sharing agreements with each partner. DHS states that 'risks are mitigated by ... foreign partners' audit and redress provisions, which are identified in the process of negotiating a data sharing agreement'.[157] Nevertheless, the willingness to share refugees' and asylum-seekers' biometric data increases the likelihood that it will fall into the wrong hands, potentially exposing a refugee to danger even in his/her asylum country.[158]

Although immigration policies may never achieve uniformity on a worldwide basis on account of the fact that there are simply too many differing national interests, policy harmonization on a regional basis is becoming more common. For instance, in Europe, the SIS (i.e. a 'list' of people who have committed an offence, are filed as 'missing' or are under observation) and EURODAC permit any visa issued by a member nation to be valid in any Schengen-zone country. Together, these systems provide an example of how regional organizations have not only deployed centralized biometric systems but have also promoted a common, harmonized framework of trans-border biometric information flows for immigration control.[159]

155 394 U.S. 721, 723–724 and 727 (1969) (holding that fingerprints obtained during an illegal detention should have been excluded).

156 US Department of Homeland Security, 'Privacy Impact Assessment for the Automated Biometric Identification System (IDENT)', 7 December 2012, at 26. Available online at: www.dhs.gov/sites/default/files/publications/privacy-pia-nppd-ident-06252013.pdf.

157 *Ibid.* at 8.

158 UNHCR, Comments on the European Commission's Proposal for a Recast of the Regulation of the European Parliament and of the Council Establishing the Criteria and Mechanisms for Determining the Member State Responsible for Examining an Application for International Protection Lodged in One of the Member States by a Third Country National or a Stateless Person ('Dublin II') (COM(2008) 820, 3 December 2008) and the European Commission's Proposal for a Recast of the Regulation of the European Parliament and of the Council Concerning the Establishment of 'Eurodac' for the Comparison of Fingerprints for the Effective Application of [the Dublin II Regulation] (COM(2008) 825, 3 December 2008), 18 Mar 2009, at 24. Available online at: www.unhcr.org/refworld/docid/49c0ca922.html.

159 Diaz, *supra*, note 679 at 20.

As of 25 May 2018, the new *European Union General Data Protection Regulation* ('GDPR') – a series of laws that were approved by the European Union Parliament and the Council of the European Union in 2016 – replaced the EU Data Protection Directive of 1995. It is a comprehensive legal framework aimed at the protection of persons from the processing of personal data and their right to informational privacy. The GDPR affects all companies, individuals, corporations, public authorities or other entities that offer goods or services to individuals in the EU or that monitor their behaviour there.[160] It applies to *all* organizations collecting or processing personal data of persons in the European Union – regardless of where they are headquartered in the world.

The GDPR introduced privacy and security restrictions on how businesses collect, store and use the *personal data* of individuals located in the EU. The GDPR defines 'Personal Data' as: 'any information relating to an identified or identifiable natural person ("data subject"); an identifiable person is one who can be identified, directly or indirectly, in particular by reference to an identifier such as a name, an identification number, location data, online identifier or to one or more factors specific to the physical, physiological, genetic, mental, economic, cultural or social identity of that person (Joshi, 2017)'. This broad definition includes all forms of personal data (including genetic, health and biometric data).

The following principles of data collection, processing, storage and use underpin the GDPR: (a) personal data shall be processed lawfully, fairly and in a transparent manner in relation to the data subject (principle of lawfulness, fairness and transparency); (b) the personal data must be collected for specified, explicit and legitimate purposes (principle of purpose limitation); (c) processing must be adequate, relevant and limited to what is necessary (principle of data minimization) as well as accurate and, where necessary, kept up to date (principle of accuracy); (d) data is to be kept in a form that permits identification of data subjects for no longer than is necessary for the purposes for which the personal data is processed (principle of storage limitation); (e) data processing must be secure (principle of integrity and confidentiality); and (f) the data controller is to be held responsible for the data (principle of accountability).

Biometric data includes physical, physiological and behavioural characteristics (Chapter I, Article 4). Article 9 sets limits on the collection and use of biometric data. There must be explicit consent by the party whose data is being collected. The consent should be freely given, which is clearly distinguishable in an intelligible and easily accessible form, using clear and plain language. Consent can be withdrawn at any time. Processing must be necessary 'for the purposes of carrying out the obligations and exercising specific

160 Nancy Harris, 'A Practical Guide to the European Union's GDPR for American Businesses', *Recode*, 16 May 2018.

rights of the controller or of the data subject in the field of employment and social security and social protection law'; or 'necessary for reasons of substantial public interest, and it shall be proportionate to the aim pursued, respect the essence of the right to data protection and provide for suitable and specific measures to safeguard the fundamental rights and the interests of the data subject'.

The Regulation also sets out various rights of the data subject, which include the right of access to information about the purpose of the collection of the data, details of the use and transfer of the data, the right to rectification of data, the right to erasure of the data or the right to be forgotten, the right to restriction of processing, the right to be informed, the right to data portability and the right to object to the illegitimate use of the data.

Yet the GDPR allows member states to introduce derogations and exemptions, for example for national defence, criminal investigations and safeguarding the general public.[161] Function creep seems somewhat unavoidable as national governments seek to enhance global interoperability between databases, which facilitate the exchange of data between national immigration, law enforcement and other public and private databases, such as those used by airline and travel agencies.

Conclusion

The present tense climate caused by wars and a fear of terrorist attacks means that the safeguarding of borders is now associated to an unprecedented extent with guaranteeing national security, and with identifying and arresting persons regarded as security risks *before* they can do harm. This means that governments are not only interested in the fact that people cross a border in a legitimate way – in possession of valid travel documents – they also increasingly want to know who will be crossing in the future.

Biometric technologies have been touted as the ideal solution to the problem of securing porous borders.[162] Critics point to the massive potential for error and the violation of international human rights standards. For instance, what happens when people are wrongly targeted as high-risk and detained on the basis of a score derived from data that is merely associated with them (an example would be 'cultural' associations resulting from the selection of Halal in-flight meals)?[163] More deeply concerning is that such efforts can be said, in some cases, to represent the continuation of repressive practices that mark certain people, or groups of people, as irredeemably *other*.[164]

161 Trend Micro, 'Balancing Security and Public Interest: The GDPR and the Public Sector', 9 April 2018. Available online at: www.trendmicro.com/vinfo/au/security/news/online-privacy/balancing-security-and-public-interest-gdpr-and-public-sector.

162 Wilson, *supra*, note 60 at 89.

163 Johnson et al., *supra*, note 711 at 64.

164 Amoore, *supra*, note 363 at 345.

Bibliography

Amnesty International, '2015 Has Seen the Worst Refugee Crisis since WWII', *Human Rights Now Blog*, 28 December 2015. Available online at: https://blog.amnestyusa.org/refugees/2015-has-seen-the-worst-refugee-crisis-since-wwii/.

Louise Amoore, 'Biometric Borders: Governing Mobilities in the War on Terror', (2006) 25 *Political Geography* 336.

BBC, 'Schengen: Controversial EU Free Movement Deal Explained', 24 April 2016. Available online at: www.bbc.com/news/world-europe-13194723.

Colin J. Bennett, 'Unsafe at Any Altitude: The Comparative Politics of No-Fly Lists in the United States and Canada', in Mark B. Salter (ed.) *Politics at the Airport* (Minneapolis: University of Minnesota Press, 2008) 51.

Dennis Broeders, 'A European 'Border' Surveillance System Under Construction', in H. Dijstelbloem et al. (eds), *Migration and the New Technological Borders of Europe* (London: Palgrave Macmillan, 2011) 40.

Tracey Caldwell, 'Market Report: Border Biometrics', *Biometric Technology Today*, May, 2015.

Chesbro on Security, 'Homeland Advanced Recognition Technology (HART)', 9 June 2018. Available online at: https://chesbro-on-security.blogspot.com/2018/06/homeland-advanced-recognition.html.

Allie Coyne, 'Govt Pushes to Collect More Biometric Data at Aussie Airports', *It-news*, 17 March 2015. Available online at: www.itnews.com.au/news/govt-pushes-to-collect-more-biometric-data-at-aussie-airports-401738.

Alan Dershowitz, *Rights from Wrongs* (New York: Basic Books, 2004).

Vanessa Diaz, 'Legal Challenges of Biometric Immigration Control Systems', (2014) 7(1) *Mexican Law Review* 3.

Huub Dijstelbloem, Albert Meijer & Michiel Besters, 'The Migration Machine', in H. Dijstelbloem et al. (eds), *Migration and the New Technological Borders of Europe* (London: Palgrave Macmillan, 2011) 1.

Wesley Dockery, 'The Syrian Conflict and its Impact on Migration', *InfoMigrants*, 14 March 2018. Available online at: www.infomigrants.net/en/post/8077/the-syrian-conflict-and-its-impact-on-migration.

Achraf Farraj, 'Refugees and the Biometric Future: The Impact of Biometrics on Refugees and Asylum Seekers', (2011) 42 *Columbia Human Rights Law Review* 891.

Gemalto, 'The Schengen Entry/Exit System: Biometrics to Facilitate Smart Borders', 2 April 2018. Available online at: www.gemalto.com/govt/coesys/eborder/entry-exit-system.

Gemalto, 'DHS's Automated Biometric Identification System IDENT – The Heart of Biometric Visitor Identification in the USA', 22 May 2018. Available online at: www.gemalto.com/govt/customer-cases/ident-automated-biometric-identification-system.

Archit Guha, 'The Illegal Immigrant Identity and Its Fragments – From Enemy Foreigner to Bangladeshi Illegal Immigrant in (Post) Colonial India', (2016) 12 *Socio-Legal Review* 108.

Nancy Harris, 'A Practical Guide to the European Union's GDPR for American Businesses', *Recode*, 16 May 2018.

Georg Hasse, 'Document Quality Issues Jeopardise Border Biometrics', *Biometric Technology Today*, January 2012.

Luke Heemsbergen & Angela Daly, 'Leaking Boats and Borders: The Virtu of Surveilling Australia's Refugee Population', (2017) 15(3/4) *Surveillance & Society* 389.

ICAO, 'Biometric Identification to Provide Enhanced Security and Speedier Border Clearance for Traveling Public', *PIO 09/03* 28 May 2003. Available online at: www.icao.int/icao/en/nr/2003/pio200309_e.pdf.

Corey Johnson, Reece Jones, Anssi Paasi, Louise Amoore, Alison Mountz, Mark Salter & Chris Rumford, 'Interventions on Rethinking "The Border" in Border Studies', (2011) 61 *Political Geography* 30.

Georgios Karyotis, 'The Fallacy of Securitizing Migration: Elite Rationality and Unintended Consequences', in Gabriella Lazaridis (ed.), *Security, Insecurity and Migration in Europe* (Abingdon: Routledge, 2016) 13.

Witold Klaus, 'Security First: New Right-Wing Government in Poland and its Policy Towards Immigrants and Refugees', (2017) 15(3/4) *Surveillance & Society* 523.

Panagiotis Loukinas, 'Surveillance and Drones at Greek Borderzones: Challenging Human Rights and Democracy', (2017) 15(3/4) *Surveillance & Society* 439.

Jennifer Lynch, 'HART: Homeland Security's Massive New Database Will Include Face Recognition, DNA, and People's "Non-Obvious Relationships"', *Electronic Frontier Foundation*, 7 June 2018. Available online at: www.eff.org/deeplinks/2018/06/hart-homeland-securitys-massive-new-database-will-include-face-recognition-dna-and.

David Lyon, 'Filtering Flows, Friends and Foes', in Mark B. Salter (ed.), *Politics at the Airport* (Minneapolis: University of Minnesota Press, 2008) 29.

Kate Lyons, Eva Thöne, Stephanie Kirchgaessner, Marilyne Baumard & Naiara Galarraga, 'Britain is One of Worst Places in Western Europe for Asylum Seekers', *The Guardian*, 2 March 2017.

M2sys, 'Biometric Border Control in 2015: Is it Making Our World More Secure?' Available online at: www.m2sys.com/blog/border-control-2/biometric-border-control-in-2015-is-it-making-our-world-more-secure/.

Shoshanna Amielle Magnet, *When Biometrics Fail: Gender, Race and the Technologies of Identity* (Durham, NC: Duke University Press, 2011).

Mark Maguire, 'Vanishing Borders and Biometric Citizens', in Gabriella Lazaridis (ed.), *Security, Insecurity and Migration in Europe* (London: Routledge, 2011).

Euan McKirdy, 'UNHCR Report: More Displaced Now Than After WWII', *CNN*, 20 June 2016.

Medium, 'US Border Cops Set to Use Biometrics to Build a Line Up of the World', 25 October 2017. Available online at: https://medium.com/@privacyint/us-border-cops-set-to-use-biometrics-to-build-a-line-up-of-the-world-c1e864d31995.

Heather Murray, 'Monstrous Play in Negative Spaces: Illegible Bodies and the Cultural Construction of Biometric Technology', (2007) 10(4) *The Communication Review* 347.

Northrop Grumman, 'Northrop Grumman Wins $95 Million Award from Department of Homeland Security to Develop Next-Generation Biometric Identification Services System', 26 February 2018. Available online at: https://news.northropgrumman.com/news/releases/northrop-grumman-wins-95-million-award-from-department-of-homeland-security-to-develop-next-generation-biometric-identification-services-system.

Sharon Pickering & Leanne Weber, 'Borders, Mobility and Technologies of Control', in Sharon Pickering & Leanne Weber (eds), *Borders, Mobility and Technologies of Control* (Dordrecht: Springer, 2006) 1 at 1.

Privacy International, 'US Border Cops Set to Use Biometrics to Build a Line Up of the World', 25 October 2017. Available online at: https://privacyinternational.org/blog/648/us-border-cops-set-use-biometrics-build-line-world.

David Ruiz, 'EFF and Other Groups Fight State Department Collection of Social Media Information ... Again', *Electronic Frontier Foundation*, 30 May 2018. Available online at: www.eff.org/deeplinks/2018/05/eff-and-other-groups-fight-state-department-collection-social-media-information.

Mark B. Salter, 'Airport Assemblage', in Mark B. Salter (ed.), *Politics at the Airport* (Minneapolis: University of Minnesota Press, 2008) i.

Mark B. Salter, 'The Global Airport', in Mark B. Salter (ed.), *Politics at the Airport* (Minneapolis: University of Minnesota Press, 2008) 1.

Bruce Schneier, 'Schneier on Security: Definition of No-Fly', 26 September 2005. Available online at: https://www.schneier.com/.

James C. Scott, *Seeing Like a State: How Certain Schemes to Improve the Human Condition Have Failed* (New Haven, CT: Yale University Press, 1998).

Michael D. Shear, 'New Order Indefinitely Bars Almost All Travel from Seven Countries', *The New York Times*, 24 September 2017.

Marcus Smith, Monique Mann & Gregor Urbas, *Biometrics, Crime and Security* (New York: Routledge, 2018).

The Conversation, 'Your Face is Part of Australia's "National Security Weapon": Should You be Concerned?' 14 September 2015. Available online at: https://theconversation.com/your-face-is-part-of-australias-national-security-weapon-should-you-be-concerned-47364.

The Economist, 'Learning to Live with Big Brother', in Peter P. Swire & Kenesa Ahmad (eds), *Privacy and Surveillance with New Technologies* (New York: International Debate Education Association, 2012) at 23. The Economist, 'Let Them Not Come', 2 April 2016. Available online at: www.economist.com/britain/2016/04/02/let-them-not-come.

The Economist, 'Raising the Drawbridge', 27 August 2016. Available online at: www.economist.com/britain/2016/08/27/raising-the-drawbridge.

TimeBase, 'Migration Amendment (Strengthening Biometrics Integrity) Bill 2015', 6 March 2015. Available online at: www.timebase.com.au/news/2015/AT082-article.html.

Trend Micro, 'Balancing Security and Public Interest: The GDPR and the Public Sector', 9 April 2018. Available online at: www.trendmicro.com/vinfo/au/security/news/online-privacy/balancing-security-and-public-interest-gdpr-and-public-sector.

US Department of Homeland Security, 'Enhancing Security Through Biometric Identification', Washington, DC, 2008. Available online at: www.dhs.gov/xlibrary/assets/usvisit/usvisit_edu_biometrics_brochure_english.pdf.

US Department of Homeland Security, 'Privacy Impact Assessment for the Automated Biometric Identification System (IDENT)', 7 December 2012. Available online at: www.dhs.gov/sites/default/files/publications/privacy-pia-nppd-ident-06252013.pdf.

US Department of State – Bureau of Consular Affairs, 'Safety & Security of U.S. Borders: Biometrics'. Available online at: https://travel.state.gov/content/travel/en/us-visas/visa-information-resources/border-biometrics.html.

UK Home Office, 'Controlling our Borders: Making Migration Work for Britain', February 2005. Available online at: https://assets.publishing.service.gov.uk/government/uploads/system/uploads/attachment_data/file/251091/6472.pdf.

UN Refugee Agency (UNHCR), 'Global Trends: Forced Displacement in 2017', United Nations High Commissioner for Refugees, 2018. Available online at: www.unhcr.org/5b27be547.pdf.

Leanne Weber, 'The Shifting Frontiers of Migration Control', in Sharon Pickering & Leanne Weber (eds), *Borders, Mobility and Technologies of Control* (Dordrecht: Springer, 2006) 21.

David Wills, 'The United Kingdom Identity Card Scheme: Shifting Motivations, Static Technologies', in Colin J. Bennett & David Lyon (eds), *Playing the Identity Card: Surveillance, Security and Identification in Global Perspective* (New York: Routledge, 2008) 163.

Dean Wilson, 'Biometrics, Borders and the Ideal Suspect', in Sharon Pickering & Leanne Weber (eds), *Borders, Mobility and Technologies of Control* (Dordrecht: Springer, 2006) 87.

Nancy A. Wonders, 'Global Flows, Semi-Permeable Borders and New Channels of Inequality', in Sharon Pickering & Leanne Weber (eds), *Borders, Mobility and Technologies of Control* (Dordrecht: Springer, 2006) 63.

Katie Worth, 'Can Biometrics Solve the Refugee Debate?' *Frontline*, 2 December 2015.

Pinar Yazgan, Deniz Eroglu Utku & Ibrahim Sirkeci, 'Syrian Crisis and Migration', (2015) 12(3) *Migration Letters* 181.

Case Law

Davis v. Mississippi, 394 U.S. 721, 723–724 and 727 (1969).

MAO v Canada (Minister of Citizenship and Immigration), 2003 FC 1406 at paras 84 and 91, [2003] F.C.J. No. 1799 [MAO].

Mohamad-Jabir v Canada (Minister of Citizenship and Immigration), [2008] IADD 44.

United States v. Flores-Montano, 541 U.S. 149 (2004).

United States v. Montoya de Hernandez, 473 U.S. 531, 537 (1985).

7 Marketplaces of surveillance

Introduction

We've heard time and again that the digital economy is 'reinventing' commerce. Another cliché for our time is that *data is the new oil.* Of course, it isn't the existence of the marketplace that is new. In every culture since ancient Babylon, humans have gathered to exchange goods.[1] By the 1400s, the weekly market had become a dominant life force in European communities, linking small-scale rural farmers to their urban neighbours, with vendors peddling everything from livestock to leather goods.[2]

Market expansion over the next several centuries brought exponential growth and more efficient manufacturing processes; but it also created complex and largely unpredictable supply chains. Economies had formerly subsisted primarily on barter and the farmer selling goods at a local market could hear first-hand what his customers wanted; thus achieving a seamless system of supply and demand. Over time, these methods gave way to the development of modern financial instruments, and ultimately, our modern consumerist society, with its mass markets and retail pricing.[3]

Today, we are witnessing the emergence of new tools, and even new kinds of markets, in search of smart and efficient businesses in a world of Internet-enabled capitalism. As we embrace wholesale changes in our capitalist system – by ushering in a 24/7 global marketplace of dynamic pricing and artificial intelligence – we are erasing many of the inefficiencies that developed over the last 500-odd years. A continuous network of consumers, vendors and manufacturers means improved efficiency and communication, real-time sales analysis, a diminished need to stockpile inventory and the eradication of many hurdles in the supply chain.[4] But how will that transform the retail experience?

Commercial networks of every kind now dominate human life and social relationships. The age of the agora – which was once a thriving marketplace and

1 Wired Staff, "Capitalist Ecoconstruction," *Wired*, March 1, 2000.

2 *Ibid.*

3 *Ibid.*

4 *Ibid.*

the centre of the athletic, artistic, spiritual and political life of the city – has given way to targeted ads. It makes little sense to ask whether the relationships that thrive in the Web-based simulated economy are an adequate substitute for traditional marketplaces, which were bound by kinship, loyalty, geography and trust. E-commerce is about markets accessible to anyone, anywhere, at any time. As consumer behaviour shifts towards personal shopping agents and bots take over the process, third parties are silently steering us towards products we want to buy while, at the same time, grabbing market share from one another by undercutting competitors' prices. Individuals have become little more than samples, data, markets and other measurements for how 'the product' should be manufactured and sold to us.

The Internet is now saturated with bots, artificial intelligence, and links to all 'things' in society. And a large part of it is managed by four leading global conglomerates – Facebook, Google, Amazon and Apple. These are the four most influential companies on the planet; and they're worth an astounding $2.3 trillion USD.[5] Together, they're responsible for an array of products and services that are woven into the daily lives of billions of people around the globe.[6] What do their unprecedented scale and influence mean for the future of the Internet economy? How does the concentration of companies at the top affect our experience and access to the Internet? To put it bluntly, we live in a massive shopping mall designed by these giants.

When it comes to social networking sites such as Facebook (which makes money from helping companies market products and services to particular demographics), the individual is caught within a web of interlocking social and commercial relationships over which he or she has very little autonomy and control.[7] The norm is widely distributed electronic openness; and you have to deliberately carve out limited zones of privacy.[8] Indeed, we've already been going down a path towards a future in which people are monitored around the clock and there's scarcely any personal privacy left.

When combined with facial recognition technologies and a web of other data, like one's Facebook or Tinder profile, government identification, workplace, medical history, and more, a single snapshot can create a detailed picture of a person that traces their entire lifespan. With credit card data you can also get picture of a person's spending habits and track their movements 24/7. China is currently leading the way when it comes to this type of omnipresent surveillance; but it's possible for western countries to follow in China's footsteps, especially since the underlying technology keeps improving.

5 Scott Galloway, *The Four: The Hidden DNA of Amazon, Apple, Facebook and Google* (London: Transworld Publishers, 2017) at 1.

6 *Ibid.*

7 Jeremy Rifkin, *The Age of Access: The New Culture of Hypercapitalism, Where all of Life is a Paid-For Experience* (New York: Penguin Putnam, 2000) at 103.

8 Mitchell, *supra*, note 33 at 29.

Why are we sharing so much online? A glance at any TV listing today shows dozens of reality-TV shows where people bare their lives in front of cameras, knowing that their actions will be broadcast to audiences around the globe. Evidently, we live in a confessional culture, whereby people are willing to expose their most intimate selves on shows like *Big Brother* and *The Bachelor* and people are drawn to this modern-day spectacle which perhaps harkens back to the public square.

But Facebook is nothing like a robust public square. While it markets itself as a free, public platform for openness, connectedness and speech, it's actually a carefully-managed top-down system with hidden rules and methods for collecting and sorting information – all for its own benefit.[9] Facebook's basic strategy involves little more than encouraging us to make it central to our lives, then using what it gleans to sell ads. Yet it also aims to know how far human beings can be steered in various ways so it can gather insights about how they're prone to vote, and which products they're likely to purchase and promote to others. Publicly, though, the company promotes an often-doubted but seemingly genuine message that its primary goal is to 'support the well-being of its users' or, even more preposterous, to truly 'improve how the world communicates'.

Facebook is invested in increasing people's engagement with the site; and it devotes tremendous resources to devising algorithms that make it easier to manipulate what people see and think.[10] It nudges users in particular directions, conducts hidden tests on them, and addicts them – just like ignorant lab rats in a behavioural experiment.[11] That's not just normal practice, it's the very foundation upon which the organization was built.[12] Meanwhile, so many of us are caught up in the 'me too' micro-fame culture of blogging, #hashtagging, and selfies that we're too busy or oblivious to notice.[13]

A clear precursor for what would eventually become a worldwide phenomenon, Andrew Niccol's film the *Truman Show* – released on 5 June 1998 – is credited with predicting the reality television phenomenon that would begin two years later with *Survivor*. It remains one of the most accurate forewarnings of modern-day popular culture, if only for how precise the sentiment behind Niccol's story proves to be years later. It's frightening to think about how obsessed consumers have become with other people's lives, but what may be even scarier is how predictable this fascination with manufactured reality and hyper-surveillance truly was more than 20 years ago when the idea was first conceived.

The film follows Truman Burbank (Jim Carey), who – unbeknownst to him – since birth has been part of an elaborate reality television show covering his every

9 Foer, *supra*, note 269 at 57.

10 danah boyd, 'Untangling Research and Practice: What Facebook's "Emotional Contagion" Study Teaches Us', (2016) 12(1) *Research Ethics* 4 at 5.

11 Foer, *supra*, note 269 at 57.

12 *Ibid*. at 5.

13 Tim Wu, *The Attention Merchants – The Epic Scramble to Get Inside Our Heads* (New York: Vintage Books, 2016) at 304.

move, entitled 'The Truman Show'. Each aspect of Truman's life is staged; his wife and friends are all actors paid to manipulate and cultivate his reality. As the first infant to be adopted and raised by a corporation, Truman is made to spend his entire life living inside an enormous television studio equipped with hundreds of hidden cameras. Each moment of his hapless life is recorded and broadcast, uninterrupted, 24/7, to an audience around the globe.

Almost everyone in this dystopian nightmare accepts the idea that a person's entire life can be dominated by a corporation. So it makes sense that every product featured on the show is also for sale to the audience – the actors' wardrobes, food products, down to the very homes they live in. The entire show – and thus Truman's whole world – is a giant marketing machine built for the sole purpose of selling products, promoting them to viewers and getting good ratings. During a conversation in the family kitchen, for example, Truman's wife Meryl suggests: 'Why don't you let me fix you some of this Mococoa drink, all natural cocoa beans from the upper slopes of Mount Nicaragua, no artificial sweeteners!' Truman replies, 'What the hell are you talking about?!? Who are you talking to?!?' to which Meryl responds – beaming into the hidden camera – 'I've tasted other cocoas, this is the best!'

It's safe to say that there has never been much reality involved in reality television; yet we watch these shows because we have a narcissistic obsession with the trivial and mundane aspects of people's lives, particularly when it comes to interpersonal relationships. The audience can detach and say, 'This is someone else. It has nothing to do with me'. Viewers delight in watching the antics of inherently absurd and problematic people causing friction, despite realizing that thoughts and emotions are never as genuine when people know they're being observed through a camera lens. Television executives love these shows for their low costs and high ratings.

At the same time, we've also witnessed the sudden increase in ordinary people's sharing intimate details of their lives with strangers on line. Thus, the *Truman Show* provided the conceptual framework for the gratuitous oversharing that comes with the explosion of reality television, the voyeuristic excesses of celebrity culture, and our insatiable appetite for even the smallest details of scandal. The outcome is always uncertain, there are certainly winners and losers, and there is plenty of surprise, conflict and outlandish behaviour – not to mention ridiculously memorable characters – to keep us hooked.

But what if – like Truman – you were the star of your own reality show and you didn't even know it? What if you woke up and found yourself a performer – or worse, a prisoner – in a manufactured world tailored to you, with your data on display, available for the scrutiny of strangers, simply because you've been too cavalier about sharing your life online?

Where it all began

Ironically, Silicon Valley's penchant for monopoly dates back to the hippie counterculture of the 1960s where it emerged from the spirit of idealism, transformation and cooperation.[14] Once the Internet was released to the masses, it was no longer just a technology – it was a movement. There was an expectation of a great transformation; and a belief in something truly extraordinary. The Internet would serve as a new global commons, liberating us from the enslavement of television and the isolating, antisocial act of reading books that tech theorists like Marshall McLuhan disdained. It would counteract the destructive forces of individualism and usher in an era of creativity and collaboration. How this might work in practice remained prophetically vague – it would take decades to see how it would unfold.[15]

Stewart Brand was a hippie for the ages. As the founder of the *Whole Earth Catalogue*, Brand was at the centre of some of the most intriguing events of the 1960s: he hung out with the writer Ken Kesey and his band of Merry Pranksters; he featured in Tom Wolfe's travelogue *The Electric Kool-Aid Acid Test*; and he was one of the organizers of the infamous Trips Festival in San Francisco, which featured 6,000 hippies, plenty of LSD, and the Grateful Dead.[16] Brand also inspired a revolution in computing which profoundly shaped the future of technology.[17]

The early network culture of the Internet had an egalitarian spirit and a left-leaning socialist mission, whereby the system – and the information it provided – was open, public and free. In his 1987 book *The Media Lab*, Brand quoted Howard Rheingold's reflection on the existence of computer-linked communities as relaxed, friendly, welcoming 'places':

> There's always another mind there. It's like having the corner bar, complete with old buddies and delightful newcomers and tools waiting to take home and fresh graffiti and letters, except instead of putting on my coat, shutting down the computer, and walking to the corner, I just invoke my telecom program and there they are. It's a place.[18]

Everything the hippie culture despised – the mindless submission of the worker, the tyranny of bureaucracy and the oppressiveness of centralized control – could be overcome in a virtual network where the individual had the freedom to find his inspiration, shape his environment and share his passions and interests with like-minded people.[19] The existence of these computer-linked communities was, in fact, predicted in 1968 by J. C. R. Linklater, one of the research directors for the US Department of Defense's Advanced Research Project Agency

14 Foer, *supra*, note 269 at 12.
15 Wu, *supra*, note 845 at 253.
16 Howard Rheingold, *Virtual Communities – Homesteading on the Electronic Frontier* (Cambridge, MA: MIT Press, 2000) at 26–27.
17 Foer, *supra*, note 269 at 13.
18 Stewart Brand, *The Media Lab: Inventing the Future at M. I. T* (London: Penguin Books, 1989) at 24.
19 Foer, *supra*, note 269 at 19.

(DARPA) – the precursor to the Internet. Linklater wrote that 'life will be happier for the on-line individual because the people with whom one interacts most strongly will be selected more by commonality of interests and goals than by accidents of proximity'.[20] As such, these digital communities could become the agorae of modern life and empower individuals to be more open, expressive and free.

Spiritual prophecies about the revolutionary potential of technologies, and the underlying manifesto they preached – which saw technology as a tool of liberation and collaboration – have been echoed by leading technology firms ever since. The spirit of egalitarianism and openness imbued within hippie culture are still apparent in the fact that big tech leaders typically eschew corner offices, preferring to sit amongst their staff in open spaces wearing the same T-shirts and jeans as those who are far beneath them on the pay grid.[21] And by and large, they continue to view themselves as powerful agents of change – liberating the masses and creating new places where communities can flourish in a new era of openness and cooperation.

Another powerful metaphor that was popular in the early days of online communities depicted the first inhabitants of cyberspace as venturing into a new electronic frontier. For instance, in the early to mid-1990s, John Perry Barlow wrote a number of columns in *Wired* magazine in which he maintained that cyberspace is an independent 'frontier' with its own rules and norms and that it would be impossible for any government to regulate it.

Like Brand, Barlow was not your stereotypical computer geek. He worked as a cattle rancher in Wyoming and also wrote lyrics for the Grateful Dead. He was the first person to use William Gibson's science fiction term *cyberspace* to describe this innovative domain.[22] Like Brand, he channelled the spiritual yearnings of his generation into musings about cyberspace; and he came off as a radical individualist who didn't care much for powerful institutions.

The hacker credo, 'information wants to be free', was a battle cry for the liberation of the Internet. These sentiments undoubtedly inspired many who designed significant social projects – without any expectation of profit – such as Linux, Wikipedia and the Creative Commons.[23] Paradoxically, they've also been trumpeted by powerful tech giants like Facebook. For example, if you walk through Facebook's headquarters in Menlo Park, California, you'll find a two-storey mural – it looks like a massive totem pole filled with abstract shapes, and in the middle, there's a single word: *hack*.[24]

Yet if we assume that information is 'disembodied' – that it floats freely through digital networks, unaffected by social, legal, political and cultural

20 Rheingold, *supra*, note 848 at 9.
21 Foer, *supra*, note 269 at 20.
22 'Cyberspace' is the term first used by William Gibson in his 1984 novel *Neuromancer*.
23 Foer, *supra*, note 269 at 26.
24 Robert McMillan, 'A 125-Year-Old Letter Dives into the True Meaning of the Word *Hack*', *Slate*, 29 January 2015.

contexts – much is overlooked.[25] The general decline of face-to-face relationships that networked technologies promote has actually led to a demand for more 'tokens of trust' – in the form of social insurance numbers, PINs, barcodes, photo IDs and increasingly, biometrics.[26] Thus, in the modern state, networked communications are increasingly dependent upon data that is said to be 'about me'.[27]

The comparison of data from different sources is now routinized, as we leave traces of our data behind whenever we engage in the routine transactions of modern society.[28] David Lyon has thus suggested that surveillance systems 'bring back' disappearing bodies, by making them visible to organizations, agencies and authorities: '[t]he existence of contemporary surveillance systems in a sense reconnects bodily persons with data about them, by constituting them as high-value consumers, terror suspects, loan defaulters, free-flight eligibles or whatever'.[29]

Another, more practical, reason for the perceived lack of control in cyberspace owes itself to the free-market optimism that animated so much thinking about the Internet, information law and policy. From the beginning, there was intense worry about the risks of state intervention and coercion, combined with astonishing inattentiveness to the ramifications of what might happen if the Internet pioneers were left alone to accumulate enormous amounts of power and wealth.[30] Much of the credit for the economic boom during the mid-to-late 1990s was attributed to e-commerce and new opportunities for selling and delivering goods and services online.[31] The idea was to let the market be free and unencumbered by government regulation that might have the effect of stifling innovation and creativity.[32]

Various calls for intervention and regulation sparked intense criticism; and the primary idea for a policy solution was simply that of 'self-regulation'. The theory was that if privacy is important to consumers, online organizations would respond and provide protection. In essence, the market would police itself and outside regulation would not be necessary. Yet the online world does not represent a perfect market; and vast power and information asymmetries need to be corrected. Nevertheless, concerns about stifling market and technological innovation trumped concerns about the commodification and misuse of personal information.

Yet the idea of the Internet as a true marketplace of ideas, or even a confessional corner, was actually quite vulnerable. The institutional forces that

25 Lyon, *supra*, note 142 at 506–507.
26 Lyon, *supra*, note 41 at 36.
27 Lyon, *supra*, note 142 at 507.
28 Bennett, *supra*, note 756 at 52.
29 *Ibid.*
30 Cohen *supra*, note 219 at 1930.
31 Priscilla Regan, 'Privacy and Commercial Use of Personal Data: Policy Developments in the United States', (2003) 11(1) *Journal of Contingencies and Crisis Management* 12 at 14.
32 *Ibid.*

ultimately overcame this utopian dream came from the Internet itself – there was nothing about its code that would keep it free, open and non-commercial forever.[33] And far from creating a practical manifestation of the counterculture's ideals, massive amounts of effort and resources have been directed towards replicating the world as it is and perpetuating its social, political and economic ills, rather than remedying it for the better.

In hindsight, we can see the first generation of Internet nomads as similar to the beatnik backpackers who set up little huts on the beach and celebrated the hidden paradise they discovered.[34] Yet once commercialization took hold – like a mega-resort storming into a tropical nirvana – online businesses came to regard the collection and exchange of user data as a legitimate interest in itself.[35] Over time, this business model proved to be enormously successful. Before long, one company – Google – became the source of all knowledge; another – Facebook – became the portal to all social connections; and a third – Amazon – became Earth's biggest store.[36]

Make no mistake about it, we're not the customers of these big tech giants; we're the product they sell to their real customers – Fortune 500 companies. This hidden marketing agenda was bluntly revealed in an open letter to customers by Apple's CEO Tim Cook in 2014, '…when an online service is free, you're not the customer. You're the product'.[37] Indeed, we are little more than 'tenant farmers' for the big tech companies, 'working their land by producing data that they in turn sell for a profit'.[38]

Facebook has invested a lot of money in developing metrics to convince its advertisers that their ads are valuable because even when users aren't clicking on them, they're seeing the product content.[39] It also allows advertisers to create their own pages, and to buy space in users' newsfeeds; and with the 'like' button feature, users can freely promote and endorse products to their friends.[40] More sneakily, Facebook's heavy investment in tracking technologies enables it to follow users around the Web and report back to their advertisers – 'she's looking at airline tickets' – which allows, for example, US Airways to bombard the user with targeted ads on Facebook advertising airfares and perhaps, even a free upgrade on her newsfeed.[41]

Largely unbeknownst to the general public, Facebook has become extremely rich from this business model, by which it cleverly mines and exploits the

33 Wu, *supra*, note 845 at 275.
34 Wu, *supra*, note 845 at 275.
35 Regan, *supra*, note 863 at 14.
36 Foer, *supra*, note 269 at 28.
37 Avi Selk, 'Apple's Tim Cook: I Would Have Avoided Facebook's Privacy Mess', *The Washington Post*, 29 March 2018.
38 Bruce Schneier, 'How We Sold Our Souls—and More—to the Internet Giants', *The Guardian*, 17 May 2015.
39 Wu, *supra*, note 845 at 300.
40 Wu, *supra*, note 845 at 300.
41 Wu, *supra*, note 845 at 300.

enormous trove of demographic data its users have given it free access to. To illustrate: in its 2017 annual financial report, Facebook revealed, 'We generate substantially all of our revenue from selling advertising placements to marketers'.[42] In fact, $39.94 billion of Facebook's $40.65 billion in total revenue — 98 percent — came from ads.

The profit-making power now held by tech giants like Facebook and Google is what keeps fierce corporate rivalry at bay – start-ups, for example, no longer aspire to displace these companies, but launch with the hope of getting bought up by the few goliaths in the marketplace.[43] Indeed, Facebook bought the five-year old, 50-employee instant messaging firm WhatsApp for a whopping 20 billion USD.[44] It also owns Instagram; and Instagram, WhatsApp and Facebook are three of the five platforms that accumulated 100 million users the fastest.[45] Apart from family, work and sleep, people spend more time on these platforms than any other activity.[46]

Facebook's motto, which is flaunted on its homepage, is that it is 'Free and Always Will Be'. Yet CEO Mark Zuckerberg has also recently disclosed that Facebook may not always be free. In his congressional testimony in April 2018, he stated that 'there will always be a version of Facebook that is free'.[47] Similarly, Facebook's chief operating officer, Sheryl Sandberg, recently told NBC that an ad-free version of the social network 'would be a paid product'.[48] This suggests that Facebook executives have thought about the future of a subscription-based service that allows users to opt out of advertisements — for a fee, with billions of dollars riding on it.

Facebook currently has two billion users, who spend on average 30 minutes per day using the service;[49] if it charged as little as $1 per hour, it could nearly double its current worth of $420 billion in a single year. Nevertheless, these admissions, made during recent investigations into Facebook's poor information-sharing and data-management practices, belie the company's self-image as an instrument for social good, promoting openness, freedom, and ease of access.

The importance of free and open networks, which appealed to many in the early days of the digital revolution, has clearly been flaunted by companies like Google and Facebook, which are subject to little regulation or market competition.[50] Hidden within this agenda – of making information freely accessible to everyone – was always a price: the collection of our personal data

42 Callum Borchers, 'Would You Pay $18.75 for Ad-Free Facebook?' *The Washington Post*, 14 April 2018.
43 Foer, *supra*, note 269 at 31.
44 Galloway, *supra*, note 837 at 7.
45 *Ibid.* at 96.
46 *Ibid.*
47 Borchers, *supra*, note 874.
48 *Ibid.*
49 Galloway, *supra*, note 837 at 96.
50 Schneier, *supra*, note 32 at 60.

in increasingly aggressive yet covert ways.[51] Like the narrative in the film *The Circle*, discussed in Chapter 3, these companies have made billions of dollars promoting the idea that transparency is an inherent good, and conversely, that secrets are intrinsically bad; yet this only extends to their user base, not to themselves. As Cory Doctorow observed: '...if it's a bargain, it's a curious, one-sided arrangement'.[52]

Cyberspace has become one of the most centralized mediums on the planet. The big tech companies that power most of the online content – Google, Amazon, Facebook and Apple – are the most powerful gatekeepers the world has ever known.[53] Indeed, 62 per cent of Americans get their news from social media – primarily from Facebook; and a third of all traffic to media sites flows through Google.[54] Of course, we lavishly reward entrepreneurship in tech culture. We elevate the executives running these companies to hero- or even God-like status. Yet it's far more than just 'entrepreneurship' at work here. We have long celebrated extremely powerful and wealthy companies, like Facebook and Google, and allowed them to become larger, richer and more powerful, without any competition or alternative for consumers.

How did this happen? The collection of user data didn't begin with Google or Facebook; in fact, it pre-dates the development of both platforms entirely. First introduced in Netscape Navigator 1.1 in 1995, cookies made it possible for servers to keep track of users' activities in ways that enabled e-commerce and soon led to targeted advertising.[55] Banner ads débuted the same month as the cookie; and although they were touted as helping to 'tailor advertising more closely to what consumers want', there were no features allowing users to modify their preferences, much less block them altogether.[56] Nevertheless, unlike the blogs and other open and creative spaces that were popular in the early days of the Internet, users channelled their energy into upgrading the value of these commercially driven platforms.[57]

By 2010, The *Wall Street Journal* reported that the 50 most-visited sites on the Internet placed more than 3,000 tracking files on users' computers, making it possible for them to track users on pages belonging to other sites and more generally, as they flitted their way across the Web.[58] This was only the beginning of the advertising business model that has become essential to the growth and shape of the Internet, and the origins of the commercial surveillance infrastructure as we now know it. Over time, through the covert technique of

51 Sarah Myers West, 'Data Capitalism: Redefining the Logics of Surveillance and Privacy', (2017) 00(0) *Business & Society* 1 at 17.
52 Cory Doctorow, 'The Curious Case of Internet Privacy', *Technology Review*, July/August 2012.
53 Foer, *supra*, note 269 at 5.
54 Foer, *supra*, note 269 at 6.
55 West, *supra*, note 883 at 8.
56 *Ibid.*
57 Wu, *supra*, note 845 at 301.
58 West, *supra*, note 883 at 9.

'attention arbitrage', the monopolists consolidated their power and influence, while rewarding us enough to keep us hooked.[59]

Of course, marketers have long been interested in siphoning data about consumers and using it to make predictions about their choices and behaviour – with the hope of eventually influencing them. The growth in the use of customer surveys and polls in the 1950s and '60s was used to render the post-war consumer understandable to researchers, political pollsters and marketers. By the 1980s, the means used to collect data about consumers shifted to the recording of credit card purchases and telephone calls.[60]

In the commercial world of the 1990s, an important change took place in the collection and use of consumer data. No longer content with survey-style data on existing customers, the goal was to find mathematical models that could identify the unknown individual – the as-yet-unencountered consumer who could be targeted.[61] Thus, the modes of identification deployed within marketing schemes and proposals – as well as in biometric identifiers, data mining and social network analysis – have less in common with historical schemes than they do with mathematical models used to identify people in other spheres.

Social media platforms are merely the latest source of insight to inform customer profiling. Awareness gleaned from user data is used to sell advertising space on their platforms, which allows marketers to locate and influence newer – and more narrowly targeted – audiences based on knowledge of their online transactions and associated patterns of behaviour.

Mass surveillance, data harvesting and targeted marketing

In recent years, greater numbers of people throughout the world have been getting on to the Internet. Thus, the idea that people will be shut out of this space simply because they can't get connected is less and less true. This is happening because governments, as well as the private sector, have encouraged participation by gradually increasing the ease of access, as well as the speed and mode of delivery, while creating the opportunity for more and more to be accomplished by electronic means.[62] People in remote villages are becoming increasingly connected, helped by rapidly diminishing technology prices. And in technically advanced societies, it is now common for large segments of the population to seamlessly engage in electronically networked interactions across all sectors of society.

We used to think of our online and offline personas separately – but they're not any more. Anyone who's online contributes a lot more data about who they are, what they like, where they shop and travel than they used to only a decade

59 Wu, *supra*, note 845 at 301.
60 West, *supra*, note 883 at 6.
61 Amoore, *supra*, note 167 at 25.
62 Nissenbaum, *supra*, note 218 at 562.

or so ago. And as we have seen, the services that collect this data are primarily driven by advertising models – they're targeting us based on the data we're freely providing every day. As the previous section showed, third-party advertising and user-tracking technologies were implemented relatively early on and became part of an industry ecosystem that increasingly treats data as a commodity to be bought, sold and shared.

As technologies progressed, those involved in the collection and aggregation of data gained increasing leverage in their ability to track users, generate profiles about them, cross-reference data with other information about them and sell it to others. Now, most of our electronic clicks, taps and swipes are captured and recorded by someone. Indeed, nearly every mundane aspect of our lives today produces a digital trace – communicating with friends and family, ordering books, buying groceries, going to work, and so on.[63] This data is then easily combined with other information from the digital or physical world.

Thus, it is now commonplace for information deemed not to be 'sensitive' to be freely compiled, transmitted and exchanged. Even data about the seemingly trivial aspects of our lives (e.g. pizza orders) has become a valuable commodity and can easily be fed into algorithms and used to predict our behaviour in lucrative ways. These practices provide the means for advertisers to reach, target and manipulate their audience.[64] For many, this comes as a major source of privacy invasion; yet because the data is eagerly shared, people are in many cases complicit in the desecration of their own confidentiality.[65]

Indeed, the aggregation of information may provide insight into an individual's behaviour, social relationships, private preferences and identity that go beyond even that obtained by accessing the content of a private communication. This data, taken as a whole, may allow very precise conclusions to be drawn about the private lives of the persons whose data has been retained. The General Assembly of the United Nations expressed similar concerns:

> [A] reality of big data is that once data is collected, it can be very difficult to keep anonymous...focusing on controlling the collection and retention of personal data, while important, may no longer be sufficient to protect personal privacy...big data enables new, non-obvious, unexpectedly powerful uses of data.[66]

Institutions in both the public and private sectors, including law-enforcement, financial, political and marketing, either take advantage of compiled data directly, or buy products from others who specialize in gathering data and organizing it

63 West, *supra*, note 883 at 2.
64 Nissenbaum, *supra*, note 218 at 590.
65 Nissenbaum, *supra*, note 218 at 565.
66 Official Records of the General Assembly, *Forty-third Session*, *Supplement No. 40* (A/43/40), annex VI, para.8.

into useful and lucrative forms.[67] For example, as an international data aggregator, Acxiom collects personal information about people from various sources, then sells it to corporations and political groups that use it for marketing and campaigning.

The information that Acxiom collects is extremely diverse and includes criteria such as: marital status; family status; ethnicity; home value; what you read; the type of car you drive; what you order over the phone or Internet; where you vacation; your hobbies; any history of mental illness you might have; patterns of alcohol consumption, and more.[68] The practice of data aggregation has a high degree of concentration around two other companies – Google and Facebook.[69] Together, they own the ten most-loaded third-party domains that appear on the million most-visited websites.[70] Thus, they play an extremely significant role in the data-tracking ecosystem.

Two factors underlie this trend: the rapid development of information technology coupled with an insatiable desire to know – 'whatever may be useful to someone, somewhere, or what may become so in the future'.[71] This practice has come to be known as 'data capitalism' – a system in which 'the commoditization of our data enables an asymmetric redistribution of power that is weighted towards the actors who have access and the capability to make sense of information'.[72] As global tech giants like Google and Facebook expanded their reach across the Internet to mine, repurpose and monetize data, they have created giant networks of surveillance and tracking, which feed into localized centres of control.[73]

The real genius behind this system is that they have convinced their customers that they are engaging in social rather than purely economic activity – or, at the very least, the two have become so blurred that it's nearly impossible to distinguish one from the other. Indeed, the targeting for commercial ends is done person by person, so it's quite easy for polarizing messages to be widely distributed and masked at the same time. New algorithms let the data infer things about us we've never disclosed. So, I may have never talked about my politics or religious beliefs online, but the things I like or the pages I visit can be used to infer my politics or my religious beliefs. The number of inferences that can be made from the data we reveal is very powerful and can be used to profile us in all sorts of ways.

On Facebook, for example, data about our preferences can be used to come up with personality and psychographic profiles. Facebook obviously collects all the data you freely give them: your political affiliation, your workplace, relationship

67 Nissenbaum, *supra*, note 218 at 587.
68 Bennett et al., *supra*, note 276 at 20.
69 West, *supra*, note 883 at 12.
70 *Ibid.*
71 Nissenbaum, *supra*, note 218 at 592.
72 West, *supra*, note 883 at 4.
73 West, *supra*, note 883 at 13.

status, favourite films and books, places you've checked in, comments you've made, photos you've shared, friends, and any and all reactions to posts. Yet, Facebook data collection actually begins before you post it – as you are crafting your message, it collects your keystrokes.[74]

This means that if you posted something like, 'I *HATE* my boss. He's such a jerk', and at the last minute baulked and wrote something like, 'Work is annoying right now', Facebook would still keep track of what you typed before you hit 'delete'.[75] Facebook keeps track of the metadata, or the data about your data. Since Facebook has so many systems and so many places where data can commingle, these connections constitute a powerful tool for understanding people, influencing their behaviour and even manipulating them. Those who are not fully aware of this are 'more easily targeted or manipulated'.[76]

The newsfeed provides a reverse chronological index of all the status updates, articles and photos that your friends have posted on Facebook. The newsfeed is meant to solve the problem of our growing inability to sift through masses of information; thus, it has been turned into a 'personalized newspaper' for users.[77] In other words, Facebook's algorithms interpret 'more than one hundred thousand signals' and sort the information, deciding what we might like to read.[78] Many users – as many as 60 per cent – are apparently completely unaware of this practice.[79]

Yet the harvesters of information are keenly aware of the qualitative shift that can occur when bits of data revealed in one context are shifted to another and compiled into profiles. At times, the shift may cross not only contextual lines but also temporal lines as information collected in the past is introduced into a current setting.[80] So the data may be willingly disclosed in 2015, but predicting what the implications of that might be down the track – say, in 2019 – can be very difficult for the individual.

Indeed, data brokers often act in ways that mask the sources of their data, including buying and combining information from other brokers, thereby making it extremely difficult for consumers to retrace the paths through which their data was collected.[81] Thus, once the data is freely handed over, its potential use is virtually limitless and consent is un-revocable. Given the uncertainty around technological developments in the future, this should make us extremely nervous. People generally resent the rampant and unauthorized distribution of information about themselves, not only when they violate the integrity of an

74 Vicki Boykis, 'What Should You Think About When Using Facebook?' 1 February 2017, Available online at: http://veekaybee.github.io/2017/02/01/facebook-is-collecting-this/.

75 *Ibid.*

76 Nissenbaum, *supra*, note 218 at 592.

77 Foer, *supra*, note 269 at 72.

78 *Ibid.* at 73.

79 *Ibid.*

80 Nissenbaum, *supra*, note 218 at 585.

81 West, *supra*, note 883 at 12.

intimate and highly personal sphere, but when they violate contextual and temporal integrity.[82]

Tech companies' heavy investments in AI are already changing our lives and gadgets and paving the way towards a more AI-focused future. Call centres, for example, have long been at the forefront of changes in labour and technology.[83] Beginning in the 1980s, a steady stream of US companies outsourced this function to countries such as India and the Philippines. More recently, voice-recognition technology has been laying the groundwork for the automation of simple tasks that once required a human on both ends, like checking a bank balance or confirming a medical appointment.[84] As you might expect, making these digital operatives more productive means that there's less work for real people to do.

Now, so-called empathy AIs are the latest thing in customer service – they're like empathy coaches for these workers, helping them become more considerate and efficient. Recently, Met Life started trying out a digital assistant called Cogito, which listens in on phone calls between clients and customer-service reps.[85] It presents a cheery notification when it detects tension or fatigue in a worker's voice. It also signals to the rep when it detects client emotions – when call agents see a heart icon, they know the software has detected a heightened emotional state, either positive or negative.[86] When tone and language suggest a caller is getting worked up, employees see a suggestion to 'calm down' and a list of soothing talking points. If a worker omits a legally required disclaimer, the system sends a reminder. In addition to nudging call agents to liven up their tone, or respond to distress in a caller's voice, Cogito's software also listens to the pace and pattern of calls.[87]

Big tech companies such as Google, Microsoft and Amazon have been enthusiastically using new advances in AI to strengthen their central business model of targeting ads or predicting your next purchase. But for many others, powerful AI has the potential to create new problems. Does technology that 'reads' human emotions erode our trust in what we think, see and hear? Does Met Life have an obligation to tell people they're being monitored by an AI? And is this another example of tech privilege, where consumers in wealthy parts of the world can rely on machines to ensure improved customer service – and where those receiving the calls (most likely low-paid service workers, often in the developing world) have to obey the commands of a faceless robot?

Secret eavesdropping by corporate, emotionally aware software may bother consumers, even those accustomed to being watched by cameras and online tracking. These technologies could also be used in shops – imagine waiting in line and something monitoring your behaviour and facial expression says, 'would you like some ice cream today? You look sad' – or maybe it won't even

82 Nissenbaum, *supra*, note 218 at 586.
83 Tom Simonite, 'This Call May be Monitored for Tone and Emotion', *Wired*, 19 March 2018.
84 *Ibid.*
85 *Ibid.*
86 *Ibid.*
87 *Ibid.*

admit that it knows you look sad. It's invisible, it doesn't require permission, and it can be used anywhere, at any time. From the perspective of the data-gatherers and marketers, this capability is one of the most exciting advances that information technology enables.

For many consumers, the ease of convenience and the disguise of benevolence provided by these systems keeps us lulled into complacency. The customer in the supermarket might happily say to herself, 'Ooh, I love it when the store reminds me to buy ice cream – it's just what I need tonight', without stopping to consider why these suggestions are being made to her in particular. In fact, technology now permits the store to keep a precise record of all of its customers' purchases and to correlate it with demographic information about them. They have the power to know everything, from our specific brand-name preferences for cereal to the probability that a particular family will buy frozen pizza on a Friday.

This commercially driven intrusion has not yet reached Orwellian heights; however, information technology has the capacity to erode many of our normative expectations about privacy and autonomy. There's the ominous, threatening surveillance state depicted in George Orwell's *1984*. Then again, there's the profligate pleasure dome in Aldous Huxley's *Brave New World*. What if both these dystopias came together to form our reality – surveillance disguised as self-gratification rather than punishment?[88]

Facebook is popular because it helps billions of people fill a void and connect with others in the otherwise vacuous online space. These seemingly benevolent technologies have become tightly integrated into the fabric of our societies – just as Orwell and Huxley predicted. Facebook, for its part, has become our online living-room: it's the place where we chat with friends, hold forth about the news, organize events, grieve over things we've lost, celebrate babies, pets, engagements, new jobs, new shoes and vacations.

While they promise to be helpful and even thoughtful, the pervasive power and persistence of advertising platforms embraced by tech giants like Facebook has become downright creepy. Some ads now seem more like stalkers than helpful friends – if, say, you've been online searching for a new pair of jeans, now those same pants begin to follow you around the Web, prodding you to take another look and luring you with progressively better deals and rewards.[89] Thanks to artificial intelligence, we can now track behaviour at a level and on a scale previously unconceivable.[90]

Rhetorically, the big tech companies peddle individuality and empowerment of the user; but they really want to see their algorithms automating our way of life in exchange for vast catalogues of our intentions, motivations and aversions.[91] Those who are happy to see these monopolies assume greater influence in our lives may wish to consider the lessons provided by the ubiquitous

88 Zeynep Tufekci, 'Data Dystopia', *Technology Review*, July/August 2012 at 10.
89 Wu, *supra*, note 845 at 323.
90 Galloway, *supra*, note 837 at 196.
91 Foer, *supra*, note 269 at 323.

Chinese-developed smartphone app known as WeChat. It may inspire us to think more about the creepiness, sleaziness and rampant tracking that many of the apps – and the tech giants supporting them – force on their users.[92]

WeChat multi has been termed the 'everything app', and a 'super app', because of its virtually limitless range of functions and platforms. This is consistent with the unimaginably large aspirations of the other leading tech monopolies: Amazon prided itself on being the 'everything store' until it expanded into drones, television shows and cloud computing. Facebook, Microsoft and Apple now want to become our 'personal assistants'.[93]

Like WeChat, these companies are openly ambitious about their plans to wake us in the morning, guide us through the day with their access to our calendar, contacts, photos and diaries; and soothe us into the evening hours when we unthinkingly turn to them for news and entertainment, catching up with friends or organizing a night out on the town.[94] They aspire to systematize the decisions we make throughout every waking moment of our lives by suggesting the news we read, the friends we connect with, the goods we buy, the food we eat and where we travel.

While it's not widely known outside China, WeChat has over one billion active monthly users in the PRC. Users can pay bills, order takeaway food, connect with friends, find dates, book a doctor's appointment, transfer money, buy products and services, donate to charity, hold video conferences, hail taxis, and more.[95] WeChat also supports nearly 20 languages including English, Spanish, Hindi, Indonesian and Russian.[96]

WeChat's rapid expansion into nearly every aspect of life in China since its launch in 2013, which has coincided with the rise of China's middle class, is astonishing; but it also raises uncomfortable questions. Many concerns have been raised about its monopoly, or near-monopoly, throughout China – far more powerful than technology 'disruptors' like Google and Facebook have ever been. Overseas Chinese, or anyone with family or relationships in China, also tend to download the app to stay in contact, since American apps are banned there.[97]

Another concern is that WeChat operates within a country ruled under a dictatorial, one-party system that has little tolerance for dissenting opinions. Not surprisingly, as with the Internet in general, WeChat has a reputation for being heavily monitored in China. Government censors use algorithms that pick up sensitive words and banned topics, including Tibet, Falun Gong, 'Tiananmen June 4', pro-democracy, and more. It should come as no surprise that WeChat's astounding rise in China was supported by the censorship of foreign apps,

92 Wu, *supra*, note 845 at 324.

93 Foer, *supra*, note 269 at 2.

94 Foer, *supra*, note 269 at 2.

95 Shannon Liao, 'How WeChat Came to Rule China', *The Verge*, 1 February 2018.

96 SBS News, 'WeChat A New Chinese Empire?' Available online at: www.sbs.com.au/news/feature/wechat-new-chinese-empire.

97 Liao, *supra*, note 927.

government subsidies, and close integration with government agencies.[98] Convenience or no convenience – the potential for surveillance, data mining, profiling, aggregation and targeting embedded within this technology is seemingly endless.

Recently, those behind WeChat have been seeking to expand internationally, and they have poured money into such efforts in places like Indonesia and Brazil.[99] WeChat has also been looking to launch an office in the UK, alongside its existing presence in Italy.[100] It has also established an office in San Francisco and is looking to grow its WeChat team in the US, targeting advertisers and payment-providers there.

But those outside China are generally unaccustomed to the idea of a single one-stop-shop app for consumers – we tend to have separate apps for the various kinds of services and features that WeChat provides. Moreover, WeChat's parent company Tencent scored a zero out of 100 for WeChat's lack of freedom of speech protection and lack of end-to-end encryption in a 2016 Amnesty International report on user privacy.[101]

In early December of 2017, the Indian Government blacklisted WeChat; yet; Australia, which is a popular destination for Chinese tourists and students, has seen at least nine of its cross-border payment service providers partner with WeChat Pay to connect Australian merchants to Chinese consumers.[102] To date, WeChat has established partnerships with a growing number of overseas merchants with the ability to handle transactions in 13 different currencies in 25 countries and regions.[103]

On every continent, governments have used both formal legal instruments and covert methods to gain access to content, as well as to metadata. As telecommunications service provision shifts from the public sector to the private sector, there has been widespread delegation – in nations throughout the West – of law-enforcement responsibilities to Internet service providers and other intermediaries under the semblance of self-regulation or cooperation. Yet very few users in Australia, Europe, the US or elsewhere are likely to tolerate sweeping surveillance and censorship on an all-in-one mobile hub for almost every aspect of life such as this. It will be interesting to see how this works in the context of WeChat's proposed expansion internationally.

98 *Ibid.*

99 C. Custer, '3 Reasons WeChat Failed Internationally (and Most Other Chinese Apps Do Too)' *TechInAsia*, 26 May 2016. Available online at: www.techinasia.com/3-reasons-wechat-failed-internationally-chinese-apps.

100 Giles Turner and Lulu Yilun Chen, 'WeChat Expands in Europe in Bid for Global Advertisers, Payments', Bloomberg, 30 March 2017.

101 Liao, *supra*, note 927.

102 Meg Jing Zeng, 'Thinking of Taking up WeChat? Here's What You Need to Know', *The Conversation*, 18 December 2017.

103 Emma Lee, 'WeChat Pay Tries to Duplicate Domestic Success Overseas With Killer Recipe: Social Networking', *Technode*, 1 March 2018. Available online at: https://technode.com/2018/03/01/wechat-pay-social-networking/.

The issue of informed consent

Are people giving their consent for these 'free' apps and services? It has been suggested that the provision of personal information by consumers is part of a conscious process through which one voluntarily surrenders information about oneself and one's relationships in return for digital access to goods, services and information. Important questions have emerged, though, about the extent to which individuals are truly aware of what they are sharing, and to what potential uses their data will be put.

Why are individuals freely sharing so much on these social media platforms? In large part, it's because we're told to – or, we're not told not to. Indeed, for the majority of social media users, there is no informed consent – we're not told about the implications of ubiquitous sharing and the possibilities of what all this data can be used for. Rather, the commoditization of data is hidden behind popular narratives that extol the social and political benefits of ubiquitous networked technologies.

The narrative behind Facebook, which is celebrated repeatedly, is that it has a proprietary claim to and special insight into human social behaviour. It's thus the bridge to new kinds of human relationships, connections and communities. In reality, it's a social media firm that analyses data and sells it. This narrative is only quietly whispered in hushed tones.

Users are caught between the desire to protect their privacy and the need to maintain meaningful relationships with others in what has become a digitally enabled social reality. Public concerns about privacy, reflected in public-opinion surveys and voiced by a number of public-interest groups, are often discredited because individuals seem to behave as though privacy is not important.[104] Although people express concern about privacy, they routinely disclose personal information because of convenience, discounts and other incentives, or a lack of understanding of the consequences.

Newsfeed algorithms reinforce certain kinds of behaviour and keep us in a feedback loop of positive and negative rewards. Positive feedback comes from friends who 'like' your posts; negative reinforcement comes when you get only a few responses to a personal disclosure, prompting you to question your self-worth and aim harder to please. Behavioural scientists call this 'intermittent reinforcement'; and it's one of the most powerful performance-modifying techniques out there.[105] For Facebook, there's nothing particularly clever or inventive about this business model – it's merely exploiting the dynamics of acceptance and rejection, buttressing deep-rooted insecurities and the sophomoric desire to be in the 'cool crowd'.[106]

Facebook, and its subsidiary Instagram, have also cleverly taken hold of consumer awareness – a driving force behind what influences us to spend money.[107]

104 Regan, *supra*, note 863 at 12.
105 Doctorow, *supra*, note 884 at 66.
106 Wu, *supra*, note 845 at 291.
107 Galloway, *supra*, note 837 at 97.

Not only are these platforms mining our preferences and choices, they're also cultivating our interests and desires. A friend posts an image of him/herself wearing J. Crew sandals in Barcelona and suddenly you want to 'own' that picture-perfect experience too.[108] In this way, Facebook influences our awareness and intentions better than any promotion or advertising conduit otherwise might.[109] It relies on the self-promotion of our friends. And by encouraging users to 'like' their brands, its advertisers accumulate enormous branded communities and generate millions upon millions of dollars' worth of free advertising. They also have the skills to leverage software and AI to detect patterns and improve their sales pitches, as well as their offerings.

A wake-up call

In 2014, Cambridge Analytica, a London-based firm that specializes in using online data to create voter personality profiles in order to target users with political messages, put out a request on Amazon's 'Mechanical Turk' platform, a global Internet marketplace enabling individuals and businesses to meet and coordinate the performance of various tasks.[110] Cambridge Analytica was seeking people who were Facebook users in the United States. It offered to pay them to download and use a personality quiz on Facebook called 'thisisyourdigitallife'.[111]

About 270,000 Facebook users responded and downloaded the app.[112] At the time, Facebook allowed app developers to access not only user data but the data of their friends. Thus, the app acquired information from these users' Facebook profiles, as well as detailed information from their friends' profiles, resulting in about 50 million Facebook profiles accessed.[113] Most of those people had no inkling that their data was harvested – they hadn't installed the app themselves.[114] Meanwhile, Cambridge Analytica began working for the Trump campaign in June 2016 and it promised that its 'psychographic' profiles could predict the personality and political leanings of every adult in the United States.[115] It also used micro-targeting to serve up pro-Trump messages that resonated with specific voters.[116]

In mid-March 2018, this scandal was exposed by *The New York Times* and the London *Observer.* Facebook made a public announcement that it was suspending Cambridge Analytica and fervently denied that this was a 'data breach'. Paul Grewal, a vice president and deputy general counsel at Facebook, wrote

108 Galloway, *supra*, note 837 at 98.
109 Galloway, *supra*, note 837 at 98.
110 Zeynep Tufekci, 'Facebook's Surveillance Machine', *The New York Times*, 19 March 2018.
111 *Ibid.*
112 *Ibid.*
113 *Ibid.*
114 *Ibid.*
115 Elizabeth Dwoskin, 'Facebook Bans Trump Campaign's Data Analytics Firm for Taking User Data', *The Washington Post*, 16 March 2018.
116 Galloway, *supra*, note 837 at 106.

that 'the claim that this is a data breach is completely false'.[117] He insisted that Facebook users 'knowingly provided their information, no systems were infiltrated, and no passwords or sensitive pieces of information were stolen or hacked'.[118] He also said that 'everyone involved gave their consent'.[119]

In her *New York Times* opinion piece on this situation, Zeynep Tufekci, an associate professor at the School of Information and Library Science at the University of North Carolina, stated:

> This wasn't a breach in the *technical* sense. It is something even more troubling: an all-too-natural consequence of Facebook's business model, which involves having people go to the site for social interaction, only to be quietly subjected to an enormous level of surveillance. The results of that surveillance are used to fuel a sophisticated and opaque system for narrowly targeting advertisements and other wares to Facebook's users. Facebook makes money, in other words, by profiling us and then selling our attention to advertisers, political actors and others. These are Facebook's true customers, whom it works hard to please.[120]

We have seen that Facebook doesn't just record every one of its users' movements on its site, it also collects their Web browsing histories, which it then sells for a substantial profit. Facebook has also recently acknowledged that it collects data – termed 'shadow profiles' – from people who don't even have a Facebook account.[121] Here's how this works: when people traverse the Internet, their Web browsers (e.g. Safari, Chrome or Firefox) send requests to the servers of various websites.[122] The browser then shares the user's IP address with the site, so it knows where to send content, as well as other information, like the type of operating system used (e.g. Windows or Android), and so on.[123]

In return, the website sends information back to the browser: content from the site and instructions for the browser to send a request to the other companies providing content or services on the site.[124] So, when a website uses one of Facebook's services, the browser also sends it the same information, including information about which website or app is being used by the individual.[125] Facebook collects that data on everyone who visits these sites, whether or not

117 Tufekci, *supra*, note 942.
118 *Ibid.*
119 *Ibid.*
120 *Ibid.*
121 Kurt Wagner, 'This is How Facebook Collects Data on You Even if You Don't Have an Account', *Recode*, 20 April 2018.
122 David Baser, 'Hard Questions: What Data Does Facebook Collect When I'm Not Using Facebook, and Why?' 16 April 2018. Available online at: https://newsroom.fb.com/news/2018/04/data-off-facebook/.
123 *Ibid.*
124 *Ibid.*
125 *Ibid.*

they're registered Facebook users. It can then use that information, which includes the individual's IP address, to show them ads encouraging them to join Facebook.[126] Some of the browsing data is also used for analytics, which means that web and app developers pay Facebook to tell them how many people visit their site.[127] Facebook also tracks non-users with the 'Like' button, which appears on apps and websites outside Facebook and allows people to indicate whether they're interested in a brand, product or digital content.[128]

The other crucial way Facebook gets information from non-users is from its contact upload feature.[129] When people sign up for Facebook, many of them choose to upload their contacts so that they can find other people to connect with. Depending on how thorough people are with recording information about their contacts, this data could include a lot more than just a phone number.[130] Given the confusing and fast-changing nature of what data may reveal and how it may be used, consent to this ongoing and extensive data collection can be neither fully informed nor consensual – especially since it is practically irrevocable.[131] Indeed, how could someone revoke their consent when they have no idea that their data's being mined in the first place?

In 2015, Facebook removed the app and demanded guarantees from Cambridge Analytica that the information had been destroyed.[132] The company certified to Facebook that they had done so, but Facebook said it received reports in March 2018 that the data was not deleted.[133] Never mind the fact that the information was used to shape voter targeting and messaging for President Trump's 2016 election campaign!

For its part, Facebook is under significant pressure to limit and be more transparent about how political operatives use its platform. Russian agents abused the company's networks to target millions of American voters with 'fake news' during the 2016 election campaign.[134] On 10 May 2018, House Intelligence Committee Democrats published downloadable files with more than 3,500 ads to their website.[135] These are Facebook ads that were purchased by the Internet Research Agency (the 'IRA'), a Kremlin-backed 'online troll farm', both before and after the 2016 presidential election.[136] The Trump campaign also made significant use of Facebook, and the social network has been criticized for having

126 Wagner, *supra*, note 953.
127 *Ibid.*
128 Simonite, *supra*, note 915.
129 Wagner, *supra*, note 943.
130 Ibid.
131 Tufekci, *supra*, note 942.
132 Dwoskin, *supra*, note 947.
133 *Ibid.*
134 *Ibid.*
135 Kurt Wagner, 'Congress Just Published All the Russian Facebook Ads Used to Try and Influence the 2016 Election', *Recode*, 10 May 2018.
136 *Ibid.*

its employees connect with Trump campaign staffers – yet Facebook has said that this was merely standard practice for large political and corporate donors.[137]

In February 2018, Special Counsel Robert Mueller indicted 13 Russian individuals linked to the IRA.[138] The indictment claims the IRA 'engaged in operations to interfere in elections and political processes', adding that the group 'posted derogatory information about a number of candidates'.[139] Clearly, Facebook was a crucial instrument for carrying out these efforts. In fact, the IRA bought thousands of ads and posted tens of thousands of other posts, promoting both sides of such contentious political issues as gun control and race relations.[140]

Since these revelations, the public and governments are finally waking up and talking about the fact that the consolidation of power in a few giant tech companies has gotten worse. In early April 2018, Facebook CEO Mark Zuckerberg appeared in front of almost half of the United States Senate. He answered questions about Facebook's data protection and privacy practices from nearly 100 different politicians in nearly ten hours of public testimony – the first real public debate about the rampant data sharing that has been allowed to continue unabated for more than a decade.

The idea that Facebook is a monopoly was raised multiple times that week. When asked who Facebook's biggest competition is, Zuckerberg didn't have much of an answer.[141] Clearly, Google competes with Facebook for advertisement dollars, and there are other social services out there – primarily Twitter – but nobody comes anywhere close to matching the size and number of services that Facebook (which also owns Instagram, WhatsApp and Messenger) provides.[142]

Some people think Facebook has grown so big that the government should break the company up. Zuckerberg has argued that breaking up Facebook would be bad for America because it would pave the way for Chinese tech companies — which don't have traditional American values – to step in and dominate: 'there are plenty of other companies out there that are willing and able to take the place of the work that we're doing', he said, pointing to Chinese tech companies, '[a]nd they do not share the values that we have'.[143] It's a ridiculous assertion in response to allegations that Facebook could have swayed the US presidential election. Furthermore, Facebook doesn't operate in China: the social network is banned there, and has been for years, which has enabled competitors – like WeChat – to thrive.[144]

137 Dwoskin, *supra*, note 947.
138 Wagner, *supra*, note 967.
139 *Ibid.*
140 *Ibid.*
141 *Ibid.*
142 *Ibid.*
143 Kurt Wagner, 'Mark Zuckerberg Says Breaking Up Facebook Would Pave the Way for China's Tech Companies to Dominate', *Recode*, 18 July 2018.
144 *Ibid.*

Where to next?

As discussed in Chapter 3, traditional privacy definitions elicit policy options that focus primarily on giving individuals 'rights of control' based largely on the thinking of Warren and Brandeis and liberal democratic notions of the right of the individual to be free from 'invasions' by the state. Yet the scale and scope of the problems now exist at a systemic level – institutions, social practices, fabric of modern life – not at the level of individual, private space. Thus, the solution must focus on the way social and institutional relationships are structured, understood, and performed.

Traditional data-protection principles, which have been wholeheartedly embraced by liberal democratic nations throughout Europe and in Canada, are based around fair information practices developed in response to concerns raised about privacy, particularly user 'consent'. The concept of consent has long been important in liberal political thought (i.e. the consent of the governed), as well as in contractual settings (i.e. informed consent to medical treatment).[145] Yet consent implies an affirmative agreement of the individual to engage in the activity in question; and it also implies that the individual has an understanding of the implications of what is being consented to.[146] The concept of consent is therefore too narrow to address the problem, especially since tech giants have long hidden their business models from their users; and consumers, for their part, mostly don't understand the risks involved when they freely give so much of their personal data away.

As with the earlier discussion of privacy, when it comes to data protection principles, there appears to be an over-reliance on liberal political thought.[147] Indeed, the entire data-protection framework is dominated by an emphasis on *personally* identifiable information. On the one hand, we grant agencies the power to collect information on individuals; on the other, we create protections against abuse of the same.[148] Yet the underlying framework rests on liberal theory: rights act as entitlements held by autonomous individuals, who themselves have the capacity for rational thought.[149]

Yet there is another aspect to privacy that can be useful here. Within democratic systems, where accountability is expected and valued, justifications are required for abuses of power. In the surveillance context, privacy provides one of the crucial values to constrain the abuse of power; and accordingly, it provides a basis for setting limits on its exercise.[150] This approach is ideally suited to the modern era, whereby people feel that they have lost all control over information about themselves and do not trust organizations to protect their privacy.

145 Regan, *supra*, note 863 at 15.
146 *Ibid.*
147 Donohue, *supra*, note 209 at 556.
148 Donohue, *supra*, note 209 at 557.
149 Donohue, *Ibid.*
150 Regan, *supra*, note 863 at 15.

Privacy regulators operating within limited spheres of statutory authority have embraced this task with enthusiasm.[151] For example, the Federal Trade Commission (FTC) in the United States, and Privacy Commissioners, operating within Commonwealth jurisdictions like Canada and Australia, have taken a leading role in exercising their authority directly over companies like Facebook. They have brought several enforcement actions against unfair or deceptive online information practices.

The Federal Trade Commission's Bureau of Consumer Protection confirmed at the end of March 2018 that it has undertaken a non-public investigation into Facebook's data practices.[152] The announcement came just over a week after *The New York Times* and *The Guardian* published their damning reports on Cambridge Analytica.[153] This isn't the first time the FTC has investigated the social network's information-sharing practices.

In 2011, Facebook agreed to settle charges that it 'deceived consumers by telling them they could keep their information on Facebook private, and then repeatedly allowing it to be shared and made public', among other things.[154] The complaint specifically referenced the fact that users' data could be obtained by third-party app developers in ways that could have caught those users unaware, which is clearly suggestive of Facebook's current debacle.

The final settlement barred Facebook from making further deceptive privacy claims, required it to obtain a user's explicit approval before changing the way it handles their data, and compelled it to receive periodic assessments of its privacy practices by third-party auditors for the next 20 years. It also demanded that users be notified explicitly if their data is shared beyond the privacy settings they have configured.

If the FTC now finds that Facebook has failed to comply with the consent decree it agreed to in 2011, it could be liable for trillions of dollars in fines.[155] Violations of the agreement could carry a financial penalty of $40,000 per violation, meaning that if the social network mishandled 50 million Americans' data, it could face fines of up to $2 trillion.[156] It's not clear, though, that the FTC would seek the maximum penalty, but even a fraction of that could put a serious dent in Facebook's coffers.

Similarly, in 2009, the then-federal Privacy Commissioner of Canada, Jennifer Stoddart, took on Facebook and forced it to change some of its policies. The Office of the Privacy Commissioner of Canada completed a detailed investigation into a complaint about the privacy practices and policies of Facebook, which was

151 Cohen *supra*, note 219.

152 Louise Matsakis, 'The FTC is Officially Investigating Facebook's Data Practices', *Wired*, 26 March 2018.

153 Katy Steinmetz, 'Mark Zuckerberg Survived Congress. Now Facebook Has to Survive the FTC', *Time*, 13 April 2018.

154 *Facebook, Inc.*, No. 092 3184 (Fed. Trade Comm'n 29 Nov 2011).

155 Matsakis, *supra*, note 984.

156 *Ibid.*

filed by the Canadian Internet Policy and Public Interest Clinic (the 'CIPPC') on 30 May 2008.[157] The case was decided by the then-Assistant Privacy Commissioner of Canada, Elizabeth Denham, who released her report on 16 July 2009.[158] This case marks a significant step in determining how Canadian privacy law influences online social networking sites, particularly a global giant like Facebook. According to Facebook, meeting Canada's requirements also satisfied those in other countries like Australia, New Zealand and many parts of Europe.[159]

Canada's *Personal Information Protection and Electronic Documents Act* (PIPEDA)[160] governs how private-sector organizations collect, use and disclose personal information in the course of commercial business. The Act covers all organizations, including foreign companies, that collect, use, or disclose 'personal information' in the course of 'commercial activity'. Section 2 defines personal information very broadly as 'information about an identifiable individual'. PIPEDA was modelled on the Canadian Standards association (CSA) Model Code for the Protection of Personal information, which contains ten 'fair information principles' that mirror those in other national and international privacy laws and guidelines.[161]

Under PIPEDA, an organization that wants to collect, use or disclose personal information about someone must first obtain that person's consent. When the personal information is particularly sensitive – medical or financial records, for example – the organization must explicitly ask for consent.[162] PIPEDA is enforced by the Privacy Commissioner of Canada, who can receive and investigate complaints from any individual or organization regarding infringements of the Act.

The central issue in the CIPPC's allegations was whether Facebook was providing 'a sufficient knowledge basis for meaningful consent' by documenting the purposes for the collection, use and disclosure of personal information, and providing that information to individual users in a 'reasonably direct and transparent' manner.[163] A key concern was that, although Facebook provides information about its privacy practices, this information was frequently confusing or incomplete.[164]

157 Elizabeth Denham, 'Report of Findings into the Complaint Filed by the Canadian Internet Policy and Public Interest Clinic (CIPPIC) Against Facebook Inc. Under the Personal Information Protection and Electronic Documents Act', 16 July 2009. Available online at: www.priv.gc.ca/cf-dc/2009/2009_008_0716_e.pdf.

158 *Ibid.*

159 9thCo, 'Canada's Privacy Act – The World's Standard For Social Networking Sites?' 15 September 2009. Available online at: www.9thco.com/insight/canadas-privacy-act-standard-for-social-networking.

160 (S.C. 2000, c. 5).

161 Bennett et al., *supra*, note 276 at 186.

162 *Ibid.*

163 Denham, *supra*, note 989.

164 Office of the Privacy Commissioner of Canada, 'News Releases – Facebook Needs to Improve Privacy Practices, Investigation Finds', 16 July 2009. Available online at: www.priv.gc.ca/media/nr-c/2009/nr-c_090716_e.asp.

The Assistant Privacy Commissioner's report recommended more transparency, to ensure that users have the information they need to make meaningful decisions about how they share personal information. Facebook was given 30 days to respond and explain how it would address these concerns. Under PIPEDA, the Privacy Commissioner could apply to the Federal Court of Canada to have her recommendations enforced. The company replied by agreeing to add important new privacy safeguards, as well as making other changes, in order to conform to Canada's privacy law. Following is an overview of the key issues raised during the investigation and Facebook's response.

Facebook agreed to amend the language of the pop-up box that users see when registering that explains the purpose of collecting the date of birth. It also agreed to make changes to the language of its privacy policy with respect to its use of personal information for advertising and has stated that it is dedicated to 'full disclosure as to the collection and use of information for advertising purposes'.[165] Facebook also committed to introducing a means whereby users would be able to select a low, medium or high privacy setting. This selection would dictate more granular default settings. Users who choose the 'high' setting would not be included in public search listings.[166]

A central allegation related to Facebook's disclosure of personal information to third parties who create applications, such as games, quizzes and classified advertisements, which run on Facebook. There are more than a million of these third-party application developers in 180 countries around the globe. When users add an application, they consent to giving the third parties access to their personal information, as well as that of their 'friends'. The Assistant Privacy Commissioner determined that Facebook did not have acceptable safeguards in place to prevent unauthorized access by third-party applications and it was not adequately ensuring that meaningful consent was obtained from these individuals prior to the disclosure of their personal information.[167]

The Assistant Privacy Commissioner recommended that Facebook implement technological measures to restrict third parties' access to only the user information essential to run a specific application.[168] In other words, there was too much personal information being shared with third-party application developers, without adequate monitoring. She also requested Facebook to ensure that users are informed about the specific information that an application requires, and what its purpose is.[169] She further recommended that users signing up for an application be asked for express consent to provide their personal information to third-party developers.[170]

165 *Ibid.*
166 Office of the Privacy Commissioner of Canada, 'News Releases – Letter from OPC to CIPPIC Outlining its Resolution with Facebook', 25 August 2009. Available online at: www.priv.gc.ca/media/nr-c/2009/let_090827_e.asp.
167 Denham, *supra*, note 989.
168 *Ibid.*
169 *Ibid.*
170 *Ibid.*

In response, Facebook agreed to redesign its application platform so as to prevent any application from accessing information until it obtains express consent for each category of personal information it wishes to access.[171] Under this model, users adding an application are advised that the application wants to access specific categories of information; and the user is able to control which categories of information an application is permitted to access. There is also a link to a statement by the third-party application developer as to how it will use the data.

Another of the Assistant Privacy Commissioner's concerns was that Facebook provided confusing information about the difference between account deactivation and account deletion (i.e. whether the users' personal information is stored on Facebook's servers or removed).[172] She also recommended that Facebook implement a retention policy under which the personal information of users who deactivated their accounts would be deleted from the site's servers after a reasonable period of time.[173] Facebook responded by agreeing to make it clear to users that they have the option of either deactivating or deleting their accounts.[174] This distinction is now explained in Facebook's privacy policy and users receive a notice about the delete option during the deactivation process.

In a subsequent, albeit separate, complaint against Facebook, on 11 August 2010, three individuals complained to the Privacy Commissioner of Canada that they received an email invitation to join Facebook, along with so-called 'friend suggestions' (i.e. a list of Facebook users and profile photos that the complainants knew).[175] The complainants alleged that the company accessed their electronic address books (or those of their friends) and used the personal information contained therein without their consent. The Office of the Privacy Commissioner of Canada concluded that Facebook failed to meet the knowledge and consent requirements under PIPEDA by failing to obtain consent for the use of a non-user's email address; failing to inform non-users of the proposed use of their email address; and failing to establish a procedure for opting out prior to the use of a non-user's email address.[176]

The complaint stemmed from a change Facebook made to its site in October 2009, whereby, in an effort to expand its subscriber base, it introduced a Friend Suggestion feature.[177] The feature allows Facebook users to upload the email addresses of non-users to their Facebook contacts and to invite people they may know to join the site. Non-Facebook users are persuaded to subscribe to the

171 Office of the Privacy Commissioner of Canada, *supra*, note 998.

172 Denham, *supra*, note 989.

173 *Ibid.*

174 Office of the Privacy Commissioner of Canada, *supra*, note 998.

175 Office of the Privacy Commissioner of Canada, 'PIPEDA Report of Findings #2012-002 – Facebook Didn't Get Non-Members' Consent to Use Email Addresses to Suggest Friends, Investigation Finds', 8 February 2012. Available online at: www.priv.gc.ca/cf-dc/2012/2012_002_0208_e.asp.

176 *Ibid.*

177 *Ibid.*

site through a series of email reminders, some of which include friend suggestions.[178] A key concept behind PIPEDA is that of ensuring an individual's control over their personal information; and control, within the framework of the legislation, is largely in relation to knowledge and consent. Consent is meaningful if the individual is clearly informed about the purposes for collecting, using and disclosing personal information.

As a result of the Commissioner's findings, Facebook now provides clear notice to non-users that their email addresses may be used to generate friend suggestions and offers them an easy-to-use opt-out mechanism.[179] The unsubscribe notice now plainly states, 'If you don't want to receive these emails from Facebook in the future, or have your email address used for friend suggestions, you can unsubscribe'.[180] Individuals who unsubscribe are added to Facebook's 'do not email' list, with their email addresses being retained only for the purpose of ensuring that the individual no longer receives messages from the site.[181]

The Canadian House of Commons conducted formal hearings on what it called 'the breach of personal information involving Cambridge Analytica and Facebook'. In early May 2018, it initiated two days of political and expert questioning in its Standing Committee on Access to Information, Privacy and Ethics (ETHI); and Facebook Canada's Global Director and Head of Public Policy, Kevin Chan, was scheduled to appear before it. The Privacy Commissioner of Canada, Daniel Therrien, issued a public statement in late March 2018, saying that his office plans to reach out to Facebook regarding the misuse of its data by Cambridge Analytica: 'Ultimately, our goal is to ensure that the privacy rights of Canadian Facebook users are protected'.[182]

The EU has also played a major role in decisions involving information privacy and has shaped the way businesses operate throughout the world. The new *European Union General Data Protection Regulation* (GDPR) regulations will give users greater control over their data, including the ability to export it, withdraw consent and request access to it. Consent must be 'explicit' for sensitive data; and the data controller must be able to demonstrate that consent was given. Data controllers must also continue to provide transparent information to data subjects; and this must be done from the time the personal data is first obtained. The law also allows individuals to withdraw their consent for companies to keep their data, particularly if the use of that information is not related to the reason that it was collected in the first place. And users have the right to ask to see the data companies have about them.

The new regulations are far stricter than their predecessors in Europe, as well as the rules in many other countries. Indeed, the law will set a new global

178 *Ibid.*

179 *Ibid.*

180 *Ibid.*

181 *Ibid.*

182 Brian Jackson, 'Canada's Privacy Commissioner Wants Answers From Facebook Regarding Cambridge Analytica Data Breach', *IT World Canada*, 20 March 2018.

standard around the importance of personal information ownership and consumer protection. Any advertising agencies doing business with clients in the EU, or companies targeting ads to potential customers there, will have to comply with the new rules – including the law's broadened definition of personal information to include computers' IP addresses. Penalties for non-compliance could be up to €20 million or 4 per cent of a company's total global revenue, whichever is greater.

In the recent senate hearings discussed above, Mark Zuckerberg said he thought the GDPR was a good idea: 'I think the GDPR, in general, is going to be a very positive step for the Internet'.[183] However, Zuckerberg made swift changes to ensure that the number of Facebook users protected by it will be considerably less. Facebook members outside the United States and Canada were historically governed by terms of service agreed with the company's international headquarters in Ireland. Yet Facebook plans to make that the case for European users only, meaning that 1.5 billion people in North America, Africa, Asia, Australia and Latin America will not fall under the rules of the GDPR. This demonstrates that Facebook is eager to reduce its exposure to the GDPR, which allows European regulators to fine companies for collecting or using personal data without users' consent. That removes a massive potential liability for Facebook, which could have meant costs of billions of dollars.

A recent case provides another illustration of why Facebook is keen to distance itself from EU law. In 2011, Max Schrems, an Austrian law student, demanded that Facebook give him all the data the company had about him – which is required by EU law.[184] Two years later, after a court battle which Facebook lost, the company sent him a CD with a 1,200-page PDF containing all the friends he could see, and items on his newsfeed, along with all the photos and pages he'd ever clicked on, and all the advertising he'd ever viewed.[185] Yes, Facebook systematically collects and saves all of this data – largely without our knowledge – and it thus has a better record of who we are and where we've been than most of us do about our own selves. But the GDPR will restrict how Facebook can collect, use and disclose this treasure trove of information from now on.

In April 2018, Zuckerberg told *Reuters* in an interview that his company would apply the EU law globally 'in spirit', but stopped short of committing to it as the standard for the social network across the world.[186] In practice, the change means that 1.5 billion affected users will not be able to avail themselves of the robust protections provided by the GDPR. They also won't be able to file complaints with Ireland's Data Protection Commissioner or in Irish courts.

183 Kurt Wagner, 'Facebook is Taking Its First Steps to Comply With Europe's Strict Data Privacy Rules', *Recode*, 18 April 2018.

184 Schneier, *supra*, note 32 at 19.

185 *Ibid.*

186 Reuters, "Facebook is Ensuring that GDPR Protection is Limited to EU Residents, the Privacy of Everyone Else is Still at its Mercy," April 19, 2018.

Instead, they will be governed by far more lenient privacy laws in the United States and potentially elsewhere.

Unlike the EU and Canada, the US has no general data protection laws. In fact, the United States has been the great exception regarding the international preference for omnibus legislation. The 1974 *Privacy Act* only addresses the personal information practices of federal entities, not state and local governments or private entities.[187] It also rests on outdated concepts – it covers identifiable information about individuals that is maintained in 'systems of records' by federal agencies.[188] Clearly, this is insufficient to address modern surveillance and information-gathering practices, which frequently occur between both public- and private-sector agencies over vast and widely dispersed networks.[189]

The legislation also appears not to apply to programmes focused on developing biometric technologies through the widespread accumulation of data that is not tied to particular individuals.[190] For example, if the government maintains a video surveillance program in which it stores the biometric information of passers-by, without correlating the information to particular individuals, this does not appear to fall within the *Privacy Act*.[191] The Act also contains a number of exceptions, which overlap, and can be said to defeat any substantive impact that it might otherwise have on surveillance technologies and systems.[192]

For instance, the statute provides a general exemption for records maintained by the CIA, national security (i.e. classified information or the identity of informers) and criminal law enforcement records.[193] This allows law enforcement agencies to exempt records relating to the identification of criminal offenders and alleged offenders, data compiled for criminal investigations, and reports developed at any stage of the criminal law process from arrest or indictment to release from supervision.[194] This would seem to exempt most, if not all, of the data discussed in the chapter on law enforcement and policing. The exceptions further permit agencies, like the Department of Homeland Security, whose automated biometric identification system incorporates information pertaining to immigration, border security, law enforcement, national security, and intelligence, to claim multiple exemptions.[195] This appears to allow for substantial further growth of these programs without any oversight, public notification or disclosure.

There have been a few recent exceptions to the general reluctance to legislate in the area of private-sector information practices. The US now regulates information privacy on a sector-by-sector basis; yet it contains only limited

187 Donohue, *supra*, note 209 at 468.
188 Bennett, *supra*, note 756 at 69.
189 *Ibid.*
190 Donohue, *supra*, note 209 at 470.
191 *Ibid.*
192 *Ibid.* at 472.
193 *Ibid.* at 472–473.
194 *Ibid.* at 473.
195 *Ibid.* at 474.

protections for sensitive information. Within the private sector, it concentrates on the data-holder and in some instances, on the type of data. Laws protect certain categories of personal data – financial data, health-care information, student data – but there is nothing similar to the broad privacy protection laws that exist in the EU and Canada.

Another key difference is that the US has not created a national data-protection commission. The closest that the United States comes to a national data-protection agency is the FTC. During the last two decades, the FTC has played an increased role in protecting privacy in the United States, and this development represents a highly significant change for privacy. At the same time, there are significant limits on the scope of the FTC's activities as protector of information privacy. The lack of a robust legal framework leaves personal information open to misuse and inevitably, it will also lead to even more invasive mass surveillance and information-sharing by private-sector entities. This makes newer technology companies a powerful voice in favour of the regulatory status quo in the United States.

Conclusion

Advertising is the Holy Grail of the Internet economy. To the extent to which companies can discover more detailed and extensive information about personal preferences and behaviours, they will make more money. In the past few years, owing to the growing availability of high-speed access and search technology, this model has become one of the fastest-growing forms of content and has revolutionized how advertisers locate and reach those individuals.

A large part of the problem is that these companies hide their business model and what they're doing from the general public and even governments at large. Data retention, surveillance, profiling and opaque targeting are now prolific. Sadly, rather than ushering in a new era of intellectual and creative freedom, the Internet has dumbed things down. With the proliferation of content such as 'Which be like Bob name applies to you?' 'What would kidnappers write in your ransom note?' 'Cats you will remember and laugh all day!', it's easy to believe that the Internet age has actually resulted in the suppression of truly valuable innovation and creativity.[196]

It seems impractical, if not impossible, that Facebook and Google would completely overhaul their businesses, tossing aside their winning advertising engines to start afresh. But it's increasingly clear that something is going to have to change. Recognition of this has prompted calls to reform existing policies and practices to ensure stronger protection of privacy.[197] The suggestion of changing Facebook's default privacy settings from opt-out to opt-in, meaning the company would need to ask for permission to collect data right away instead

196 Wu, *supra*, note 845 at 326.

197 Office of the United Nations High Commissioner for Human Rights, *supra*, note 637 at para.19.

of collecting it by default, seems as if it would be most dangerous to Facebook. It would severely limit the amount of data they can collect about people, thus hurting their business model.

When it comes to regulation, each country will ultimately take a different view – it may thus be impossible to find global standard – but citizens need to be educated and aware of the risk that they'll be tracked. Mark Zuckerberg openly stated that he thinks the new EU privacy regulations are a good thing; and he promised Congress that Facebook will roll out the strict GDPR privacy regulations that are now required in the EU. While, in theory, that kind of approach might limit the desire for more formal regulation in the US – if Facebook is seen as already 'regulating' itself. But the fact that he is now seeking to scale back these requirements should leave everyone asking for more legislative changes, particularly changes that hit closer to home.

Bibliography

9thCo, 'Canada's Privacy Act – the World's Standard for Social Networking Sites?' 15 September 2009. Available online at: www.9thco.com/insight/canadas-privacy-act-standard-for-social-networking.

Louise Amoore, 'Governing by Identity', in Colin J. Bennett & David Lyon (eds), *Playing the Identity Card: Surveillance, Security and Identification in Global Perspective* (New York: Routledge, 2008).

David Baser, 'Hard Questions: What Data Does Facebook Collect When I'm Not Using Facebook, and Why?' 16 April 2018. Available online at: https://newsroom.fb.com/news/2018/04/data-off-facebook/.

Colin J. Bennett, 'Unsafe at Any Altitude: The Comparative Politics of No-Fly Lists in the United States and Canada', in Mark B. Salter (ed) *Politics at the Airport* (Minneapolis: University of Minnesota Press, 2008) 51.

Colin J. Bennett, Kevin D. Haggerty, David Lyon & Valerie M. Steeves (eds) *Transparent Lives: Surveillance in Canada (The New Transparency Project)* (Edmonton: Athabasca University Press, 2014).

Callum Borchers, 'Would You Pay $18.75 for Ad-Free Facebook?' *The Washington Post*, 14 April 2018.

danah boyd, 'Untangling Research and Practice: What Facebook's "Emotional Contagion" Study Teaches Us,' (2016) 12(1) *Research Ethics* 4.

Vicki Boykis, 'What Should You Think About When Using Facebook?' 1 February 2017. Available online at: http://veekaybee.github.io/2017/02/01/facebook-is-collecting-this/.

Stewart Brand, *The Media Lab: Inventing the Future at M. I. T.* (London: Penguin Books, 1989).

Julie E. Cohen, 'What Privacy is For', (2013) 126(7) *Harvard Law Review* 1904.

C. Custer, '3 Reasons WeChat Failed Internationally (and Most Other Chinese Apps Do Too)' *TechInAsia*, 26 May 2016. Available online at: www.techinasia.com/3-reasons-wechat-failed-internationally-chinese-apps.

Elizabeth Denham, 'Report of Findings into the Complaint Filed by the Canadian Internet Policy and Public Interest Clinic (CIPPIC) Against Facebook Inc. Under the Personal Information Protection and Electronic Documents Act', 16 July 2009. Available online at: www.priv.gc.ca/cf-dc/2009/2009_008_0716_e.pdf.

Cory Doctorow, 'The Curious Case of Internet Privacy', *Technology Review*, July/August 2012.

Laura K. Donohue, 'Technological Leap, Statutory Gap', (2012) 97 *Minnesota Law Review* 407.

Executive Office of the President of the United States, 'Big Data and Privacy: A Technological Perspective', May 2014. Available online at: https://bigdatawg.nist.gov/pdf/pcast_big_data_and_privacy_-_may_2014.pdf.

Franklin Foer, *World Without Mind – The Existential Threat of Big Tech* (New York: Penguin Press, 2017).

Scott Galloway, *The Four: The Hidden DNA of Amazon, Apple, Facebook and Google* (London: Transworld Publishers, 2017).

Brian Jackson, 'Canada's Privacy Commissioner Wants Answers From Facebook Regarding Cambridge Analytica Data Breach', *IT World Canada*, 20 March 2018.

Emma Lee, 'WeChat Pay Tries to Duplicate Domestic Success Overseas With Killer Recipe: Social Networking', *Technode*, 1 March 2018. Available online at: https://technode.com/2018/03/01/wechat-pay-social-networking/.

Shannon Liao, 'How WeChat Came to Rule China', *The Verge*, 1 February 2018.

David Lyon, 'Biometrics, Identification and Surveillance', (2008) 22(9) *Bioethics* 499.

David Lyon, 'Filtering Flows, Friends and Foes', in Mark B. Salter (ed.), *Politics at the Airport* (Minneapolis: University of Minnesota Press, 2008) 29.

Louise Matsakis, 'The FTC is Officially Investigating Facebook's Data Practices', *Wired*, 26 March 2018.

Robert McMillan, 'A 125-Year-Old Letter Dives into the True Meaning of the Word *Hack*', *Slate*, 29 January 2015.

William J. Mitchell, *ME ++* (Cambridge, MA: MIT Press, 2004).

Helen Nissenbaum, 'Protecting Privacy in an Information Age: The Problem of Privacy in Public', (1998) 17 *Law and Philosophy* 559.

Office of the Privacy Commissioner of Canada, 'News Releases – Facebook Needs to Improve Privacy Practices, Investigation Finds', 16 July 2009. Available online at: www.priv.gc.ca/media/nr-c/2009/nr-c_090716_e.asp.

Office of the Privacy Commissioner of Canada, 'News Releases – Letter from OPC to CIPPIC Outlining its Resolution with Facebook', 25 August 2009. Available online at: www.priv.gc.ca/media/nr-c/2009/let_090827_e.asp.

Office of the Privacy Commissioner of Canada, 'PIPEDA Report of Findings #2012-002- Facebook Didn't Get Non-Members' Consent to Use Email Addresses to Suggest Friends, Investigation Finds', 8 February 2012. Available online at: www.priv.gc.ca/cf-dc/2012/2012_002_0208_e.asp.

Office of the United Nations High Commissioner for Human Rights, 'The Right to Privacy in the Digital Age', 30 June 2014.

Reuters, 'Facebook is Ensuring that GDPR Protection is Limited to EU Residents, the Privacy of Everyone Else is Still at its Mercy', 19 April 2018.

Howard Rheingold, *Virtual Communities – Homesteading on the Electronic Frontier* (Cambridge, MA: MIT Press, 2000).

Jeremy Rifkin, *The Age of Access: The New Culture of Hypercapitalism, Where all of Life is a Paid-For Experience* (New York: Penguin Putnam, 2000).

SBS News, 'WeChat A New Chinese Empire?' Available online at: www.sbs.com.au/news/feature/wechat-new-chinese-empire.

Bruce Schneier, *Data and Goliath: The Hidden Battles to Collect Your Data and Control Your World* (New York: W. W. Norton & Co., 2015).

Bruce Schneier, 'How We Sold Our Souls—and More—to the Internet Giants', *The Guardian*, 17 May 2015.
Avi Selk,'Apple's Tim Cook: I would Have Avoided Facebook's Privacy Mess', *The Washington Post*, 29 March 2018.
Tom Simonite, 'This Call May be Monitored for Tone and Emotion', *Wired*, 19 March 2018.
Katy Steinmetz, 'Mark Zuckerberg Survived Congress. Now Facebook Has to Survive the FTC', *Time*, 13 April 2018.
Wired Staff, 'Capitalist Ecoconstruction', *Wired*, 1 March 2000.
Zeynep Tufekci, 'Data Dystopia', *Technology Review*, July/August, 2012.
Zeynep Tufekci, 'Facebook's Surveillance Machine', *The New York Times*, 19 March 2018.
Giles Turner & Lulu Yilun Chen, 'WeChat Expands in Europe in Bid for Global Advertisers, Payments', *Bloomberg*, 30 March 2017.
Kurt Wagner, 'Facebook Is Taking its First Steps to Comply With Europe's Strict Data Privacy Rules', *Recode*, 18 April 2018.
Kurt Wagner, 'This Is How Facebook Collects Data on You Even If You Don't Have an Account', *Recode*, 20 April 2018.
Kurt Wagner, 'Congress Just Published All the Russian Facebook Ads Used to Try and Influence the 2016 Election', *Recode*, 10 May 2018.
Kurt Wagner, 'Mark Zuckerberg Says Breaking Up Facebook Would Pave the Way For China's Tech Companies to Dominate', *Recode*, 18 July 2018.
Sarah Myers West, 'Data Capitalism: Redefining the Logics of Surveillance and Privacy', (2017) 00(0) *Business & Society* 1.
Tim Wu, *The Attention Merchants – The Epic Scramble to Get Inside Our Heads* (New York: Vintage Books, 2016).
Meg Jing Zeng, 'Thinking of Taking up WeChat? Here's What You Need to Know', *The Conversation*, 18 December 2017.

Case Law

Facebook, Inc., No. 092 3184 (Fed. Trade Comm'n 29 Nov 2011).

8 Conclusion

Over the past hundred years or so, a steady stream of new technologies has progressively challenged our cultural and legal attitudes towards privacy. Historically, privacy concerns were raised around the threats posed by photography and telephony; today, our apprehensions typically focus on data aggregation, online profiling, electronic surveillance, social media – and, of course, the use of biometrics. The legal and policy questions raised by these tools substantially differ from those in the past.

Yet every significant new technology in recent history has gone through a similar cycle. There's a window at the birth of a new technological tool when things are in flux – it's open and decentralized, somewhat chaotic and largely unpredictable. The rules of the game, power balances, and especially how the technology will be governed, are open for lively debate. Invariably, though, power begins to consolidate and centralize. It gets harder to turn back the clock as our use of the technology comes to be seen as 'just the way it is'. This can have dramatic consequences for our society and personal freedom.

Facial recognition represents the first of a series of next-generation biometrics, such as hand geometry, iris, vascular patterns, hormones and gait, which, when paired with surveillance of public space, give rise to unique and novel questions of law and policy. They give both public and private entities the ability to ascertain the identity of multiple people at a distance in either public or private spaces – absent notice and consent – in a continuous and ongoing manner. They also allow for the linking and matching of data in new ways to engage in profiling and risk assessment across all sectors of society. There is very little possibility for the individual to know how her information is being used and how decisions are being made about her.

When it comes to advances in biometrics, and AI in particular, we can point to a few key criteria that have enabled their rapid integration into multiple sectors of modern society. In short, these advances happened as a result of four key factors: Moore's Law – the fact that roughly every two years there's a doubling of computing performance; vast increases in the amount of data that we have; the fact that algorithms are getting much better; and there has been a massive increase in the amount of funding going into biometric technologies and AI. We now have the necessary computing power, reams of data, sophisticated algorithms, and a lot of people working on advancing these technologies.

Alongside these advances, and perhaps because of them, governments throughout the world have given both public- and private-sector agencies the authority to collect, analyse, and share personally identifiable information on an unprecedented scale.[1] At the heart of these measures are other activities – known as 'profiling', 'matching', 'data aggregation', and 'data mining' – in which diverse records and sources of information are aggregated to produce databases with complex patterns of information about individuals.[2] It must be stressed, though, that biometric systems and devices are not foolproof and they don't guarantee absolute security.

There are many risks associated with their use, and possible abuses that come with their acceptance into mainstream society. For example, biometric devices do not provide equal opportunities for every individual who comes into contact with them. There will always be some who cannot be enrolled or detected by a particular biometric sensor. In other cases, they are not integrated into society in a way that is designed to provide equal outcomes for *all* individuals. Rather, they are used to stigmatize and disenfranchise individuals, particularly those who are already in the poor and marginalized sectors of society.

The perceived need for heightened security in the wake of large-scale terrorist events, like the 9/11 attacks, has provided great impetus for the uptake of biometric security systems throughout the world. Various claims have been made about the reliability and usefulness of these systems, particularly for national security. Yet few limits have been imposed on the exercise of these powers. While privacy law traditionally responds to the threat of governmental intrusion into the personal and intimate realms, it has yet to respond adequately to these new developments.

If traditional surveillance involves the tracking of one or a few suspects by police officers, what happens when a person 'emerges' as a surveillance target as a result of a computer analysis? In the traditional context, police have not been constrained by the Fourth Amendment as long as their investigations neither interfered with an individual's movements, nor extended beyond public spaces. Yet this surveillance discretion may mean something different in the big-data context. The very quality of public life may be different when governments covertly watch everyone and store all of the resulting data. Moreover, this information is inherently private and sensitive and is subject to theft and misuse by hackers and others.

We have seen that countries in the West, like Canada and the United States, have been steadily expanding the constitutional right to privacy over many decades. And robust data-protection laws underpin privacy rights in the European Union and Canada. Together, these regimes provide protections against privacy

1 Donohue, *supra*, note 209 at 462.
2 Nissenbaum, *supra*, note 218 at 596.

and data abuses on the part of both the public and private sectors. They provide a system of integrity that can be agreed upon as the baseline for the ways in which personal information should be collected, shared and used. This informs thinking about what will happen to such data in the future and what could possibly go wrong. And it provides a mechanism to hold public and private entities accountable when their obligations are not met.

Yet legislative developments in the area of biometrics have not kept up with technological ones. Only a handful of hearings has even questioned the use of biometrics in the national security or law enforcement context. Scholarship about privacy within the North American legal academy is beset by liberal political theory, particularly the notion of 'the self' as innately autonomous. Within this framework, privacy preserves the space around the individual to defend against the pressures of societal and technological change. Yet people can often be pseudo-anonymized through aggregated data.

Accordingly, the traditional approach is no longer adequate to address contemporary networked surveillance measures within the modern liberal democratic state. Biometric technologies now demonstrate far-reaching capabilities that are significantly different from those which the government has held at any point in recent history. The shift from discipline to control is central to the growing use of networked technologies that permit surveillance of mobile populations.

Surveillance practices have been moving away from the targeted scrutiny of individuals within relatively closed spaces and institutions to widespread monitoring for the purpose of identifying and pre-empting adverse behaviour. Police largely do not understand or investigate either the technology's effectiveness or its side effects.[3] Thus, it's hard to say in the abstract what stronger regulatory solutions may be required, or how significant a problem the technology poses, until more information about its implementation is available.

This is especially important as the functions of surveillance and policing are increasingly offloaded to third parties whose motivations and concerns may not always agree with those of a publicly accountable body. Companies like Accenture and Northrop Grumman are being awarded contracts for tens of millions of dollars to develop surveillance and security measures. IBM spent billions acquiring data analytics companies in order to develop and market predictive tools to the police.[4] Similarly, Microsoft and the N.Y.P.D. will profit from every police department that adopts a 'total domain awareness system'. COMPAS is also owned by a private company and, in states like Wisconsin, sentencing relies upon a proprietary code available for independent testing, but for which the algorithms are kept secret. This prevents defendants from knowing how decisions are made about their incarceration or release from prison.

In the commercial sector, covert monitoring, tracking and data aggregation are used to infer and predict individual preferences for products and services.

3 Selbst, *supra*, note 382 at 168.
4 Joh, *supra*, note 313 at 66.

At the same time, though, we have shown alarming disregard for our own online privacy and security, and no amount of legal protection or commercial goodwill is going to protect us if we continue to disclose so much of our personal information with the world indiscriminately. There needs to be a cultural shift towards the protection of personal data, as a matter of individual responsibility, in order to deal with the threat of big data in the modern age.

Nevertheless, the absence of a robust statutory framework for the protection of biometric data in the majority of jurisdictions examined in this book is a cause for concern. The most powerful of those looked at appears to be the new GDPR rules in the European Union. However, this framework, like other data protection statutes examined herein, falls short for focusing on individual consent and access to data. Like the constitutional approaches reviewed earlier, this framework remains limited by liberal democratic notions of the autonomous, rational individual who can make choices about the data that he or she is disclosing. As we have seen, most people are unaware of the extent of the information they're disclosing, and the purposes for which it will be used, much less the fact that it may be shared indiscriminately between private and public sector entities for a variety of uses far into the future.

Just as the tech giants introduced radically new business models that affected how we live our lives; governments can raise the cost of surveillance and data collection with new laws that radically change how these business models can operate. We need independent oversight by courts and regulatory bodies, analysing and debating the actions of those who wield enormous power. For this to happen, we need a concerned public to sit up and take notice of what has already been going on for some time. Fortunately, that seems to have happened, at least to some extent, in the wake of the Cambridge Analytica scandal.

A good way to make companies improve the security of our data is to make them responsible for safeguarding it. Privacy must be built into new systems and tools, not added as an afterthought. We need restrictions upon how our data can be used, especially on ways that differ from the purposes for which it was collected. But we cannot simply trust companies to abide by these standards. This is likely to be as effective as the 'self-regulation' approach in the early days of the Internet that led to the abusive monopolies we now face.

We need to hold companies accountable for their actions – and make them answerable to us – by subjecting them to hearings, fines and public scrutiny. Regular audits can ensure that companies are following the rules and make them liable to penalties if they don't. By raising the costs of data misuse, we can also force companies to expend money and effort on protecting the privacy of those whose data they've acquired *before* misuse can occur.

Along these lines, if legislation is proposed in the biometrics context, the ten principles described in Table 8.1 should be implemented (see Table 8.1).

The future is inevitable. It's no longer necessary, or even appropriate, to question whether we can or cannot stop the technological advances occurring all around us. Instead, we need to shift our focus towards asking how we can best adapt to the societal changes that that they bring. We've seen, for example, that

Table 8.1 10 Principles for Biometric Data Collection

1 Limit the Collection of Biometrics

The collection of biometrics should be limited to the minimum necessary to achieve the stated purpose. If a legitimate aim can be achieved by not collecting this data or collecting it in a less restrictive and privacy-infringing manner, that option should be pursued.

2 Define Clear Rules on the Legal Process Required for Collection

A legal framework should be established that gives government agencies, commercial entities, and private citizens clear guidelines for when and how biometric information can be collected, accessed and used. This includes whether a specific legal process (e.g. a court order or warrant) is required prior to collection. Other standards can be used to safeguard the privacy of individuals against incursions by entities in either the public or private sectors. Agencies could be required to conduct privacy impact assessments when developing or procuring information technology systems that include personally identifiable information. For example, the United Kingdom recommends 'equality impact assessments' as part of the 'public sector Equality Duty', which requires attention to discrimination concerns in all activities by public bodies.[1] And the European Union's GDPR requires data-protection impact assessments whenever data processing 'is likely to result in a high risk to the rights and freedoms of natural persons'. The recitals suggest that discrimination is one such high-risk concern.

3 Limit the Amount and Type of Data Stored

For biometrics such as DNA, which can reveal a great deal of highly sensitive and intimate information about the person, rules should limit the amount of data stored. Also, different kinds of biometric data should be stored in separate databases. This data should also not be stored together with non-biometric data that might increase the scope of harm that may result if a data breach occurs.

4 Limit Retention

Retention periods should be defined by statute and should be limited to no longer than necessary to achieve the goals of the program. Notice should be given to the individual, wherever possible, and there should be clear and simple methods for the individual to request the removal of his or her biometric data from the system.

5 Define Clear Rules for Use and Sharing

Biometrics collected for one purpose should not be used for another purpose. For example, biometrics collected for use in a criminal context should not automatically be shared with another agency for use in an immigration context. Also, information collected for a welfare scheme or for a driving licence should not automatically be shared and used for law-enforcement purposes without proper legal safeguards and the consent of the individual.

6 Implement Security Measures to Avoid Data Compromise

Traditional security features, like encryption and backup, are paramount. There must also be limits around who has access to the data and for what purposes. Digital time stamps and the application of digital signatures can also enhance the strength of security and help detect any changes that are made to the data. Biometric data should also be anonymized and stored separately from other self-identifying information. A plan must be put in place in case the data are compromised for risk mitigation, notification and recovery. This plan must be tested and updated, where necessary, and must be communicated to all those responsible for securing the data.

(*Continued*)

7 Mandate Notice Provisions
Clear rules should define notice requirements to alert people to the fact that their biometric data has been collected, the purpose for collecting the data, the scope of storage, use and distribution, and that adequate protection is being provided to safeguard it from misuse. Note that consent and awareness are not the same. An individual might be aware that data is being acquired but not consent to it. Or he may be completely unaware that a biometric is being captured. For example, a sensor attached to a keyboard could monitor typing patterns without interacting with the user. If, for example, an online learning provider wanted to use this method to ensure that students who sit an exam are the same as those who submitted a quiz, the students must be told this in advance. Similarly, concertgoers and sporting match attendees should be notified when they purchase their tickets that police may be conducting biometric surveillance of the crowd during the event. There also needs to be information provided on how to request removal of the biometric data from the relevant database.

8 Define and Standardize Audit Trails and Accountability
All database transactions should be authorized and logged, including access to and searches of the system, as well as any data transmissions. Independent audits of the system, in terms of ensuring security, accuracy and accountability, should be conducted regularly. There must be a process for update, modification, and training in the event of any changes to the system following an audit.

9 Ensure Independent Oversight
Every entity that collects or uses biometric data must be subject to independent and meaningful oversight. This body must have statutory authority to make its findings public, such as in the event of a breach. The oversight body must also have the authority to hold accountable those responsible for any misuse or breach of the data.

10 Ensure Measures for Penalty and Redress
Data subjects should have a meaningful private right of action. The independent body overseeing the biometric data must also have a statutory right to penalize those responsible for misusing or breaching data, such as through substantial fines and, where necessary, referral to a court of law for civil or criminal charges to be pursued.

---

[1] https://assets.publishing.service.gov.uk/government/uploads/system/uploads/attachment_data/file/5700/2140142.pdf

in the United States, algorithms are now being used to help judges make decisions. This is a line that many of us don't want to cross – we don't want to wake up and discover that we're living in a society where we're locking people up because of a decision made by an algorithm in the dark.

Yet proponents argue that algorithms are much more reliable than people. People, they say, are inherently flawed, biased, discriminatory and prone to making mistakes. Yet this is one of the most important decisions we make in our society. The most serious criminals have normally been judged by a jury of their peers; and this long-standing common-law tradition has been relied on for hundreds of years. Isn't this something we should hold on to despite the fact that technology now allows those decisions to be made by machines?

In this sense, perhaps, we can say that 'the future' is not so inevitable after all. It's merely the result of the decisions we make today. Biometric technologies are value-neutral. They can – as we have seen throughout this book – be used for good or for bad. There are many wonderful things they can do: they can work towards eliminating diseases; they can help eradicate poverty; they can tackle global migration problems and terrorism threats. Equally, though, the same technology can be used for bad: it can be used to increase discrimination and inequality; it can transform warfare to the detriment of entire regions and populations; and it can be used to make our lives much, much worse.

Fortunately, we get to make these choices, which is both a great responsibility and a privilege.

Bibliography

Laura K. Donohue, 'Technological Leap, Statutory Gap', (2012) 97 *Minnesota Law Review* 407.

Elizabeth E. Joh, 'Policing by Numbers: Big Data and the Fourth Amendment', (2014) 89 *Washington Law Review* 35.

Helen Nissenbaum, 'Protecting Privacy in an Information Age: The Problem of Privacy in Public', (1998) 17 *Law and Philosophy* 559.

Jeffrey Rosen, 'The Naked Crowd', *The New York Times*, 22 February 2004.

Andrew D. Selbst, 'Disparate Impact in Big Data Policing', (2017) 52 *Georgia Law Review* 109 at 114.

Index

Page numbers in **bold** indicate a table on the corresponding page

For Product Safety Concerns and Information please contact our EU
representative GPSR@taylorandfrancis.com
Taylor & Francis Verlag GmbH, Kaufingerstraße 24, 80331 München, Germany

www.ingramcontent.com/pod-product-compliance
Ingram Content Group UK Ltd.
Pitfield, Milton Keynes, MK11 3LW, UK
UKHW022131190926
475702UK00013B/1742
* 9 7 8 1 0 3 2 2 4 1 4 2 5 *